Power in the Global Information Age

"As these essays demonstrate, Joseph S. Nye combines clear-sighted realism about power with an uncanny sense for emerging global trends – from interdependence to 'soft power.' His insights on turning theory into ethically purposeful practice make this book a 'must' for students of world politics."

Robert O. Keohane, Duke University, USA

Joseph S. Nye Jr. has been one of the most brilliant and influential international relations scholars of his generation and one of the few academics to have served at the very highest levels of US government. This book collects together many of his key writings for the first time as well as some important new material and a concluding essay, which examines the relevance of international relations in practical policymaking. It contains essays on core issues such as:

- America's post-Cold War role in international affairs
- hard and soft power
- the ethics of foreign policy
- interdependence
- the information revolution
- globalization
- governance
- terrorism

This unique volume is essential reading for all those with an interest in American foreign policy and international relations.

Joseph S. Nye Jr. is Dean of the John F. Kennedy School of Government. Professor Nye has been on the faculty at Harvard since 1964, during which time he also served as Assistant Secretary of Defense for International Security Affairs, Chair of the National Intelligence Council, and Assistant Secretary of State for Security Assistance, Science and Technology.

Power in the Global Information Age

From realism to globalization

Joseph S. Nye Jr.

 Routledge
Taylor & Francis Group

LONDON AND NEW YORK

First published 2004
by Routledge
11 New Fetter Lane, London EC4P 4EE

Simultaneously published in the USA and Canada
by Routledge
29 West 35th Street, New York, NY 10001

Routledge is an imprint of the Taylor & Francis Group

© 2004 Joseph S. Nye Jr. for selection and editorial matter,
essays as detailed in the acknowledgements.

Typeset in Times New Roman by
Newgen Imaging Systems (P) Ltd, Chennai, India
Printed and bound in Great Britain by
TJ International Ltd, Padstow, Cornwall

British Library Cataloguing in Publication Data
A catalogue record for this book is available from the British Library

Library of Congress Cataloging in Publication Data
A catalog record for this book has been requested

ISBN 0–415–70016–7 (hbk)
ISBN 0–415–70017–5 (pbk)

Contents

Acknowledgments

The author and publishers would like to thank the following for granting permission to reproduce material in this work:

Massachusetts Institute of Technology Press Journals for permission to reproduce Joseph S. Nye Jr., 'Old wars and future wars: causation and prevention', *The Journal of Interdisciplinary History* 18:4 (Spring 1988). Copyright 1988 by the Massachusetts Institute of Technology and the editors of *The Journal of Interdisciplinary History*.

Johns Hopkins University Press for permission to reproduce 'Neorealism and neoliberalism' by Joseph S. Nye Jr., *World Politics* vol. XL, no. 2 (January 1988).

Massachusetts Institute of Technology Press Journals for permission to reproduce Joseph S. Nye Jr., 'Conflicts after the Cold War', *The Washington Quarterly* 19:1 (Winter 1996). Copyright 1995 by the Center for Strategic and International Studies (CSIS) and the Massachusetts Institute of Technology.

Joseph S. Nye Jr., 'The changing nature of power in world politics' reproduced with permission from *Political Science Quarterly* 105:2 (Summer 1990).

Joseph S. Nye Jr., 'Soft power' reproduced with permission from *Foreign Policy* #80 (Fall 1990). Copyright 1990 by Carnegie Endowment for International Peace.

Taylor and Francis (www.tandf.co.uk/journals) for permission to reproduce 'The information revolution and American soft power' by Joseph S. Nye Jr., *Asia-Pacific Review* (2002) vol. 9 no. 1.

Joseph S. Nye Jr., 'The new Rome meets the new barbarians' reproduced with permission from *The Economist*, March 2002.

Harvard University Press for permission to reproduce 'Nationalism, statesmen, and the size of African States' *New States in the Modern World*, Martin Kilson ed. (Cambridge, MA: Harvard University Press, 1975).

Joseph S. Nye Jr., 'Ethics and foreign policy' reproduced with permission from *The Aspen Quarterly*, 1985.

Joseph S. Nye Jr., 'NPT: the logic of inequality' reproduced with permission from *Foreign Policy* #59 (Summer 1985). Copyright 1985 by Carnegie Endowment for International Peace.

Joseph S. Nye Jr., 'Independence and interdependence' reproduced with permission from *Foreign Policy* #22 (Spring 1976). Copyright 1976 by Carnegie Endowment for International Peace.

Johns Hopkins University Press for permission to reproduce 'Transgovernmental relations and international organizations' by Robert O. Keohane and Joseph S. Nye Jr., *World Politics* (October 1974).

Robert O. Keohane and Joseph S. Nye Jr., 'Globalization: what's new? what's not? (and so what?)' reproduced with permission from *Foreign Policy* #118 (Spring 2000). Copyright 2000 by Carnegie Endowment for International Peace.

Joseph S. Nye Jr., 'Globalization's democratic deficit' reproduced with permission from *Foreign Affairs* 80:4 (July/August 2001). Copyright 2001 by the Council on Foreign Relations.

1 Hard and soft power

International politics has long been described in terms of states seeking power and security in an anarchic world. States form alliances and balance the power of others in order to preserve their independence. Traditionally, we spoke of states as unitary rational actors. "France allied with Britain because it feared Germany." There was little room for morality or idealism – or for actors other than states. When I first studied the subject, towering figures like E. H. Carr and Hans Morgenthau were warning against the misguided idealism that had helped produce the catastrophes of the first half of the twentieth century.[1]

As a first approximation in most situations, the simple propositions of realism are still the best models we have to guide our thinking. That is why I start this collection of essays with three essays on the power and limits of realism. Realist models are parsimonious, intuitive, sometimes historically grounded, and often provide useful rules of thumb for policy makers. For example, when I was responsible for East Asian policy in the Clinton Administration Defense Department, I relied partly on realism to help redesign a floundering policy. At that time, many people considered the US–Japan security treaty to be an obsolete relic of the Cold War. Unlike Europe, where a web of institutions had knit previous enemies together, East Asian states had never come fully to terms with the politics of the 1930s, and mistrust was strong. Some Americans feared Japan as an economic rival; others feared the rise of Chinese power, and felt that the United States should play the two against each other. Still others urged the containment of China before it became too strong.

As I looked at the three-country East Asian balance of power, it seemed likely that it would eventually evolve into two against one. By reinforcing rather than discarding the US–Japan security alliance, the United States could ensure that it was part of the pair rather than be isolated. From that position of strength, the Americans could afford to engage China economically and socially and see whether such forces would eventually transform China. Rather than turning to military containment, which would confirm China as an enemy, the US pursued engagement while it consolidated its alliance with Japan in the triangular balance, secure in the knowledge that if engagement failed to work, there was a strong fallback position.[2] This strategy involved elements of liberal theory about the long-term effects of trade, social contacts, and democracy but it rested on a hard core of realist analysis.

As much as I admire the parsimony of realist models, I have always been interested in the aspects of world politics that the Occam's razor of realism shaves away. As a graduate student, I remember taking a course from Morgenthau and being impressed by the simple clarity of his realism. But I also remember asking him questions about ideas and social interactions that he tended to sweep aside. I never felt I received adequate answers. Decades later, scholars interested in how ideas shape identities and how social forces lead states to redefine their national interests labeled their new approach "constructivism." In some ways, as the essays in Parts 3 and 4 illustrate, I was interested in constructivism well before the term was invented.

Perhaps that is why I entered the field of international politics through a side door rather than the main entry. I started in comparative politics in what many regarded as a peripheral area. At that time I wrote my thesis on whether the ideas of Pan-Africanism, so prevalent in the early 1960s, would help the leaders of newly independent states in East Africa hold together their common market. Economic rationality pointed in the same direction. Their ensuing failure was not because of realism as much as social forces within each state. My observations on these issues appear in the essay below on "Nationalism, statesmen, and the size of African states."

Field work in East Africa led me to regional integration theories as I tried to make sense of what I found, and testing those theories in turn led to further field work in Central America and Europe. I found myself focusing on the impact of trade, migration, social contacts, and ideas in changing identities, attitudes, and definitions of national self-interest. Regional integration theory flourished in the 1960s when there was a good deal of optimism that the example of European economic integration would be followed in other parts of the world. It was a good laboratory for developing ideas outside the realist mainstream, and some of the insights carried over into my work on interdependence and regimes, but the field dried up when the optimism about regional integration declined.[3] That experience serves as a reminder of the way that theorizing in our field is affected by current events in the world.

In 1968, Robert O. Keohane and I were among a group of young scholars invited to join the editorial board of the journal *International Organization*. I had always considered the journal's focus on legal and formal institutions such as the United Nations to be rather dull, and Keohane and I said so at the first meeting. We argued that the world was full of international organization with a small "i" and small "o" which the journal totally ignored. We were invited to demonstrate what we meant. The result was a special issue on "transnational relations and world politics." We edited a set of essays that highlighted the role of trade, money, multinational corporations, NGOs, the Catholic Church, terrorists, and others.[4]

We argued that the realist approach to world politics discarded too much important information. As the little diagram below illustrates, realists focused on government-to-government interactions with domestic societies having an impact

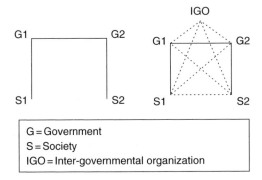

G = Government
S = Society
IGO = Inter-governmental organization

Figure 1.1

only through their governments. But we felt that direct transnational interactions of citizens and groups with other government and inter-governmental organizations often created interesting new coalitions and outcomes in world politics. Rather than the simple "inverted U" relationship in the first image above, our volume presented evidence that a complex star shaped web of relationships was evolving.

Our book was generally well received, but the common reaction by realists was that we had shown a spotlight on marginal issues, and lacked any theory to show how these aspects related to the "real" issues. At best, we had illuminated some oddities. Now, as I will argue below and as the essays in Parts 2 and 4 illustrate, transnational relations can no longer be ignored by realists. On September 11, 2001, a transnational terrorist organization killed more Americans than the state of Japan did in December 1941. The national security strategy of the United States now states that "we are menaced less by fleets and armies than by catastrophic technologies falling into the hands of the embittered few." Instead of strategic rivalry, "today the world's great powers find ourselves on the same side – united by common dangers of terrorist violence and chaos."[5] The "star" of transnational relations depicted in the second image above has gone from an amusing detail to a critical picture.

Keohane and I subsequently published *Power and Interdependence*, designed to show how interdependence (military, economic, ecological, social) can serve as a source of power.[6] In some settings, military instruments are trumps, but in others economic interdependence may be more useful. The oil embargo of 1973 and President Nixon's delinking of the dollar from gold meant that there was some growing interest in these ideas. The first two articles in Part 4 are illustrative of our concern at that time.

We developed an ideal type that we called complex interdependence, by reversing three realist assumptions: that states were the only significant actors, that force was the dominant instrument, and that security was the primary goal. We argued that as some parts of world politics began to approximate the conditions of complex interdependence (e.g. US–Canada and intra-European relations), we should expect to see new political processes, coalitions, and outcomes that would be anomalous from a traditional realist perspective. We did not discard realism, but we argued that in some instances, "marginal" dimensions from a realist view could become central to good explanation. These insights stood us in good stead in terms of predicting how Europe would evolve after the Cold War ended. While some realists were predicting that Germany would break away from the European Union, develop nuclear weapons, and ally with Russia, we felt that the institutions of the European Union would hold together and Brussels would serve as a magnet that would orient Central Europe westward.[7]

While Keohane went on to explore and develop the neo-liberal theory of institutions, I took a detour into practical policy work as a deputy undersecretary in the Carter Administration State Department. I was responsible for developing and implementing policy on the non-proliferation of nuclear weapons. It was shortly after the 1973 oil crisis, and there was a widespread belief that plutonium would be the energy source of the future. Governments were subsidizing reprocessing plants to extract plutonium from spent nuclear fuel and building experimental breeder reactors to produce plutonium. France had sold a reprocessing plant to Pakistan. The Carter Administration argued that the real costs of plutonium were disguised by the subsidies, and that spreading a fuel that was an ingredient of nuclear weapons created grave risks.

We were bitterly opposed by the nuclear industry at home and abroad. I found it ironic to be the subject of personal attacks by a transnational coalition whose common interests in nuclear energy were greater than national differences between them. A 1977 international conference in Persepolis, Iran that condemned Carter's policies represented more the views of nuclear agencies and organizations rather than most foreign ministries. I remember thinking that "this is what I wrote about," but I never expected to experience it so directly! Part of our policy response was to design and organize a high profile multi-year inter-governmental study of plutonium economics and proliferation risks as a means of slowing the momentum of the transnational nuclear elites, and to spread more new information as an alternative way of framing the issue. This was a policy issue where I was able to build upon the insights developed in my academic work.

The intensity of my two years of policy focus on nuclear proliferation led to a decade of academic concern about the role of nuclear weapons and whether institutional arrangements could help control them. It also led to a fascination with a set of moral questions. How could one justify the possession of nuclear weapons – by the superpowers or by anyone? The question remains relevant to this day, and my answer is reprinted in the essay "NPT: the logic of inequality."[8] This in turn led me to ask broader questions about the role of morality in international politics more generally. Much of what I published in that decade focused on such issues, and I still stand by the views reprinted in "Ethics and foreign policy." The moral dilemmas and framework remain relevant, and a strong case can be made that the moral issues in world politics are likely to become more prominent as the information revolution and democratization spread power to larger numbers of citizens around the world.[9]

Toward the end of the 1980s, as the Soviet nuclear superpower declined, the conventional wisdom was that the United States would follow suit. Paul Kennedy's *The Rise and Fall of the Great Powers* made the bestseller list.[10] Some analysts believed that geo-economics was replacing geo-politics and that Germany and Japan would become the new challengers to the United States in world politics. Some books even predicted a coming war with Japan. I felt these predictions were mistaken, and that the United States had a number of sources of power other than its nuclear status. I argued that the United States was likely to remain on top in military and economic power, but also in a third power resource that I called soft power. I had always been interested in the way that culture and ideas could contribute to power. I developed the concept of soft power to refer to the power of attraction that often grows out of culture and values and is too frequently neglected.

As the essays in Part 2 explain in greater detail, military power and economic power are both examples of "hard" command power that can be used to get others to change their position. Hard power can rest on inducements ("carrots") or threats ("sticks"). But there is also an indirect way to get the outcomes that you want that could be called "the second face of power." A country may obtain its preferred outcomes in world politics because other countries want to follow it, admiring its values, emulating its example, aspiring to its level of prosperity and openness. In this sense, it is just as important to set the agenda and attract others in world politics as it is to force them to change through the threat or use of military or economic weapons. This soft power – getting others to want the outcomes that you want – co-opts people rather than coerces them. The ability to establish preferences tends to be associated with intangible power resources such as an attractive culture, political values and institutions, and policies that are seen as legitimate or having moral authority. If I can get you to want to do what I want, then I do not have to force you to do what you do **not** want. If a country represents values that others want to follow, it will cost less to lead.

I first developed the concept of "soft power" in *Bound to Lead*, a book I wrote in 1989. In the ensuing decade and a half, I have been pleased to see the term enter the public discourse, being used by the U.S. Secretary of State, the British Foreign Minister, political leaders, and editorial writers as well as academics around the world. At the same time, however, I have felt frustrated to see it often misused and trivialized as merely the influence of Coca-Cola and blue jeans. It is far more than that. The ability of a country to attract others arises from its culture, its values and domestic practices, and the perceived legitimacy of its foreign policies.

In the early 1990s I was trying to explore the dimensions of soft power and what was being called "a new world order" when I was again lured into policy work after Bill Clinton's election. When I returned to academia, neo-liberal institutionalism and constructivism had become widely accepted as a legitimate subsidiary approaches. Many scholars were turning their attention to the information revolution and globalization. I felt that the new work on globalization seemed to ignore the earlier literature on interdependence, and that information technology was making soft power more relevant than ever. Keohane and I agreed that much of the writing on these topics was re-inventing the wheel. We regretted the lack of cumulative knowledge in the field, and felt that we should try to relate our earlier work on interdependence and institutions to the new work on globalization and governance. This led to a renewed period of collaboration at the end of the decade, some of which is represented by the essays in Part 4.

At the same time, I felt a personal challenge to update the predictions I had made about American power a decade earlier. I had challenged the then conventional wisdom that the United States was in decline, but I feared that the new conventional wisdom of unipolarity and American domination was mistaken in a different way. While the United States would enjoy unprecedented military power, it was not nearly as dominant on economic issues (where Europe acted collectively). And the information revolution and globalization were empowering non-state actors on transnational issues in ways far greater than anything encountered in the 1970s. The result was a complex three-dimensional set of issues in world politics each possessing a different structure in the distribution of power. While the distribution of power on military issues was unipolar, it made no sense to use traditional terms like unipolarity and hegemony to describe the distribution of power on economic and transnational issues where the United States needed the help of others to obtain its preferred outcomes. I described this world in some detail in *The Paradox of American Power: Why the World's Only Superpower Can't Go It Alone*. The heart of the argument is represented by the essays in Part 2.

As mentioned earlier, much of this change became blindingly clear after September 11, 2001 when a global network of non-state actors attacked the United States. Globalization is more than just an economic phenomenon, and it had been shrinking the natural buffers that distance and two oceans traditionally provided. September 11 also dramatized how the information revolution and technological change have elevated the importance of transnational issues, and empowered non-state actors to play a larger role in world politics. A few decades ago, instantaneous global communications were out of the financial reach of all but governments or large organizations like transnational corporations or the Catholic Church. At the same time, the US and the USSR were secretly spending billions of dollars on overhead space photography. Now commercial one-meter resolution photos are cheaply available to anyone, and the Internet enabled 1500 NGOs to inexpensively coordinate the "battle of Seattle" that disrupted the World Trade Organization.

Most worrying are the effects of these deep trends on terrorism. Terrorism is nothing new, but the "democratization of technology" has been increasing the lethality and agility of terrorists over the past decades, and the trend is likely to continue. In the twentieth century, a pathological individual like Hitler or Stalin needed the power of a government to be able to kill millions of people. If twenty-first-century terrorists get hold of weapons of mass destruction, that power of destruction will for the first time be available to deviant groups and individuals. Traditional state-centric analysts think that punishing states that sponsor terrorism can solve the problem. It can help, but it does not remove the effects of the democratization of technology empowering individuals. After all, Timothy McVeigh in the United States and the Aum Shinrykio in Japan were not state sponsored. This "privatization of war" is not only a major historical change in world politics; the potential impact if terrorists obtained nuclear weapons could drastically alter the nature of modern cities and contemporary civilization.

In the aftermath of the successful American military campaign in Afghanistan, some analysts concluded that the traditional realist view of force and unilateral American responses remained sufficient. The United States should exercise more control and not shrink from the duties of empire. Some have compared the United States to the Roman and British empires.[11]

The temptation to make such comparisons is strong. Not since Rome has one country been so large compared with all other nations as the United States is today. America's defense expenditure is equal to nearly all other countries combined; its economy is larger than the total of the next three countries, and its culture – from Hollywood to Harvard – has greater global reach than any other. America, like Rome, is less likely to succumb in battle with another empire than to suffer a death of a thousand cuts by hordes of new barbarians.

But Americans should resist the temptation to see themselves as the new Romans. The politics of primacy should not be confused with empire. Empire involves greater control over other peoples. The United States is more powerful compared with other countries than Britain was at its imperial peak, but the US has less control over what occurs in other countries than Britain did. For example, when I lived in East Africa in the waning days of the British empire, Kenya's schools, taxes, laws, and elections – not to mention external relations – were controlled by British officials. The United States has no such control outside its borders today.

Devotees of the new imperialism say not to be so literal. "Empire" is merely a metaphor. But the problem with the metaphor is not merely that it distorts American history. More importantly, it will distort the perceptions of those who shape American foreign policy today. The concepts we use have an influence on policy. The metaphor of empire implies a control from Washington that is unrealistic, and reinforces the prevailing strong temptations towards unilateralism.

America in the twenty-first century is the strongest country since Rome, yet it cannot achieve many of its goals by acting alone. In the economic area, international financial stability is important for American prosperity, but the United States needs the cooperation of others to achieve it. The United States cannot achieve its objective of a new trade round without the cooperation of Europe, Japan, and other countries. The information revolution and globalization are creating issues that are inherently multilateral. Global climate change will affect the quality of life in the United States, but three-quarters of the problem arises outside American borders. Diseases originating in distant parts of the globe, such as AIDS or West Nile fever or SARS, cross borders with ease, and must be attacked in cooperation with other countries.

In the current war on terrorism, the American military easily toppled the Taliban government in Afghanistan, but it destroyed only a quarter to a third of the al Qaeda network with its cells in more than fifty countries. Unilateral military solutions would be out of the question because of cells in friendly countries. Success in the war on terrorism requires years of patient civilian cooperation with others in intelligence sharing, police work, and tracing of financial flows. Such a war cannot be won unilaterally with orders from imperial headquarters.

America's disproportionate size at this stage in world politics means that the United States will often have to take the lead – witness the campaign against terrorism. But the American preponderance of power will be generally be more acceptable and legitimate in the eyes of other countries when its policies are embedded in multilateral frameworks. Sometimes the largest country must take the lead because it is difficult for others to do so, but it matters greatly whether it appears to be acting on narrow self-interest or a broad approach that incorporates the interests of others.

American success in dealing with the new challenges will depend not just on its military and economic might, but on the soft power of its culture and values, and on pursuing policies that make others feel that they have been consulted and their interests taken into account. As the German editor Joseph Joffe has said, "unlike centuries past, when war was the great arbiter, today the most interesting types of power do not come out of the barrel of a gun. . . . Today there is a much bigger payoff in 'getting others to want what you want,' and that has to do with cultural attraction and ideology and agenda setting and holding out big prizes for cooperation, like the vastness and sophistication of the American market. On that gaming table, China, Russia and Japan, even the West Europeans, cannot match the pile of chips held by the United States."[12] The United States could squander this soft power by heavy-handed unilateralism.

The world has changed dramatically since the first of these essays was written. In three decades, what Realists had once been dismissed as marginal clutter is now part of the central focus of analysts and practitioners. Analysts and policy makers are today learning to deal with matters that were largely regarded as peripheral when I entered the field of international politics. Some traditional realists resist the changes and try to squeeze the new reality into old models. Other analysts neglect the past as they breathlessly search for new concepts. Yet some of the old concepts remain relevant and many of the moral dilemmas surrounding nuclear and other weapons of mass destruction are more relevant than ever today. The purpose of looking at the essays reprinted here is to help accelerate that search, to see what of the explorations of the past can contribute to an understanding of the present. Some wheels need to be reinvented; some merely updated and repaired. If these essays help in that process, their publication will be warranted. In the final section, I end on a personal note. By doing so, I hope to provide younger readers with an illustration of how academic ideas, political opportunities, and serendipity become interwoven over a lifetime. I wish them well in their own explorations.

Notes

1   E. H. Carr, *The Twenty Years' Crisis, 1919–1939: An Introduction to the Study of International Relations* (New York: Palgrave, 2001); Hans Morgenthau, *Politics Among Nations: The Struggle for Power and Peace* (New York: McGraw-Hill, 1985).

2 The details are described in Yoichi Funibashi, *Alliance Adrift* (New York: Council on Foreign Relations Press, 1999).

3 See Ernst Haas, *The Obsolescence of Regional Integration Theory* (Berkley, CA: Institute of International Studies, University of California, 1975).

4 Robert O. Keohane and Joseph S. Nye, *Transnational Relations and World Politics* (Cambridge, MA: Harvard University Press, 1972).

5 National Security Strategy of the United States, September 2002 (http://www. whitehouse.gov/nsc/nss.html).

6 Robert O. Keohane and Joseph S. Nye, Jr., *Power and Interdependence* (Boston: Little, Brown, 1977).

7 Stanley Hoffmann, Robert Keohane and Joseph Nye, *After the Cold War: International Institutions and State Strategies in Europe 1989–1991* (Cambridge, MA: Harvard University Press, 1993).

8 Also relevant is Joseph S. Nye, *Nuclear Ethics* (New York: The Free Press, 1986).

9 John Arquilla and David Ronfeldt make this point in *The Emergence of Noopolitik: Toward an American Information Strategy* (Santa Monica: RAND, 1999).

10 Paul Kennedy, *The Rise and Fall of the Great Powers: Economic Change and Military Conflict from 1500 to 2000* (New York: Random House, 1987).

11 See, for example, Andrew Bacevich, *American Empire: The Realities and Consequences of US Diplomacy* (Cambridge, MA: Harvard University Press, 2002).

12 Josef Joffe, "America the Inescapable," *Portland Oregonian*, June 22, 1997, p. D1.

Part 1

The power and limits of realism

2 Old wars and future wars*

Causation and prevention

History is the study of events that have happened only once; political science is the effort to generalize about them. These caricatures sometimes seem an apt description of mutual reactions when members of the two professions discuss the origins and prevention of major wars. It might be amusing were it not that the next major war could be the last. Nuclear war is too serious to leave to either historians or political scientists alone.

As Kenneth Waltz argues, conflict may be endemic in human behavior, but war has its origins in social organization. Nonetheless, general theories of the causes of war can be misleading. "It is assumed, for instance, that there is a class of events involving human behavior that can be legitimately subsumed under a single term 'war.' True, the events have a common observable factor – organized violence perpetrated by groups of people upon each other. But that is near the extent of the commonality."[1] This volume does not search for a common set of causes of all violence from tribal vendettas to world wars. Instead, it focuses on the upper end of the scale.

Since the development of the modern state system in Europe some four centuries ago, there have been ten general wars involving a majority of the major powers and a high level of battle deaths.[2] Some of these wars stand out in terms of their consequences for the hierarchy and structure of the system of states. Robert Gilpin refers to them as hegemonic wars. Historians do not agree on the exact set of such wars, but at a minimum most would include the Thirty Years' War (1618–1648); the French Revolutionary and Napoleonic wars (1792–1815); and the two world wars of the twentieth century (1914–1918, 1939–1945). Each of these wars is discussed below as well as the earlier wars of the Ottoman Empire for control of eastern Europe. By looking at major wars of the past, we learn about the potential causes and prevention of major war in our own time.

Historians and political scientists tend to approach this task differently. Political scientists strive to generalize and develop theory; historians probe the layers of complexity and the potential pitfalls of overly simple analogies. Each has strengths and weaknesses. Poor political science runs the risk of false simplicity; poor history describes causality through irrelevant detail and confused complexity.

Some theory is unavoidable. Like John Maynard Keynes' practical man of affairs, unknowingly the mental prisoner of some scribbler whose name he has long forgotten, so the historian faced with an infinite supply of facts must follow some general principle to select and make order of them. As Waltz argues, a theory separates a particular domain (such as international politics) from its surroundings and gives a picture of the connections among its parts. Bueno de Mesquita adds that such mental constructs specify a simplified, ordered view of reality in order to reveal internally consistent and externally useful general principles.

There are different views about how to judge theory in the social sciences. The model of the natural sciences is not fully applicable where there is no laboratory to hold variables constant, and in which human choices are not fully predictable. Nonetheless, one can speak of the range and power of different theories. Theories of limited range cover a narrow domain of cases or a limited period. Their generalizations hold only within carefully specified limits. The explanatory power of a theory is a more complex concept and involves two dimensions often at odds with each other: parsimony and descriptive fit. Parsimony is the ability to say a lot with a little. It is the principle of Occam's razor: shave away unnecessary detail. However, parsimony is only one dimension of power. Inventing parsimonious explanations is easy; inventing parsimonious explanations with a reasonable descriptive fit is rare. Explanatory power requires accounting for behavior with few anomalies. Since theory (by definition) is not pure description, there will always be problems of descriptive fit. Some anomalies are inevitable. The most powerful theories are the least procrustean in their treatment of anomalies. They also encompass more corroborated empirical content than their alternatives.[3]

Successful prediction is one sign of a powerful theory, but determining success is often ambiguous. When theories predict general categories of behavior rather than specific events, there is room for interpretation of how successful (or unsuccessful) a theory has been. For the same reasons, it is difficult to falsify such theories. Proponents challenge interpretations and introduce auxiliary hypotheses to save their theories. Yet a good theory should specify conditions which, in principle, could falsify it. For example, Darwinian theory is not good at predicting the evolution of particular species, but the discovery of mammal bones in the Precambrian strata of rocks would falsify it.

Most theories in social science are of limited range and modest power. In part the weakness of the theories reflects the nature of the domain. As a political philosopher has counseled, "A rational social scientist might well learn to relax and to enjoy the rich diversity and uncertainty that mark his calling. . . ."[4] As Maier argues, post-Enlightenment historians do not seek to identify the constant traits sought by Enlightenment historians or by some contemporary political scientists. Instead, they map complicated and unanticipated causal chains, not foreseeable individual reactions. They see history as a temporal process of development, rather than as a warehouse of examples. This indeterminacy does not make history useless to policymakers.

For history to provide insights applicable to present conduct, it must explain why other outcomes did not prevail – not in the sense that they could not, but in the sense that they might well have. . . . By exploring what conditions would have been needed for alternative outcomes to materialize, history can assume a heuristic role. It thereby suggests how freedom of action is foreclosed or seized.[5]

Such a method of counterfactual argument cannot assign precise probabilities, but it does raise the historian out of total immersion in the particularity of one time and place. This counterfactual reasoning is also an area of common ground with political scientists. Such "post-diction" represents a means (in the absence of a laboratory) of estimating the range and power of theories.

In practice, there is a long tradition of theorizing about international politics and the causes of war. Thucydides' *History of the Peloponnesian War* was more than a descriptive account of battles. Gilpin discusses Thucydides' interest in setting forth a general account of how such wars occur. This theory led Thucydides to select and emphasize certain facts rather than others.[6] Thomas Hobbes was indebted to Thucydides and his focus on power. Indeed, the preponderant school of thinking – both academic and practical – in modern European history has stressed the fundamentally anarchic nature of the international system and the struggles and balances of power among states that result. This "realist" tradition became dominant in the United States after 1945. Theorists such as Hans Morgenthau were well read in history and wanted to warn their countrymen against reverting to the idealism and isolationism that they believed helped to bring on World War II.

As Waltz describes Morgenthau never developed a fully coherent theory, and there are a number of ambiguities intrinsic to classical realism. Terms such as power and balance are used loosely. Some theorists hold that war is more likely when power is nearly balanced, whereas others argue that it is more likely when one side has a preponderance of power. Still others point out that the balance of power is a principle for maintaining the independence of states, not peace.[7] These articles represent theories which refine different aspects of the mainstream realist tradition. They all focus on states that act rationally in response to incentives created by their environment – defined as the international system of states. In that sense, they are analogous to microeconomic theories in which firms respond rationally to market incentives.

Waltz's neorealist theory portrays power as a means rather than a goal deeply rooted in human nature. It predicts that states will act to balance the power of others in order to preserve their independence under the anarchic situation in which they find themselves. It does not try to predict particular wars, but the general propensity to war. It focuses attention on the structure (distribution of power) of the system. Waltz argues that bipolar systems are more stable and peaceful because they involve less uncertainty than multipolar systems. The opponents and their relative power are clearer, and shifts in alliances make less difference.

Waltz's theory has the virtue of broad range and great parsimony, but its explanatory power is less impressive than might first appear. The theory is static. Since changes in the structure of the system are rare, other causes must be invoked to explain most wars.[8] Waltz defines bipolarity very narrowly as involving the power of the two largest states, not two tightly knit coalitions. By this definition, neither the Greek city-state system at the time of the Peloponnesian War nor Europe in 1914 was bipolar. Historians are hard pressed to find cases before 1945 to test the theory. Further, as Waltz admits, the peace of the bipolar world since 1945 owes a great deal to the existence of nuclear weapons, which he calls a feature of the units in the system rather than its structure. Nonetheless, because diffusion of power is occurring and a multipolar system may evolve in the future, Waltz's theory focuses attention on important questions about the propensity to make war under such conditions.

Bueno de Mesquita's theory also had broad range and great parsimony. Moreover, there is something commonsensical about an expected utility theory that says states go to war when they expect to do better than by remaining at peace. This explanation is not the same as saying that states go to war when they expect to win. As Scott Sagan shows, Japan chose war in 1941 not because it expected to win, but because even a modest prospect of success was better than sure defeat if the American oil embargo was allowed to take its course. By refusing to assume that states have similar reactions to risk, Bueno de Mesquita is able to resolve differences among realists about whether a balance or a preponderance of power is more likely to produce war. Power itself is neither a necessary nor a sufficient condition for a rational realist to choose war or peace. The distribution of power (Waltz's structure) has no direct bearing on the likelihood of war independent of different utilities.

Bueno de Mesquita admits some limitations to his theory. He aggregates utilities at the level of the state, but they may not remain consistent under the pull of domestic politics. And leaders may have different psychological reactions to taking risks to avoid losses as compared with achieving gains even though the expected utility is the same. Moreover, in strategic interaction, states may bluff rather than act on their true utilities. Even more fundamental is the debate over the power of the theory. For some historians, his use of what he calls "stylized facts" compresses the temporal flow of history and represents parsimony purchased at the expense of descriptive fit. Others argue that the theory lacks power because it says so little about where utilities come from and how preferences are shaped and change over time. It says little about what variables of international politics are relevant. In a sense, it is not a theory of international politics at all, but a model borrowed from microeconomics and applied to international politics. If one believes that the rational-actor assumptions of microeconomics have not done all that well when applied to macroeconomic policy, then one might be skeptical about the promised power of the theory even if problems such as intransitive preferences and non-rational psychological responses are overcome. Nonetheless, the microeconomic metaphor directs the attention of historians to important questions about rationality and war.

Gilpin theorizes about hegemonic wars resulting from changes in the preponderance of power as a result of uneven growth among states. Essentially, he updates Thucydides' variant of realism. The theories he develops are dynamic but incomplete. They deal with wars which have major structural effects on the international system, but, as Gilpin points out, they do not specify whether the nation in decline or the challenger is likely to start the war, nor what the consequences will be. Nor is it easy to identify hegemonic wars in such a way that the argument is nontautological. Although Gilpin sees hegemonic wars occurring at roughly 100-year intervals, he is skeptical of the causation adduced in cyclical theories.

Gilpin's own argument is that states act rationally to try to change the system to advance their interests in response to shifts in the distribution of power, but unanticipated consequences can give rise to hegemonic wars that no one wanted. This admission of uncertainty improves the descriptive fit, but weakens the parsimony and overall explanatory power of the theory. Given the effects of uneven growth and the role of declining power in the onset of World War I, as described by Williamson, Gilpin's theory also brings attention to important issues. But a powerful theory must explain why and when dogs do not bark as well as when they do. A powerful hegemonic transition theory would explain the absence of war between the United States and Britain in the 1890s and the relatively pacific withdrawal of Spain after the seventeenth century. It would also suggest what to watch for in the relationship between the United States and East Asia in coming decades.

Jack Levy, Robert Jervis, and George Quester concentrate on perceptions and domestic politics. They make no claims to powerful or parsimonious general theories. As Levy points out, the complexity of the linkage between domestic political factors and the causes of war has made historians feel at home with their line of work but has discouraged broad theorizing by political scientists. Marxist and liberal theories about economic structure and war have not held up well under the test of events. A version of liberal theory that explains why democracies do not fight *each other* is interesting but limited in range.[9] Scapegoat theories relating internal conflict to external conflict have generally been poorly formulated and tested.

Jervis explicitly admits that there are so many kinds of misperceptions with so many different effects that it is impossible to develop an overal theory of misperception as a cause of war. Nonetheless, he argues that misperception often plays a large role, and that certain modest propositions can be developed. Many historians agree. Blainey has argued that "it is not the actual distribution or balance of power which is vital; it is rather the way in which national leaders *think* that power is distributed. . . . War is a dispute about the measurement of power. War marks the choice of a new set of weights and measures."[10] Excessive military optimism is frequently associated with the outbreak of war. Jervis points out that it is especially dangerous when coupled with political and diplomatic pessimism. Jervis' observation makes a useful auxiliary hypothesis to the power transition theories that Gilpin addresses.

Quester's discussion of brinkmanship and crises of resolve is an illustration of how both perceptions and the logic of war change sequentially under certain conditions. Both parties may start out in a game such as "chicken," in which both are better off if there is no war. But the process of crisis escalation and the belief that war is inevitable and imminent may transform the game into one of Prisoner's Dilemma, in which it is better to strike first than to be struck first. As Quester points out, wars of attrition or contests of endurance encourage the "rationality of irrationality." Each side pretends indifference to disaster in order to win the contest of resolve in the game of chicken. But there is danger that the pretense could become reality as the game changes or unforeseen events occur. Charles Maier and Bueno de Mesquita describe how each step in War War I seemed to be a rational choice to the participants as the sequence unfolded. As Maier puts it, "From one point of view the war was 'irrational,' risking national unity, dynasties, and even bourgeois society. Many of the European statesmen . . . claimed to understand that such long-term stakes were involved . . . they did not think they were in a position to act upon these long-term forebodings. Rather, they saw themselves confronted with decisions about the next step."[11] Although each step may be rational in a procedural sense of relating means to ends, the substantive outcome may be so distorted that one should refer to it as irrational.

None of the political theories discussed above is very powerful, but each suggests interesting questions for historians to consider as they map the complex causality of major wars and try to structure counterfactual arguments that illuminate the range of choice and the limits that statesmen face. In addition, the various theories suggest different attitudes and problems regarding the prevention of a major nuclear war.

The implications of Waltz and Bueno de Mesquita's theories are optimistic. For Waltz, the stability of the bipolar structure is reinforced by the prudence which nuclear weapons engender at the level of the individual states. In terms of expected utility theory, a major nuclear war should be very difficult to start. There would be no political goals which leaders could hold commensurate with the absolute magnitude of destruction that their nations would suffer. This situation is the crystal-ball effect.[12] In 1914, if one could have shown Europe's leaders a crystal ball with a picture of the devastation in 1918, they might have drawn back from war rather than become trapped in the sequence that Maier describes. An elementary knowledge of the physical effects of nuclear weapons serves as today's crystal ball.

Gilpin agrees that a nuclear balance of terror has created a new basis of international order among the superpowers in contrast with the earlier balance of power. But he argues that change in the nature of warfare has not necessarily altered the nature of international politics. Struggles for hegemony continue, and one cannot rule out the possibility of hegemonic war in the nuclear age. "The theory of hegemonic war does not argue that statesmen 'will' a great war; the great wars of history were seldom predicted, and their course has never been foreseen."[13] Jervis, Quester, and others tend to reinforce Gilpin's cautionary note. Misperceptions and situational irrationality can occur in the nuclear age. Crystal balls can be clouded by misperception or shattered by accident.

How likely are such dangers? Howard argues that it is difficult to find any historical cases of accidental war. Blainey argues that unintended war is also rare. It is not enough to say that "neither side wanted war." Like Bueno de Mesquita, he argues that "every preference for war or peace is attached to a price. . . . What was so often unintentional about war was not the decision to fight but the outcome of the fighting."[14] In one sense, Blainey is correct. Someone decides. There are no purely accidental wars. But the important questions are how the preferences for war or peace are shaped, and how the compression of time in nuclear crises may magnify the effect of nonrational factors.

A nuclear war is unlikely to start by accident or by purely rational calculation. But the intersection of rational and nonrational factors may greatly increase risks in a crisis.[15] Nonrational factors include psychological stress clouding judgment (witness Joseph Stalin in June 1941); organizational complexity (for example, the straying of a U-2 reconnaissance flight over the Soviet Union at the height of the Cuban missile crisis); misdirected or misunderstood communications; and accidents (which may have greater effects on perceptions in a nuclear crisis when there is less time to correct them). Under the influence of such nonrational factors, situationally constrained rationality could persuade a leader who believed nuclear war to be imminent and inevitable that it would be better to strike first than be struck first.

The fact that such scenarios are possible and that the consequences would be devastating lead one back to the proposition that major war in the nuclear age is too important to leave to the political scientists or historians alone. Their strengths and weaknesses complement each other as they turn to history as a substitute for a laboratory. Historians should pay heed to questions about rationality, perceptions, crises, and power transitions raised by some of the most interesting political theorists. Political scientists must pay heed when historians challenge their stylized facts, warn against the loss of temporal context and sequences, and point out the dangers of mistaking theory for reality. Both need to cooperate in formulating the counterfactual arguments that can illuminate the range and limits of choice for policy.

Notes

* This was written as the introduction to a set of essays on war. I am indebted to Stephan Haggard, Robert O. Keohane, Charles S. Maier, and Robert I. Rotberg for comments on an earlier draft.

1 Anatol Rapoport, "Approaches to Peace Research," in Martin Nettleship, R. Dale Givens, and Anderson Nettleship (eds.), *War: Its Causes and Correlates* (The Hague, 1975), 44.

2 Jack S. Levy, "Theories of General War," *World Politics*, XXXVII (1985), 372.

3 Imre Lakatos, "Falsification and the Methodology of Scientific Research Programmes," in *idem* and Alan Musgrave (eds.), *Criticism and the Growth of Knowledge* (London, 1970), 91–180; Harry Eckstein, "Case Study and Theory in Political Science," and Donald J. Moon, "The Logic of Political Inquiry," in Fred Greenstein and Nelson Polsby (eds.), *Handbook of Political Science* (Reading, Mass., 1975), I, 131–209; VII, 79–138.

4 Judith N. Shklar, "Squaring the Hermeneutic Circle," *Social Research*, LIII (1986), 473.

5 Charles S. Maier, "Wargames: 1914–1919," *Journal of Interdisciplinary History*, XVIII (1988), 821.

6 Donald Kagan, *The Outbreak of the Peloponnesian War* (Ithaca, 1969).

7 Edward Vose Gulick, *Europe's Classical Balance of Power* (New York, 1955), 30.

8 See Robert O. Keohane (ed.), *Neorealism and its Critics* (New York, 1986), 158–203.

9 Michael Doyle, "Kant, Liberal Legacies, and Foreign Affairs," *Philosophy and Public Affairs*, XII (1983), 205–235, 323–353.

10 A. Geoffrey Blainey, *The Causes of War* (New York, 1973), 114.
11 Maier, "Wargames," 840.
12 Joseph S. Nye, Jr., *Nuclear Ethics* (New York, 1986), 61.
13 Robert Gilpin, "The Theory of Hegemonic War," *Journal of Interdisciplinary History*, XVIII (1988), 611–612.
14 Michael Howard, *The Causes of War* (Cambridge, Mass., 1984), 12. Blainey, *Causes of War*, 15, 144.
15 See Graham Allison, Albert Carnesale, and Nye (eds.), *Hawks, Doves, and Owls* (New York, 1985), 206–222.

3   Neorealism and neoliberalism*

International relations theory is constrained by the fact that history provides a poor substitute for a laboratory. In world politics, a relatively small number of states play major roles, along with many other entities that seek to influence events. Even if one focuses on state behavior, one is confronted by few independent events and by multiple causes of behavior at different levels of analysis. Furthermore, strategic interaction is inherently indeterminate, and states often have incentives to deceive observers. To use an analogy from another social science, multiple causality makes some aspects of international relations more like macroeconomics than like microeconomics, and strategic indeterminacy means that the relevant analogy in microeconomics would be the troubled area of oligopoly theory.

Moreover, most theorists of international relations suffer from being in the middle of events, rather than viewing them from a distance. Thus it is not surprising that international relations theory has always been strongly affected by current political concerns. This is true even for the Realists with their parsimonious efforts to state eternal truths. Thucydides, the founding father of Realism, presented a structural account of the origins of the Peloponnesian War in part because of the lessons he wished to teach his fellow citizens.[1] When Hans J. Morgenthau wrote his post-war classic, *Politics Among Nations*, he was clearly intent on instructing *his* fellow citizens about the importance of avoiding the idealist and isolationist fantasies of the interwar period. Even the neorealist structural theories of Kenneth Waltz can best be read as exhortations to policymakers and fellow citizens about how they *ought* to respond to the structure of power rather than as accurate accounts of how the two superpowers behave.

The changing context of theory

In the early 1970s, many theorists, reflecting current concerns, overreacted to the traditional theories of Realism. There was widespread repugnance to the Vietnam War, and detente seemed to reduce the importance of the nuclear competition. At the same time, international trade grew more rapidly than world product. Transnational corporations not only developed patterns of international production, but in some instances played dramatic political roles as well. All this occurred against a backdrop of declining U.S. economic predominance – from one-third to less than one-quarter of world product. President Nixon and Secretary of State Kissinger spoke of the development of a five-power world, and futurologists such as Herman Kahn predicted the imminent arrival of a multipolar international system.[2]

On top of all this came the oil crisis of 1973. Some very weak states extracted enormous resources from the strong. Even Hans Morgenthau described what he called an unprecedented divorce of military and economic power based on the control of raw materials.[3] The vulnerability of the Western societies at a period of high commodity prices encouraged many of the less developed countries to believe that a greater transformation of power had occurred than was actually the case. A number of theorists reflected these concerns. Among the modernist writers of the 1970s, a representative view was that

> the forces now ascendant appear to be leaning toward a global society without a dominant structure of cooperation and conflict – a *polyarchy* in which nation-states, subnational groups, and transnational special interests and communities would all be vying for the support and loyalty of individuals, and conflicts would have to be resolved primarily on the basis of ad hoc bargaining in a shifting context of power relationships.[4]

By the late 1970s the mood began to change both in the United States and in the United Nations. East-West concerns started to supplant North-South issues at the top of foreign policy agendas. The experience of the Carter administration reflects the changes in American opinion: while campaigning in 1976, Jimmy Carter promised to reduce the defense budget, but by 1980 his position was closer to that of his rival, Reagan, than to his own previous position. The election of Ronald Reagan to the American presidency accentuated these trends. American policy focused on East-West confrontation and scaled down North-South issues and the role of multilateral institutions. The defense budget increased in real terms for five straight years, and the United States became more willing to use military force, albeit against extremely weak states such as Grenada and Libya. Arms control was downgraded and the modernization of nuclear forces was seen as restoring an "edge" for additional utility of military force. This shifting agenda of world politics saw a resurgence of Realist analysis, for history seemed to have vindicated the Realist model.

While some analysts in the 1970s tended to overstate the obsolescence of the nation-state, the decline of force, and the irrelevance of security concerns, some in the early 1980s unduly neglected the role of transnational actors and economic interdependence. Contrary to the tone of much political rhetoric and some political analyses, the world of the 1980s is not a return to the world of the 1950s. Just as the decline of American power was exaggerated in the 1970s, so was the restoration of American power in the 1980s. Looking carefully at military and economic indices of power resources, one notes that there has been a far greater change in psychology and mood than in these indicators of power resources. The diffusion of power, as measured by shares in world trade or world product, continues. Economic interdependence, as measured by vulnerability to supply shocks, has eased in a period of slack commodity markets, but this could change if markets tighten again and growth of economic transactions continues. Sensitivity to exchange-rate fluctuations has remained high. The costs of the great powers' use of force seem higher than in the 1950s – measured, for instance, by the ease with which the U.S. overthrew governments in Central America and Iran then as contrasted with the 1980s. Moreover, despite rhetoric, relations between the superpowers do not show a return to the Cold War period. Not only are alliances looser, but transactions are higher, and relations between the superpowers reflect a fair degree of "learning" in the nuclear area.[5]

Realism and Liberalism

In a sense, the contrast between the 1970s and the 1980s is merely the latest instance of a recurring dialectic between the two main strands in what has been called the classical tradition of international relations theory. Realism has been the dominant strand;[6] the second is the Liberal or Grotian tradition that tends to stress the impact of domestic and international society, interdependence, and international institutions. In their simplest forms, Liberal theories have been easily discredited. The proposition that the gains from commercial transactions would overcome the problems inherent in the security dilemma and make war too expensive were belied in 1914. Hopes that a system of international law and organization could provide collective security, which would replace the need for self-help inherent in the security dilemma, were disappointed by 1939. Nonetheless, the sharp disagreement between Realism and Liberal theories is overstated. In fact, the two approaches can be complementary. Sophisticated versions of Liberal theory address the manner in which interactions among states and the development of international norms interact with domestic politics of the states in an international system so as to transform the way in which states define their interests. Transnational and interstate interactions and norms lead to new definitions of interests, as well as to new coalition possibilities for different interests within states.

How states define their interests, and how their interests change, has always been a weak area in Realist theory. One of the most thought-provoking questions in international relations is how states learn. How do national interests become defined, and how do those definitions change? Can cooperation be learned? Realist theories maintain that states learn by responding to structural changes in their environment; to put it in game-theory terms, they adjust their behavior to changes in the payoff matrix. When mutual interests or a long shadow of the future suggest that rewards for cooperation are great, states may adopt new strategies in pursuit of their interests. In that case, Realists admit that cooperation can be learned. Although this is sometimes a satisfactory and parsimonious explanation of changing state behavior, it is often incomplete because it says little about how interests themselves are formulated or redefined. It does not show why the same situation may be perceived in totally different ways by successive governments or different leaders. A Bismarck, a Kaiser, and a Hitler can formulate different answers to similar geopolitical situations. Nor does Realist theory note how groups within societies can use partners in transnational coalitions or transnational norms and institutions to advance or retard the learning of new interests by their own governments.

Realist theory is better at explaining interactions than interests. A theory of interests defined solely in terms of power is an impoverished theory of interests. Here Liberalism can help. The more sophisticated variants of Liberal theory provide a useful supplement to Realism by directing attention to the ways in which domestic and international factors interact to change states' definitions of their interests. To say that states act in their self-interest is merely tautological (or "change" is reduced to merely a change in means) unless we have a reasonable account of how such interests are perceived and redefined. Both Realism and Liberalism can contribute to such an account.

The major developments in the Liberal tradition of international relations theory in the post-1945 period occurred in studies of regional integration. These studies did not explicitly refer to classical Liberalism; they were generally called "neofunctionalist." Nevertheless, their focus was clearly on issues emphasized in the Liberal tradition. Karl Deutsch concentrated on the development of pluralistic security communities – groups of states that developed reliable expectations of peaceful relations and thereby overcame the security dilemma that Realists see as characterizing international politics. Ernst Haas focused on the uniting of Europe and the transformation of the Franco-German hostility into a postwar economic and political community. Subsequent scholars extended these perspectives on economic, social, and political interdependence and integration to other regions.[7] What these studies had in common was a focus on the ways in which increased transactions and contacts changed attitudes and transnational coalition opportunities, and the ways in which institutions helped to foster such interaction. In short, they emphasized the political processes of learning and of redefining national interests, as encouraged by institutional frameworks and regimes.

In a sense, the development of regional integration theory outstripped the development of regional communities. Predicted changes materialized more slowly than had been expected, which may account for the declining academic interest in the subject during the 1970s. The transformation of Western Europe into a pluralistic security community is real, however, and many of the insights from integration theory were transferred in the early 1970s to the growing and broader dimensions of international economic interdependence. Studies in transnational relations and interdependence broadened conceptions of how national interests are learned and changed. Some studies explicitly addressed the conditions under which assumptions of Realism were sufficient, or needed to be supplemented by a more complex model of change.[8] Rather than focusing primarily on formal and universalistic organizations such as the United Nations, they devoted much attention to the role of international institutions. The concept of regime was borrowed from international law and broadened to incorporate the whole range of norms, rules, and procedures that constrain states' behavior and around which the actors' expectations converge within a given issue.[9] A rich set of studies applied the concept of regimes to a broad range of behavior in international political economy. But in the climate of the early 1980s, it seemed that the Liberal legacy was relevant only to the peripheral literature on political economy and had little to contribute to the central theory of the field. Kenneth Waltz's *Theory of International Politics*, published in 1979, was a well-timed and elegant restatement of Realism that explicitly cast doubt on the relevance of the writings on interdependence.[10]

The two books reviewed here provide a good opportunity to look at the latest turns in the classic dialectic between Realism and Liberalism. Richard Rosecrance's *The Rise of the Trading State* is clearly in the Liberal tradition. Rosecrance argues that an open trading system offers states ways to transform their positions through economic growth rather than through military conquest. All states can benefit from the enhanced growth. "The basic thrust of trade today is entirely different from what it was in the 1830s, the 1880s, and the 1930s" (p. 227). What is different in the world since 1945 "is that a peaceful trading is enjoying much greater efficacy than ever before. . . ." The main thesis of this book is that a new "trading world of international relations offers the possibility of escaping . . . a vicious cycle and finding new patterns of cooperation among national states" (p. ix).

Robert O. Keohane, in *Neorealism and Its Critics*, features four core chapters of Waltz's influential book and four criticisms of that work. In addition, he includes Waltz's first published reply to his critics. It is rare to have such clear intellectual dialogue in a single volume, and the whole issue is nicely framed by the editor's introductory essay.

Neorealist theory

As Keohane points out, the significance of Waltz's work is not in elaborating a new line of theory, but in the systematization of Realism, which Robert W. Cox (one of the critics) has termed "neorealism." While Hans J. Morgenthau may be the most influential of the postwar Realists, his aspirations to create a science of international politics were marred by inconsistency in his use of the concepts of power and balance. Moreover, by basing international politics on human nature's drive for power, Morgenthau explained too little by explaining too much. Human nature does not adequately account for variation.

Waltz provides a more elegant theoretical basis for Realism. He avoids references to humans pursuing power as an end; pursuit of power as a means is sufficient for his theory. Balance-of-power behavior by states is predicted from the structure of the international system. A system is a set of interacting units having behavioral regularities and identity over time. Its structure defines the ordering of its parts. Structure involves an ordering principle, specification of the functions of different parts, and the distribution of capabilities. In international politics, the ordering principle is anarchy, interpreted as the absence of a higher government above states. The specification of differentiation drops out because states perform similar functions. Thus, the distribution of capabilities (multipolarity, bipolarity) predicts variations in states' balance-of-power behavior. Waltz provides not merely a systemic theory to predict the behavior of the units (states), but a parsimonious *structural* systemic theory.

In a sense, Waltz did for the classical Realists what they never did for them-selves. His structural theory provides a simple deductive basis for what was hitherto a heterogeneous set of views about the importance of power politics. In the eyes of the critics, however, Waltz's virtues and faults are two sides of the same coin. Parsimony has been purchased at too high a price. Robert Cox and Richard K. Ashley complain that Waltz's neorealism has sacrificed the interpre-tive richness of classical Realism as a critical theory in order to transform it into a positivistic problem-solving theory. Although that may be true, neither essay provides a compelling alternative, and Waltz in his reply is quite happy to let their remarks roll off his back.

Keohane and John G. Ruggie launch more telling criticisms. Keohane points out that Waltz's spare structural definition of system ignores international economic processes and institutions that can also have strong effects on states' behavior. Ruggie argues that Waltz has not only ignored changes in the density of interactions in systems, but has been too quick in assuming that the differentiation in units can be dropped as a characteristic of the structure of the international system. In the short term, states may be the dominant units and play a similar functional role, but over long periods other units may grow in importance, and roles may alter. Ruggie points to the evolution of the concept of territoriality at the end of the feudal era to illustrate such generative changes, and argues that Waltz's theory is too static to explain such changes.

Waltz replies that "a structural theory of international politics can fix ranges of outcomes and identify general tendencies. . . . We cannot hope to predict spe-cific outcomes" (p. 344). He would not deny the importance of change at the unit level. "Realist theory by itself can handle some, but not all, of the prob-lems that concern us. . . . Yet some successful predictions can be made without paying attention to states" (p. 331). Structural analyses "tell us a small num-ber of big and important things" (p. 329). If we add more variables, theoretical acuity gives way to rich and dense description. Many unit-level factors, such as density of interactions, demographic trends, resource constraints, national ideolo-gies, and political systems, can affect systemic outcomes. Indeed, in the case of nuclear weapons, "a unit-level change has much diminished a structural effect" (p. 327). But it is a mistake to mingle structural and unit levels. Just as "economists get along quite well with separate theories of markets and firms" (p. 340), we shall have to get along with separate theories of international politics and of states.

Waltz has a valid point about the selectivity of theory and the costs of mixing unit and structural characteristics. But his reply to his critics is not entirely sat-isfactory. First, as Keohane points out in his Introduction, many economists are unhappy about the disjunction between the assumptions of microeconomics and what is known about the behavior of firms. Moreover, oligopoly theory tends to be indeterminate, and efforts to establish a rational-expectations micro-basis for macroeconomics have been problematic. In the words of one economist, the danger for a clinical profession is that "the models become more real than more explicitly descriptive reality."[11]

Second, Waltz accuses Ruggie of reductionism – the explanation of the whole by explaining the behavior of the parts. That is neither good nor bad *per se*. In a parsimonious systemic explanation, the behavior of the parts is handled by assumptions of rationality and the constraining conditions produced by the structure of the system. "Socialization and competition are two aspects of a process by which the variety of behavior and outcomes is reduced." Systems theories explain why different units behave similarly; unit theories explain why different units behave differently despite similar placement in a system. But Waltz's own assignment of characteristics to the systemic and unit levels seems odd. It is easy to understand why characteristics of a particular leader or political culture or domestic regime fit at the unit level. In his words, "a theory about foreign policy is a theory at the national level."[12] But why are demographic trends, transnational flows, and military technology that affect all (or many) states assigned to the unit level? It is particularly odd to see nuclear technology described as a unit characteristic that has had "system-wide" pacific effects (p. 327). Waltz has no way of knowing whether the vaunted stability of the bipolar system is caused by a structural or a unit-level characteristic. Moreover, by assigning everything except the distribution of capabilities to the unit level, that category becomes a dumping ground hindering theory building at anything but the structural level. The result may be theoretical parsimony, but parsimony is not the only way by which one judges good theory. Good theory also requires a good explanatory fit.

A third problem with Waltz's reply to his critics relates to his handling of false predictions. Waltz correctly states that a few false predictions do not falsify a theory. He admits that he will often need to supplement his sparse neorealist theory with foreign policy explanations in order to account for anomalous cases. But sometimes his handling of anomalies runs the risk of being retrogressive in Lakatos's terms – i.e., it explains less and directs researchers away from new information.[13] In response to Keohane's evidence that Canada, a weak state, has often prevailed over the United States, Waltz introduces a power-activation hypothesis: "I suspect that American officials hardly cared about the outcomes or even noticed what they might be" (p. 333). But aside from the danger of tautology, such a reply ignores the evidence that the cases Keohane cites were at the presidential level, and that some, such as oil trade in 1974, were highly visible and politicized.

Some anomalies are forgiven for any theory that has a broad explanatory power and that points to the discovery of new empirical information. But Waltz's theory does not score well on those criteria: it describes a system as stable if it remains anarchic and there is no consequential change in the number of political units. By this definition, the multipolar system was stable for 300 years until World War II reduced it to the current bipolar system, which has been stable because no third state has been able to develop capabilities comparable to those of the United States and the Soviet Union.[14] But this portrayal of history by the theory leaves an enormous number of important changes unaccounted for, and lends credence to the charge that it is too static. There are so few strands in the web of Waltz's theoretical net that even very big fish slip through it. The change from a flexible alliance system to two rigid alliances before 1914 is not a shift from multipolarity to bipolarity for Waltz. Only the strength of single units counts in measuring bipolarity under his definitions. Thus, his theory tells us little about the onset of World War I. Instead, it disclaims any intent to predict particular wars. Neither is it clear that Waltz's theory tells us about what causes stability in the current world. There has been only one bipolar system as defined in Waltz's theory. Thus he has to test his conclusions about stability against evidence drawn from a sample of *one*. Waltz cannot determine which behavior is caused by structure and which by nuclear weapons (assigned by him to the unit level).

Moreover, Waltz's theory leads him to conclusions that seem to bury rather than uncover new information about the behavior of states. For example, he argues that "in a bipolar world, military interdependence declines even more sharply than economic interdependence. Russia and America depend militarily mainly on themselves."[15] But it is an odd definition of military interdependence that blurs the change from the 1930s to a world in which the U.S. and U.S.S.R. can each destroy the other in thirty minutes. Even if Waltz means his statement to refer only to the formation of alliances, he has a hard time explaining the enormous efforts which both sides devote to their "unnecessary" alliance structures. Waltz may be right that "a five percent growth rate sustained for three years increases the American gross national product by an amount exceeding one-half of West Germany's GNP, and all of Great Britain's," but that alleged evidence for low military interdependence leaves the anomaly of actual U.S. behavior unexplained. In extolling the virtues of economic growth as a path to power, Waltz sounds a bit like Rosecrance; but, unlike the latter, he uses a restricted definition of inter-dependence to argue that economic interdependence is declining in the modern world.[16] Once again, Waltz's theoretical lens focuses so tightly on bipolarity that it tends to generate anomalies and to direct attention away from the discovery of new information.

It is not true that Waltz's theory is completely static, for changes in the structure predict changes in unit behavior. But change at the structural level seems to have occurred only once in three hundred years for Waltz. That leaves an awful lot of the stuff of international politics to be explained at the unit level. Waltz would admit as much, but he is then left with a theory that is so spare that nothing seems to move. The charge that Waltz has explained less about more of what concerned traditional Realists seems justified. It is ironic that Robert Gilpin appears in the Keohane volume in a cameo role as the author of a brief reply to Ashley's scattergun criticism of neorealism. Gilpin's own work represents an updating of Thucydides' classical Realist theory of hegemonic transition, which has disappeared in Waltz's nearly static neorealist world. Like Thucydides, Gilpin focuses on the ways in which uneven growth leads to cycles of rising and declining hegemonic states and the onset of great systemic wars.[17] Whatever its own problems, Gilpin's version of Realism is dynamic and focused on explaining the major changes in world politics that slip through the coarse net of Waltz's neorealist theory. Gilpin achieves this, however, by eschewing a purely structural theory and reaching deep into the unit level of analysis.

The revival of Liberal theories

Partly in reaction to the inadequacies of neorealism, a number of theorists have begun to resurrect Liberal theory. While admitting the diversity of Liberal theories, they argue that the core of Liberalism is a concern for liberty. That philosophical perspective is often correlated with such features as an interest in limited government, institutional restraints, and open contacts (including trade) across borders.[18] Michael Doyle has pointed out different historical strands of Liberal thought in Schumpeter's economic theories of pacifism, Machiavelli's republican theories of imperialism, and Kant's liberal international confederation based on republican governments and transnational contacts.[19] Robert Keohane has identified three major causal strands of classical Liberal theory: (1) commercial Liberalism, which asserts the pacific effects of trade; (2) democratic Liberalism, which asserts the pacific effects of republican government (at the unit level of analysis); and (3) regulatory Liberalism, which asserts the importance of rules and institutions in affecting relations between countries.[20] One might add a fourth: sociological Liberalism, which asserts the transformative effect of transnational contacts and coalitions on national attitudes and definitions of interests. Many of these Liberal causal theories were central to the neofunctionalist theories of regional integration developed in the 1950s and 1960s.

By and large, Rosecrance's *The Rise of the Trading State* fits mainly in the category of commercial Liberalism. His argument rests more upon the beneficial effects of trade than on the other three potential components of a neoliberal theory. Rosecrance's view (p. 218) that "if nuclear war can be ruled out, economic processes will progressively act to reshape the international world" bears a strong family resemblance to Richard Cobden's (1846) belief that "if we can keep the world from actual war, and I trust Trade will do that, a great impulse will from this time be given to social reforms."[21]

Rosecrance does not share all of the illusions of the classical free trade Liberals. He is fully aware that high levels of trade and other transactions did not prevent the outbreak of World War I, and that trade was often associated with conflict in earlier eras. But he argues that the world was different then: "the nineteenth and early twentieth century represent the apex of the military political system" (p. 88). In Rosecrance's view, "it was not until after 1945 that large-scale territorial expansion began to evolve as too costly – too dangerous and too uncertain as a general strategy of national advancement." As that lesson dawned, "one would have reached 'the Japanese period' in world politics . . ." (p. 20).

Even if Rosecrance proves to be correct in his projections, it is unclear to what extent the causation is due to factors stressed by Liberal or by Realist theories. Perhaps what happened after 1945 is that nuclear technology transformed a balance-of-power system into a balance of terror that encourages prudence about any territorial expansion that could raise nuclear risks. In this situation, Japan has found a more successful path to become the second-most-powerful economy in the world than it did in the 1930s. But it has done so while sheltered under the American nuclear umbrella and spending only one percent of its GNP on defense.

Rosecrance admits that hegemonic stability theory may have some relevance, but he argues that it does not explain "why there has not *already* been a marked decline in international economic cooperation ... well after the onset of decline in American economic and military power" (p. 57). The answer may lie in the success of economic regimes (which Rosecrance discusses only briefly); or in the exaggeration of the decline of American power; or in Waltz's theory of the stability of bipolarity; or in the paralysis of the territorial conquest system caused by nuclear risk.[22] Causation remains unclear in Rosecrance's account.

Because Rosecrance is cautious, there are really two versions of his argument – a strong form and a weak form. The strong form is close to classic commercial liberalism. "Since 1945, the world has been poised between ... [a] territorial system ... composed of states that view power in terms of land mass ... and [a] trading system ... based on states which recognize that self-sufficiency is an illusion," Rosecrance writes (p. 16). "A major crossroads is now approaching. ... In the past the military-political world was efficient. It was cheaper to seize another state's territory by force than to develop the sophisticated economic and trading apparatus needed to derive benefit from commercial exchange with it" (p. 160). "The current equipoise ... can scarcely be maintained," Rosecrance argues (p. 165). "The worst aspects of the Westphalian system with its emphasis on territoriality, sovereignty, and a spurious independence, are likely to be mitigated in the years ahead" (p. 211). "The increasing deconsolidation of traditional states and the decline of national loyalty as they seek to serve such purposes gradually undermines the military-political system" (p. 214).

But this strong liberal theory is eroded by the more cautious form of the argument. Dualism is proffered as "the minimum possible approach to an international theory" (p. 60).[23] Which strategy will be dominant cannot be predicted at present. One can commend Rosecrance for his cautious judgments when faced with a confusing reality, but such caution does not enhance theoretical development. One wishes Rosecrance had gone further in specifying the relationship between the Liberal and Realist components of the dualistic theory he suggests in the weak form of his argument. Perhaps if he had gone beyond commercial liberalism and explored more deeply the effects of transnational contacts on domestic political coalitions, or looked more carefully at the effects of regimes on learning (even in the security area where he discounts regimes), he might have begun to suggest such connections. Since he did not, we are left with a suggestive work, but one that hardly provides the neoliberal theory needed to accompany Waltz's neorealism.

Directions for future research

What do these works suggest for future research programs in international relations? Taken on its own terms, Waltz's theory is too static to provide a rich agenda of research questions. But it may be more fruitful when coupled with the rational-actor approach that has received increasing attention in recent years.[24] Neither game theory nor expected utility are really theories of international politics because they need to import theoretical assumptions about context.[25] Here Waltz's structural theory can be helpful, but only if handled with care.

Rational-choice theories can be parsimonious and powerful, but as research strategies, they run risks that are reinforced by the sparse structure of neorealism. How preferences are formulated and how learning occurs may be more important than the actual choice, yet both rational choice and neorealism are weak in this dimension and tend to turn attention in other directions. Moreover, while there is no *a priori* reason why game theory cannot be applied to transnational actors as well as to unitary state actors, such analyses are rare. The benefit of marrying rational choice with neorealist approaches is a double parsimony. The danger is that each already has a negative heuristic that directs attention away from preference formation and transnational interactions. Theorists who would make the marriage must be alert to such costs and open to the insights to be gained from other variants of Realist as well as Liberal theory.

Rosecrance's work suggests a number of interesting avenues for those who wish to develop neoliberal theory. Many of the questions he raises in the area of commercial Liberalism suggest both historical and contemporary research about the interconnection between power and nonpower incentives with which states are confronted. But the indeterminacy of his work also suggests the limits of commercial liberalism alone. Much more attention needs to be paid to the effects of norms and institutions, both in the economic and in the security area. More can be done with the ways in which transnational contacts and coalitions affect attitudes, learning, and formulation of preferences. A careful rereading of neofunctionalist integration theory can suggest numerous hypotheses. Finally, neoliberal theory should not neglect the unit level of analysis. Michael Doyle's work on the possible causal relationship between democratic governments and foreign policy choices is highly suggestive.[26]

Above all, it is important to pay more attention to the ways in which Liberalism and Realism relate to each other. One way is to be less restrictive in the basic assumption of anarchy. Alker attacks the metaphor of "anarchy" and argues for Hedley Bull's concept of an "anarchic society," which admits the absence of any formal government above states, but does not define anarchy as the absence of communication, cooperation, and governance.[27] In *Power and Interdependence*, Robert Keohane and I suggested that systemic theory could be enriched without (or before) retreating to the particularisms of the unit level of analysis by adding the concept of systemic process.

Systems have two dimensions: structure and process. We used the term "structure" in the neorealist sense to refer principally to the distribution of capabilities among units. "Process" refers to the ways in which the units relate to each other. In the metaphor of a poker game, the structure refers to the players' cards and chips, while the process refers both to the formal rules and the informal customs or conventions that affect interactions among the players. Variations in the ability of the players to calculate odds, infer the strength of opponents' hands, or bluff are at the unit, or actor, level.[28]

Factors such as the intensity of international interdependence and the degree of institutionalization of international rules do not vary from one state to another on the basis of their internal characteristics. Therefore, they should not be termed unit-level factors according to Waltz's own definition. Making the unit level a grab bag for all unexplained variance is an impediment to the development of theory. Not only does it complicate the task of analysis by confusing unit-level factors referring to domestic political and economic arrangements with factors at the level of the international system; it also leads neorealist analysts to forgo the opportunity to theorize at a systemic level about nonstructural determinants of state behavior.

At the systemic level, in addition to the distribution of power, states experience constraints and opportunities because of changes in levels of world economic activity, technological innovation, shifts in patterns of transnational interactions, and alterations in international norms and institutions. These systemic processes affecting state choices can be categorized as non-power incentives and the ability to communicate and cooperate. Nonstructural incentives alter calculations of national interest without necessarily affecting the distribution of power among actors. For instance, the destructiveness of nuclear weaponry, which Waltz assigned to the unit level, is better portrayed as a feature of systemic process that produces incentives not to engage in warfare regardless of whether the structure is bipolar or multipolar. Similarly, reduced costs of communications and transportation may increase the benefits of transnational business and encourage state policies of greater economic openness, without any changes in the structure of power.

The ability to communicate and cooperate can provide opportunities for the redefinition of interests and for the pursuit of strategies that would not be feasible in a world where the only information available to states was about other states' preferences and the power resources at their disposal. Just as allowing players in Prisoners' Dilemma games to communicate with one another alters the nature of the game, so a systemic process that increases the capability of states to communicate and to reach mutually beneficial agreements can add to the repertoire of state strategies and thus alter political outcomes.

These two aspects of systemic process – non-power incentives and variations in the capacity to communicate and cooperate – have traditionally been empha-sized by Liberal theory. Liberal theorists often stress the ways in which trade and economic incentives may alter states' behavior. Similarly, Liberal theorists often stress the effects of increased transnational (and transgovernmental) contacts on attitudes and abilities to communicate. Institutions and norms have always played a role in Liberal theory.

This is not to say that Liberal theory has addressed all processes at the sys-temic level. For example, most Realists have been concerned about technological changes even when they do not alter the distribution of power. And there is much in Liberal theory about the effect of domestic politics that does not belong at the sys-temic level. However, the addition of the process level to the concept of structure in defining international systems provides an opportunity to develop a "neoliberal" systemic theory that moves toward a synthesis rather than a radical disjunction between Realism and Liberalism. Neorealism would be most appropriate at the structural level of systemic theory; neoliberalism would more often be fruitful at the process level.

The time has come to transcend the classical dialectic between Realist and Liberal theories of international politics. Each has something to contribute to a research program that increases our understanding of international behavior. Perhaps work in the 1990s will be able to synthesize rather than repeat the dialectic of the 1970s and the 1980s.

Notes

* This was written as a review essay of the two books discussed. I am grateful to Robert Beschel, Sean Lynn-Jones, Andrew Moravcsik, and David Welch for comments.
1 Donald Kagan, *The Outbreak of the Peloponnesian War* (Ithaca, NY: Cornell University Press, 1969).
2 Herman Kahn and B. Bruce-Briggs, *Things to Come* (New York: Macmillan, 1972).
3 Hans J. Morgenthau, "The New Diplomacy of Movement," *Encounter* 43 (August 1974), 52–57, at 56.
4 Seyom Brown, *New Forces in World Politics* (Washington: Brookings Institution, 1974), 186.
5 Joseph S. Nye, Jr., "Nuclear Learning and U.S.-Soviet Security Regimes," *International Organization* 41 (Summer 1987), 371–402.
6 K. J. Holsti, *The Dividing Discipline: Hegemony and Diversity in International Theory* (Boston: Allen & Unwin, 1985).
7 Karl Deutsch *et al.*, *Political Community and the North Atlantic Area* (Princeton: Princeton University Press, 1957); Ernst Haas, *The Uniting of Europe* (Stanford, CA: Stanford University Press, 1958); Joseph S. Nye, Jr., *Peace in Parts* (Boston: Little, Brown, 1971).
8 Robert O. Keohane and Joseph S. Nye, Jr., *Power and Interdependence* (Boston: Little, Brown, 1977).
9 Stephen Krasner, ed., *International Regimes* (Ithaca, NY: Cornell University Press, 1983).
10 Waltz, *Theory of International Politics* (Reading, MA: Addison-Wesley, 1979).
11 Francis M. Bator, *The State of Macroeconomics* (Kennedy School Discussion Paper 1520, Cambridge, MA: 1986), 19.
12 Waltz (fn. 10), 77, 72.
13 Imre Lakatos, "Falsification and the Methodology of Scientific Research Programmes," in Imre Lakatos and Alan Musgrave, eds., *Criticism and the Growth of Knowledge* (Cambridge: Cambridge University Press, 1970).
14 Waltz (fn. 10), 162.
15 *Ibid.*, 168.
16 Waltz ignored the criticism of narrow definitions of interdependence in terms of vulnerability alone that was published in *Power and Interdependence* (fn. 8). Had he considered a more complex treatment of interdependence, he might have come to different conclusions about its decline.
17 Robert Gilpin, *War and Change in World Politics* (New York and Cambridge: Cambridge University Press, 1981).
18 Stanley Hoffmann, "Liberalism and International Affairs," in *Janus and Minerva* (Boulder, CO: Westview Press, 1987). Hoffmann points out a terminological difficulty: many Realists are liberal in their domestic political preferences.
19 Michael Doyle, "Liberalism and World Politics," *American Political Science Review* 80 (December 1986), 1151–69.
20 Robert O. Keohane, "Economic Limits of Modern Politics: International Liberalism Reconsidered," unpub., 1986.
21 Cobden, quoted in Kenneth Waltz, *Man, the State, and War* (New York: Columbia University Press, 1959), 104.

22 For alternative explanations, see Robert O. Keohane, *After Hegemony* (Princeton: Princeton University Press, 1984), and Bruce Russett, "The Mysterious Case of Vanishing Hegemony: or Is Mark Twain Really Dead?" *International Organization* 39 (Spring 1985), 207–31.

23 Rosecrance mistakes the argument in *Power and Interdependence* as being similar to his own. Keohane and I did not establish "dualistic categories: power and interdependence . . . power is the preeminent goal of a state-centric universe, but interdependence is a characteristic that only applies when states as entities have lost control" (p. 62). On the contrary, we argued the need to see asymmetrical interdependence as a source of power. Rosecrance seems to confuse the ideal type of complex interdependence developed in chapter 2 of our work with our larger argument about interdependence.

24 See Bruno Bueno de Mesquita, *The War Trap* (New Haven: Yale University Press, 1981), and the special issue of *World Politics* 38 (October 1985), *Cooperation under Anarchy*, Kenneth A. Oye, ed. (also published under that title by Princeton University Press, 1986).

25 Note the assertion by Duncan Snidal, "The Game *Theory* of International Politics," *ibid.*, 25–57.

26 Doyle, "Kant, Liberal Legacies, and Foreign Affairs," *Philosophy and Public Affairs* 12 (Summer 1983), 205–35.

27 Hayward R. Alker, Jr. "The Presumption of Anarchy in World Politics," unpub., 1986. See also Hedley Bull, *The Anarchical Society* (London: Macmillan, 1977).

28 See Robert O. Keohane and Joseph S. Nye, Jr., "Power and Interdependence Revisited," *International Organization* 41 (Autumn 1987), 725–53, for a fuller discussion of the concepts that are introduced here.

4   Conflicts after the Cold War*

"War" is a term that covers a myriad of activities. Through much of history, war has been the norm rather than the exception in relations among nations. For example, there have been wars among the great powers for 60 percent of the years since 1500.[1] Ten of these wars were general or "world" wars involving nearly all the great powers. Although not the most prevalent, these are by far the most devastating wars and have the strongest effects on the international system. If we divide today's wars into the three categories of great power, regional, and internal wars, the first is the least likely, but still the most important.

Each of the major great power wars since 1500 was followed by a period of uncertainty in which statesmen attempted to change the international system or adapt it to prevent a recurrence of great power war. We are at present in a new period of uncertainty after the equivalent of a major great power "war" – the Cold War. This is very different from past postwar periods for several reasons. First, in some ways it is the most uncertain transition of all because there has been no single, decisive military confrontation or postwar negotiation. Second, the rise and fall of great powers and technological, economic, and cultural change have all accelerated. Third, future conflicts may have very different sources from those of the recently concluded Cold War, which was partly rooted in ideological tensions that are unlikely to reappear, and these conflicts may be altered or constrained by the presence of weapons of mass destruction.

This article briefly reviews the likelihood of these three types of conflict after the Cold War. One encouraging conclusion is that the conflicts with the greatest potential for devastation – great power conflicts over the global balance of power – are the least likely given the deterrent effects of nuclear weapons and the decreasing importance of territorially defined resources. Still, such conflicts cannot be ruled out entirely because the potential remains for misunderstandings, security dilemmas, and internally unstable great powers.

Regional balance of power conflicts like the Persian Gulf War are more probable than world wars and could have wide and lasting regional or global implications, although they are less likely than in the past to catalyze direct military clashes between the great powers. Their prevalence will depend in large part on the constraining role played by the United States as the largest external power.

Communal conflicts, scattered around the globe and often taking place within states, are likely to be the prevalent form of conflict. Almost all of the approximately 30 significant conflicts since the end of the Cold War have been internal. The most likely locations of these conflicts are the regions of collapsed empires – Africa and the rim of the former Soviet Union. Although most of these conflicts are not immediately damaging beyond their respective borders, they can spread geographically, induce humanitarian intervention, and cumulatively create longterm and global threats to international security. Thus, although great power conflicts are less likely than ever before to arise out of global or regional balance of power considerations, the great powers will continue to face difficult choices on how to prevent communal conflicts from occurring or from escalating in intensity, spreading geographically, and proliferating in number.

American leadership is a key factor in limiting the frequency and destructiveness of all three kinds of conflicts. This does not mean that the United States could or should get involved in every potential or ongoing conflict. Its role must be proportionate to its interests in each conflict, and the nation cannot afford the military, economic, and political costs of being a global policeman. Instead, where it has important interests, the United States must continue to aspire to a role more like the sheriff of the posse, enabling international coalitions to pursue interests that it shares whether or not the United States itself supplies the bulk of the military forces involved.

Preventing the last war: continuity and change in the sources of conflict

There are two basic schools of thought that purport to explain wars: Realism and Liberalism.[2] Both perspectives are essential to understanding post-cold war conflicts. Realists argue that wars arise from the efforts of states to acquire power and security in an anarchic world, or one in which there is no ultimate arbiter of order other than self-help and the force of arms. In this view, power transitions, disequilibriums in the balance of power, and competition over allies, territory, and other power resources are the root of causes of war. Also, security dilemmas arise when states try to promote their own security through arms buildups, creation of alliances, or efforts to acquire buffer states. This causes other states to feel insecure, leading to arms races, rigidifying alliances, and competition over strategic territory and resources. In the Realist view, strong international institutions can only exist when the balance of power is satisfactory to leading states, so these institutions are effective only when they are not needed, and needed only when they are not effective.

Liberals argue that conflicts and their prevention are determined not only by the balance of power, but by the domestic structures of states, their values, identities, and cultures, and international institutions for conflict resolution. In this view, trade is important, not because it prevents war between states, but because it may lead states to define their interests in ways that make war less likely, encouraging them to seek gain through commerce rather than conquest. Moreover, the domestic structures and values of states greatly affect their propensity for international conflict. In particular, the most striking correlation to emerge from recent studies of war is that liberal democracies have rarely, if ever, fought with other democracies, even though democracies have frequently fought with nondemocratic states. In contrast to Realists, Liberals argue that international institutions can help prevent conflict by stabilizing expectations, creating a sense of continuity and a feeling that current cooperation will be reciprocated in the future, providing information on whether states are abiding by international norms, and establishing mechanisms for conflict resolution.

Neither of these schools of thought is adequate by itself in understanding the causes of conflict after the Cold War. The Realist emphasis on the balance of power is necessary but not sufficient when long-term societal changes are eroding the norms of state sovereignty. The Liberal view that peace has broken out among the major liberal democracies is accurate, but it is not a panacea when many states, including great powers, are not liberal democracies. Yet both schools of thought point to important realities, and it is necessary to address the international, domestic, and institutional dimensions of conflict. Drawing upon each school of thought, then, what are the most likely sources of conflict after the Cold War?

Global balance of power conflicts

As historians and political observers since Thucydides have noted, rapid power transitions are one of the leading causes of great power conflict. Such power transitions were a deep structural cause of historically recent great power conflicts, including the rise and fall of Napoleonic France, Germany's rise before each World War, and the relative rise and resulting rivalry of the United States and the Soviet Union after World War II. Power transitions can lead to preemptive strikes by declining powers against their rising competitors, or to aggression by rising powers who feel their role in the system is lagging behind their military prowess. In addition, wars can result from security dilemmas between rising powers and counterbalancing coalitions, as in World War I. Similarly, wars can arise from uncertainties over how fast-changing military balances might play out in battle – wars are less likely when it is clear to all which side would win.

There is a strong consensus that we are in a period of rapid power transitions. There is considerable debate over the direction and magnitude of these transitions, however, and the center of gravity of this debate has shifted in recent years. Such debates are indicative of the unpredictability that makes such transitions a potential source of conflict. In the late 1980s, many commentators, following the lead of Paul Kennedy's best-selling *Rise and Fall of the Great Powers*, argued that the United States was in a period of long-term decline relative to other leading powers.[3] At that time, I argued that the U.S. decline relative to other states was only natural as they recovered from the devastation of World War II, and that by the 1970s America's relative decline had leveled off, with the nation at its prewar share of about 22 to 25 percent of world gross national product (GNP).[4] Moreover, I argued that of all the leading powers, only the United States had a diverse and deep range of power resources across all the key dimensions of power, including military power, economic power, and "soft power," the broad appeal of cultural, ideological, and institutional factors.

The intervening five years have largely reaffirmed these observations. The Soviet Union and Russia have declined farther and faster than almost anyone expected in 1990. China has risen faster than most anticipated, with a long period of double-digit economic growth. Japan and Germany have not become the full-fledged superpowers that many predicted at the 1990 summit in Houston of the group of seven industrialized countries (G-7). Unpredictable lurches and lags in growth are likely to continue, but the central reality of the global balance of power is the same as it was in 1990: the United States is the only true superpower, with global assets in all the dimensions of power.

This does not mean that a unipolar world has replaced the bipolar balance of the Cold War. There are many important security, economic, and political goals that the United States cannot achieve by itself. Neither is the world multipolar, as every great power but the United States lacks one or more key power resource. Instead, power is distributed in a complex three-dimensional pattern. Military power is largely unipolar, with the United States the only country with both intercontinental nuclear weapons and large, modern, air, naval, and ground forces capable of deploying around the globe. Economic power is tripolar, with the United States, Europe, and Japan representing two-thirds of world product. China's growth may make economic power quadripolar after the turn of the century. At the level of transnational relations that cross borders outside the control of government, and that include actors as diverse as bankers and terrorists, power is widely dispersed.

Just as important as these changes in the distribution of power are changes in the nature of power and the processes through which it can be exercised. Some Liberals argue that economic power has replaced military power as the central medium of international politics, but this is greatly overstated. Realists rightly argue that economic instruments still cannot compare with military forces in their coercive and deterrent effects. Economic sanctions, for example, did not compel the Iraqis to withdraw from Kuwait. In addition, all it takes is one good security crisis to send stock and commodity markets spinning, set off capital flight, stifle investment, and raise the risk premium on the full range of economic transactions. Economic instruments have grown slightly in importance relative to military ones, but this was already true by the 1970s.[5] The main change has been in the fungibility of military power itself. Nuclear weapons have so greatly raised the potential costs of conflict that the great power states that have them have worked hard to prevent any direct military conflicts among themselves, including conventional conflicts that could escalate to the nuclear level.

Taken together, these changes in the balance and nature of power indicate that the most dangerous kind of conflict – a direct clash among two or more of the five major power centers of the United States, Russia, China, Europe, and Japan over the fundamental shape of the international system – is very unlikely. None of the paths through which power transitions have historically led to conflict is very likely to open up. There is no temptation for the United States to overreact to rising powers because it is not in a steep power decline, as some pessimists suggested a few years ago. Rising powers today have fewer incentives for territorial aggression than they have had throughout most of history because the route to prestige, power, and economic success in the modern era lies in high-technology production and human capital.

Whereas World War II armies could seize territory and factories and convert them from commercial to military production fairly quickly, it is enormously difficult to convert highly specialized modern production lines.[6] Nor do countries aspire to increase their economic production by taking over neighboring software or service industries in the same way that past aggressors coveted agricultural land or raw materials deposits. Indeed, transnational economic ties are such that it is increasingly difficult to tell whether a particular company is "American" if its headquarters are in one country, its production facilities in several others, and its raw material inputs, distribution system, and export markets in still others. Iraq's invasion of Kuwait is one of the increasingly rare cases in which a state seized territory in the hope of gaining resources that could increase its economic and military power. Finally, uncertainty over the balance of power and arms races represent perhaps the most likely dangers, but even these are muted in an era in which nuclear weapons are the ultimate deterrent and satellite intelligence quickly informs a potential counterbalancing coalition of a rising power's military capabilities. All of these factors help explain why there were no large-scale and direct military clashes between American and Soviet troops despite more than 40 years of intense rivalry, and why the hegemonic power transition of the decline and breakup of the Soviet Union took place without even a small risk of great power war of the kind that has accompanied the decline of most empires throughout history.

Perhaps even more important than these Realist considerations, two of the leading power centers – Japan and Europe – consist of democratic states that are allied with the United States and that largely share its view of world order. It is often said that democracies do not fight each other. A more accurate formulation is that *Liberal* democracies do not fight each other. As the political scientist Karl Deutsch argued, a "pluralistic security community," or an island of peace, has emerged among the United States, Europe, and Japan.[7] Shared values, stable expectations, and interlocking institutions have become so powerful among these three power centers that wars among them, including wars among European powers that have fought with one another over several centuries, are unthinkable. Anyone today who warned of impending military conflict among the Scandinavian countries would be considered a lunatic, but in past centuries, wars among these states were commonplace.

The low likelihood of direct great power clashes does not mean that there will be no tensions between them. Disagreements are likely to continue over regional conflicts, like those that have arisen over how to deal with the conflict in the former Yugoslavia. Efforts to stop the spread of weapons of mass destruction and means of their delivery are another source of friction, as is the case over Russian and Chinese nuclear cooperation with Iran, which the United States steadfastly opposes. The sharing of burdens and responsibilities for maintaining international security and protecting the natural environment are a further subject of debate among the great powers. Furthermore, in contrast to the views of classical Liberals, increased trade and economic interdependence can increase as well as decrease conflict and competition among trading partners. The main point, however, is that such disagreements are very unlikely to escalate to military conflicts.

Uncertain transitions among the great powers: China and Russia

The key uncertainties in the long-run continuation of this island of peace among the great powers are long-term developments in China and Russia. Of all the great powers, these two states' long-term growth rates and domestic politics, the indices of greatest concern to Realists and Liberals respectively, are hardest to predict. Even so, the general analysis of great power interests outlined above applies to U.S. relations with both China and Russia. Although the three powers have many disagreements, their vital national interests are not at odds. In addition to the post-cold war constraints on great power conflict noted above, these three powers have no direct territorial disagreements of the kind that led to great power wars in the past.

There remains a residual risk for the United States of greater tension with Russia and China in the long term if they misunderstand the realities of the post-cold war world outlined above, or if domestic political instabilities – ideological blinders, internal power struggles, military-industrial-governmental interest groups, or ethno-nationalism – push their foreign policies in extreme directions. Yet to treat China and Russia as adversaries would become a self-fulfilling prophecy, particularly at a time when China faces a leadership transition and Russia has a presidential election scheduled in 1996. Both powers are preoccupied with their domestic political and economic situations, and they are more concerned about joining the world economy, and having a voice in international political affairs commensurate with their status as great powers, than about throwing their weight around the globe in ways that would only cause their neighbors to band together against them. Still, these two states retain considerable potential for either bolstering or undermining security and stability in their respective regions, where their interests are greatest. Thus, efforts by the democratic great powers to engage them in the international community and to urge them to make their intentions and military forces transparent are the best means of limiting the potential for conflicts.

If China's recent growth rates continue, its economy will become the world's second largest soon after the turn of the century. Even if China does not increase its defense budget as a percentage of its gross domestic product (GDP) – currently about 4 to 5 percent of GDP according to most estimates – the sheer magnitude of its growing GNP ensures that China will have impressive military capabilities. In the past five years, China's inflation-adjusted defense spending has grown by an estimated 40 percent.

Assessments by regional experts are mixed on whether China will behave expansively outside the Chinese cultural area. Some emphasize China's assertive pursuit of its territorial claims in the Spratly Islands and its saber-rattling missile tests near Taiwan. Others note that in the early 1990s China has normalized its relations with Indonesia, Singapore, Vietnam, and the Republic of Korea, and agreed to partici-pate in multilateral organizations like the Association of Southeast Asian Nations (ASEAN) Regional Forum (ARF). In the face of such ambiguities and uncer-tainties, it would be unwise to push China into a corner through a preemptive containment strategy. Such a strategy would be difficult to reverse, whereas if the United States begins with a strategy of engagement, together with its allies it can always fall back on containment if China's actions make this necessary.

Despite some tensions and setbacks, engagement has had several key successes. Chinese behavior on the proliferation of weapons of mass destruction and means of their delivery has moderated over the past decade. China is a member of the Nuclear Non-Proliferation Treaty and has indicated its support for the Comprehensive Test Ban ratification in 1996. In addition, China has participated in a number of multilateral regional dialogues, including the Asia-Pacific Economic Cooperation (APEC) and the ARF, and it has normalized its relations with South Korea and others. When Secretary of Defense William J. Perry visited China in October 1994, he began a dialogue on confidence-building and transparency in the region. Notably, China's neighbors share the U.S. preference for engagement. The only country that can bring about the encirclement of China by a coalition seeking China's containment is China itself.

As for Russia, official figures, though dubious, indicate that Russia's industrial production has dropped by as much as half since 1991. Nonetheless, Russia could emerge as an economic power in the long term. Russia's conventional forces are far less capable than those of the Soviet Union, and its nuclear capabili-ties are being reduced in accordance with arms-control agreements. Still, Russia remains the second most powerful military force in the world. It has the poten-tial to influence regional balances through its policies on exports of conventional arms and nuclear technology. As with China, Russia's ultimate intentions are unpredictable. Russia's military operation in Chechnya provides an ambiguous indicator of the ultimate direction of its foreign policy. On the one hand, it demon-strated a willingness to use force to resolve political problems. On the other, its actions aroused great domestic opposition in Russia itself, which was openly expressed in the Russian media and parliament. Similarly, Russia has at some times been a constructive contributor in the "contact group" of states seeking peace in the Balkans, while at other times it has disruptively criticized United Nations (UN) and North Atlantic Treaty Organization (NATO) efforts, even if mostly for domestic political purposes. Given these mixed signals, and with its upcoming presidential election and continuing but difficult transition toward a market economy, the United States can best encourage Russia's longterm emer-gence as a constructive member of the international community through a policy of engagement.

Russia is already involved in most aspects of the new security architecture emerging in Europe. It is an active participant in the Organization for Security and Cooperation in Europe (OSCE), it has signed an ambitious partnership agreement with the European Union (EU), and it has joined the Partnership for Peace (PFP) and recently approved its formal plan for PFP activities. As outlined in the U.S. Department of Defense's report *United States Security Strategy for Europe and NATO*, NATO and Russia have agreed to develop a far-reaching cooperative relationship both within the PFP and outside it, and NATO and Russia are considering how they could establish a long-term relationship embodied in a formal agreement.[8] A close and cooperative relationship between NATO and Russia is important to the successful construction of an inclusive European security architecture. NATO's enlargement, while ultimately inevitable, will necessarily be gradual given the requirement of ratification by NATO's 16 parliaments, thereby allowing time to demonstrate to Russia that NATO can contribute to the mutual interest of Russia and the United States in a stable Europe. Moreover, the emphasis that NATO enlargement and the PFP place on democratization, civil-military reforms, civilian control of the military, transparency, and close military-to-military relations should further reassure Russia of NATO's intentions. In addition to these European ties, Russia, with U.S. support, is becoming more deeply involved in the political side of the G-7 process and moving closer to membership in the World Trade Organization.

This inclusive European security architecture, and the U.S. policy of engagement with China, are very different from the punitive settlement of World War I. Instead, they are similar to the Concert of Europe formed after the Napoleonic wars, which attempted to include even those great powers that had recently been adversaries in the management of the international system. This approach is based on the recognition that Russia and China will remain important players in world politics and that the prospects for international security are much brighter with their cooperation. Still, success will depend not only on international mechanisms and the balance of power, but also on domestic political developments in the states with the potential to disrupt the system. Even in the worst-case post-cold war scenario, however – the emergence of an aggressive regime in a great power at the same time that it experiences rapid growth – a strong counterbalancing coalition of democratic great powers, nuclear deterrence, and the limited benefits of territorial conquest would continue to make direct great power conflict unlikely.

Regional balance of power conflicts

A more likely and near-term risk than great power conflicts is that of attempts by rising regional powers to acquire weapons of mass destruction and establish regional hegemony. Wars initiated by these regional powers may draw in the great powers, although the latter will probably see aspiring regional hegemons as shared threats rather than potential allies. This was exemplified when Iraq's seizure of Kuwait posed a threat to world oil markets. In other regions, however, like South Asia, great power interests and constraints are weaker after the Cold War.

Deterring regional powers from aggression requires that the great powers seek to contain aspiring regional hegemons, and that they maintain sufficient forward military forces to do so. In particular, three states have capabilities to upset regional power balances, have shown a willingness to do so in the past, and continue to be governed by insular and autocratic rulers: North Korea, Iraq, and Iran.

North Korea's history of aggression and its isolation from the rest of Asia have made it a source of regional instability. Despite severe economic problems, North Korea continues to devote a large share of its national resources to maintaining and improving one of the world's largest military forces. Given its history of aggression, the development of nuclear weapons by North Korea would threaten the regional balance of power and could spark a regional arms race. In this context, the October 1994 Agreed Framework is an important step in reducing the North Korean nuclear threat. Still, the Framework will take a long time to implement, and North Korean conventional forces continue to pose a potential threat to the South. As explained in the Department of Defense's report *United States Security Strategy for the East Asia-Pacific Region*, to help deter this threat the United States continues to maintain about 37,000 troops in South Korea, and 100,000 troops in Asia as a whole.[9] In addition, the United States has undertaken dialogues with Japan and Korea to reaffirm its alliances for the post–cold war era.

In the Middle East, Iran and Iraq continue to pose the foremost threats to regional stability. Despite losing more than half its forces in the Gulf war, Iraq continues to have the largest military forces in the Gulf region. Iraq's ominous troop movements in October 1994 demonstrated its continuing capacity to threaten the region. Iran also harbors ambitions of hegemony over the Persian Gulf and has pursued its goals using every available means, including terrorism and subversion. Although its conventional forces remain limited, its recent purchases of submarines, attack aircraft, and anti-ship missiles are worrisome. Most dangerous of all are Iran's efforts to develop weapons of mass destruction.

Although U.S. Gulf allies are working to contain the Iraqi and Iranian threats, they cannot do so alone. The United States is thus continuing to strengthen its rapid deployment capabilities in the region. In 1979, when the Rapid Deployment force was created, it would have taken three months to get a division of heavy ground forces into the region. When Iraq invaded Kuwait in 1990, the U.S. military was able to get seven combat brigades, three carriers, and numerous aircraft into the Gulf in three weeks. In October 1994, when Iraqi forces again moved toward Kuwait, the first heavy ground units to the Gulf, in Operation Vigilant Warrior, arrived in three days, and a total of 150,000 troops were poised to deploy quickly if necessary. Whereas the Gulf war demonstrated the ability of the United States to defeat Iraq, Vigilant Warrior showed its ability to deter it.

As noted in the Department of Defense's report, *United States Security Strategy for the Middle East*, Operation Vigilant Warrior also demonstrated the importance of maintaining U.S. forces capable of responding to two major regional conflicts (MRCs) that occur nearly at the same time.[10] Although some have criticized the "two MRC" standard as a basis for planning U.S. forces because they see it as an unlikely scenario, the deterrent encounter with Iraq in October 1994 took place at the same time that the nuclear negotiations with North Korea were at a difficult phase. Had the United States lacked sufficient forces to respond to contingencies in both arenas nearly simultaneously, it would have lost leverage with both these regional powers and they might have been tempted to exploit U.S. difficulties. Sizing the force to two MRCs also ensures that the United States has a sufficient capability to deal with the residual risk of great power conflict.

The sources of communal conflicts

Communal conflicts over competing identities, territorial claims, and political institutions are, of course, not unique to the modern era. What has changed, however, is the complex interplay of transnational, national, and subnational identities with rapid and far-reaching social, technological, and economic changes. This potent mix can spark latent tensions into sudden conflict because of instantaneous communications.

The rapid rise and fall of great powers, the end of the Soviet empire and the demise of communism, and the technological and communications revolution have led not to the end of history, as some have argued, but to the return of history in the form of clashes over identity among individuals, groups, and nations. Such clashes can happen at three levels – over transnational identities, like Islam; national identities, as in Russia; and subnational identities based on religious, ethnic, or linguistic divisions, as in Africa or the former Yugoslavia. These have challenged conflict management institutions on each level – transnational, national, and subnational.

Technological change has had transnational and contradictory effects. It has made the economy global but made politics more parochial. It has globalized communications, but instead of creating a global village, as Marshall McLuhan predicted, this has created global villages. "Village" connotes community, but it also connotes parochialism. Individuals are now more vulnerable to the vagaries of international labor, currency, and commercial markets. With state sovereignty eroded through global interdependence, the political efficacy and legitimacy of many governments is less assured. Many groups have had their sense of identity and community challenged by economic dislocation and the collapse of communism. They have become susceptible to the parochial political appeals of political entrepreneurs who hope to seize power in states whose governments have been weakened by the collapse of communism or the ebb and flow of the global economy. In this context, it is not surprising to find former Communist apparatchiks suddenly transformed into ethnic demagogues. With modern technology, such demagogues can now communicate their hateful messages more easily to both wide and select groups.

The result has not been a clash between Toynbee's world civilizations, as Samuel P. Huntington has argued.[11] Huntington is correct that communalism and competing identities are a major source of conflict after the Cold War, but he captures only one dimension or level of analysis of clashing identities. There are more clashes among competing identities *within* grand civilizations than between them. The Iran–Iraq War, for example, was between states within the Islamic world. Moreover, Huntington calls Africa a "civilization," yet the largest number of current wars are within Africa.

Closer to the mark are Freud's observations on the "narcissism of small differences" – the tendency to focus on the 10 percent that is different between individuals instead of the 90 percent that is the same. We have seen these small differences exaggerated by combatants in Somalia, Northern Ireland, and elsewhere, including conflict between family or clan groupings. Even in Rwanda, the site of the worst genocide since the Holocaust, the differences between Hutu and Tutsi were far from absolute. Many intermarriages had occurred. But once Rwanda's politics became polarized into a zero-sum "kill or be killed" atmosphere, genocide tore its society apart.

Bosnia, which is often depicted solely as a civilizational clash, includes many other elements: for example, Serbs who define themselves as Bosnians and have stayed in Sarajevo side-by-side with Bosnian Muslims. In many cities of the former Yugoslavia, neighbors paid little attention to their own or others' "ethnic" identity until propaganda created a frenzy of ethnic conflict and a Hobbesian zero-sum politics. As one Bosnian-Croat officer told me during a battle between Muslims and Croats in Mostar, "Before the war I could not tell on sight who was a Muslim, but now the uniforms make it easy." In a sense, the war in the former Yugoslavia represents the victory of the countryside and villages, where identities changed slowly compared to the assimilation that had advanced in the cities.

Domestic politics and communal conflicts

Just as domestic politics and values affect the likelihood of conflict among the great powers, they also have a powerful influence on the likelihood of communal conflicts within or between states, and on the propensity for other regional or great powers to become involved in these conflicts. Communal conflicts often arise in states undergoing a legitimacy crisis because of two related dynamics. First, established mechanisms for mediating such conflicts lose force in delegitimized states, just as the practice of a rotating presidency broke down in Yugoslavia after the collapse of communism. Second, those who aspire to attain power within delegitimized states are tempted to appeal to ethnic or other identities as a means of establishing a new claim to legitimacy.

Again, the case of Yugoslavia is a clear example, as Slobodan Milosevic transformed himself from a Communist apparatchik to a born-again ethno-nationalist. It is thus not surprising that many communal conflicts have arisen within the former Soviet empire, where the identity crises are sharpest and have multiple roots in the collapse of Communist governments, the economic dislocation of individuals, and the reemergence of ethnic identities long suppressed or mediated by Communist regimes.

A second category of states susceptible to communal conflicts includes so-called "failed states," which refers in this context to states that either have never had a strong central government, or whose moderately strong central government has been undermined by economic or political developments. Afghanistan fits the former pattern, many states in Africa fit the latter, and some, like Somalia, have elements of both. By definition, in such states power is contested and political and economic problems provide opportunities for ethnic scapegoating. Thus, even though the end of the bipolar contest over the developing world has led to the withdrawal of foreign troops from Afghanistan, Angola, Cambodia, and elsewhere, communal conflicts in these states have taken the place of conflicts between factions backed by the United States and those sponsored by the Soviet Union.

A very different set of domestic pressures affects the democratic great powers that are not themselves at risk of experiencing communal conflicts. The instantaneous and all-intrusive nature of modern communications imparts conflicting impulses to the leading democracies. On the one hand, graphic televised reports of humanitarian abuses by combatants in communal conflicts can galvanize a strong impulse to act. On the other, equally graphic coverage of peacekeepers killed, wounded, or taken hostage can stimulate public pressure to withdraw from conflicts that do not directly threaten the democracies' vital security interests. Even worse, such pressures will inevitably fall unevenly on those states that feel the closest cultural or geographic ties to suffering populations, and those whose troops take casualties, leading to tensions over definitions of missions, rules of engagement, and burden sharing. Moreover, both the victims and perpetrators of humanitarian abuses are well aware of the power of media coverage, and they seek to exploit it to their own ends, with victims publicizing or even exaggerating their plight and aggressors seeking to inflict casualties upon or take hostages from the contributing states that they see as most vulnerable to such blackmail. This underscores the difficulty for the leading democracies of engaging in consistent, coordinated, and long-term approaches to communal conflicts.

Likelihood and consequences of communal conflicts

While generally less threatening to U.S. interests than global or regional balance of power conflicts, communal conflicts are the most likely kind of post-cold war conflict and have thus far proved the most frequent. Less than 10 percent of the 170 states in today's world are ethnically homogenous. Only half have one ethnic group that accounts for as much as 75 percent of their population. Africa, in particular, is a continent of a thousand ethnic and linguistic groups squeezed into some 50-odd states, many of them with borders determined by colonial powers in the last century with little regard to traditional ethnic boundaries. The former Yugoslavia was a country with five nationalities, four languages, three religions, and two alphabets. As a result of such disjunctions between borders and peoples, there have been some 30 communal conflicts since the end of the Cold War, many of them still ongoing.

Communal conflicts, particularly those involving wars of secession, are very difficult to manage through the UN and other institutions built to address interstate conflicts. The UN, regional organizations, alliances, and individual states cannot provide a universal answer to the dilemma of self-determination versus the inviolability of established borders, particularly when so many states face potential communal conflicts of their own. In a world of identity crises on many levels of analysis, it is not clear which selves deserve sovereignty: nationalities, ethnic groups, linguistic groups, or religious groups. Similarly, uses of force for deterrence, compellence, and reassurance are much harder to carry out when both those using force and those on the receiving end are disparate coalitions of international organizations, states, and subnational groups.

Moreover, although few communal conflicts by themselves threaten security beyond their regions, some impose risks of "horizontal" escalation, or the spread to other states within their respective regions. This can happen through the involvement of affiliated ethnic groups that spread across borders, the sudden flood of refugees into neighboring states, or the use of neighboring territories to ship weapons to combatants. The use of ethnic propaganda also raises the risk of "vertical" escalation to more intense violence, more sophisticated and destructive weapons, and harsher attacks on civilian populations as well as military personnel. There is also the danger that communal conflicts could become more numerous if the UN and regional security organizations lose the credibility, willingness, and capabilities necessary to deal with such conflicts.

Preventing and addressing conflicts: the pivotal U.S. role

Leadership by the United States, as the world's leading economy, its most powerful military force, and a leading democracy, is a key factor in limiting the frequency and destructiveness of great power, regional, and communal conflicts. The paradox of the post-cold war role of the United States is that it is the most powerful state in terms of both "hard" power resources (its economy and military forces) and "soft" ones (the appeal of its political system and culture), yet it is not so powerful that it can achieve all its international goals by acting alone. The United States lacks both the international and domestic prerequisites to resolve every conflict, and in each case its role must be proportionate to its interests at stake and the costs of pursuing them. Yet the United States can continue to enable and mobilize international coalitions to pursue shared security interests, whether or not the United States itself supplies large military forces.

The U.S. role will thus not be that of a lone global policeman; rather, the United States can frequently serve as the sheriff of the posse, leading shifting coalitions of friends and allies to address shared security concerns within the legitimizing framework of international organizations. This requires sustained attention to the infrastructure and institutional mechanisms that make U.S. leadership effective and joint action possible: forward stationing and preventive deployments of U.S. and allied forces, prepositioning of U.S. and allied equipment, advance planning and joint training to ensure interoperability with allied forces, and steady improvement in the conflict resolution abilities of an interlocking set of bilateral alliances, regional security organizations and alliances, and global institutions.

The United States has already had several important successes in leading international security coalitions while at the same time sharing burdens and responsibilities with its allies. U.S. leadership of the Desert Storm coalition, which involved international contributions of more than 240,000 troops and $70 billion, was one such success. More recently, in the fall of 1994 when Iraq again moved troops south toward Kuwait, prepositioning agreements with allies in the region were a key factor in allowing the United States to mobilize 150,000 U.S. troops quickly and deter any Iraqi aggression. In Macedonia, the United States and others have engaged in a preventive deployment that has thus far deterred the spread of conflict from the former Yugoslavia, and American diplomacy has made progress toward resolving the Greek–Macedonian dispute. In Haiti, the United States provided most of the troops for the initial intervention, yet others also contributed and the operation took place with the backing of the UN Security Council and has subsequently been turned over to a UN force. On the Korean peninsula, the United States has reached an agreement with North Korea to dismantle its nuclear weapons program, and its South Korean and Japanese allies will pay the great majority of the financial costs of implementing this agreement.

Defense Secretary Perry has distinguished vital, important, and humanitarian national interests and identified appropriate U.S. options on each level. When its vital interests are threatened and it cannot protect them by means short of force, the United States is ready to use force, unilaterally if necessary, to defend them. When U.S. interests are important but not vital, the United States has to weigh the costs and risks of using force, and must also consider more carefully whether it can bring together a multinational coalition rather than acting alone. When U.S. interests are primarily humanitarian, the use of U.S. military capabilities in a non-combat mode is appropriate when a humanitarian catastrophe threatens to overwhelm relief agencies, when the response requires capabilities that are unique to the U.S. military, and when the risk to American troops is minimal.

An important consideration in each of these three categories, and especially when U.S. interests are less than vital, is whether U.S. participation can win public and congressional support. Contrary to conventional wisdom, the U.S. public does not become weak-kneed at the risk of high casualties when vital interests are at stake – witness the high level of public support for the Desert Storm operation despite early predictions of thousands of casualties. Unless vital or important U.S. interests are involved, however, it can be counterproductive to send U.S. ground troops, who can become symbolic political targets, when peacekeepers from other states can serve equally well. To incur significant casualties where interests are few could jeopardize public support for the forward presence abroad that is crucial for deterring global or regional balance of power conflicts that could inflict grave damage to U.S. vital interests in the long run. The comparative advantages of the United States in many peacekeeping operations often lie in air and naval forces, logistics, transport, and intelligence assets. Thus, it is a measure of successful sharing of international responsibilities that the vast majority of UN peacekeepers have not been Americans.

Although the United States cannot single-handedly resolve the many communal conflicts that have erupted, it can work to make international institutions better able to deal with these conflicts. The Clinton administration is working to create a web of security cooperation, from bilateral alliances, to regional alliances and security organizations, to global organizations like the UN. At times, this will involve building new alliance structures, as in the enlargement of NATO and the revitalization of the U.S.–Japan alliance, or regional security organizations, as in the reinvigorated OSCE and the ARF. In other cases, it will require creating and leading ad hoc coalitions, like the Desert Storm coalition that defeated Iraq in the Gulf war. Sometimes, as in the Gulf war, the United States may work primarily through the UN to advance its diplomatic interests while at the same time retaining leadership of the military component of the operation as the leading contributor. In other cases where U.S. interests and forces are not as directly engaged, allies who have greater interests will naturally step into the lead. The key is to take the steps necessary to make ad hoc coalitions of the willing effective, such as developing agreed-upon mechanisms for burden-sharing, interoperability of forces, and decision-making mechanisms on missions and rules of engagement. This approach enables some states to act even when not all are willing to contribute, and, for those states most willing to contribute to internationally recognized missions, to lead the military component of the operation.

Those who sing the siren song of unilateralism without being willing to invest in international infrastructure fail to understand what makes U.S. leadership possible. They would unilaterally change the rules for paying for UN peacekeeping operations, for example, in which roughly seven foreign troops have served for every American peacekeeper deployed over the last year. The end result of such unilateralism would be the same as that of neo-isolationism: abandonment of the United States by its allies and friends in the face of cumulating threats.

Conclusion

Technological, social, and political change have made the sources of modern conflicts very different from those of the past. A good illustration of this is the changing role of the Balkans in World War I, World War II, and the present conflict in the former Yugoslavia. The great powers clashed over the Balkans in both World Wars, in part out of concern that Balkan conflicts with communal roots could upset a multipolar balance of power that was already complicated and rapidly shifting. In the present Balkan conflict, global balance of power considerations have played little role. The great powers have contributed peacekeeping forces out of humanitarian concerns and an interest in containing the conflict. The danger that the conflict will spread arises not from balance of power considerations as in the past, but from the possibility of escalating conflicts over identity that drag in neighboring states.

Realists, usually the pessimists when it comes to international politics, have it right that the balance of power, the nature of military technology, and the importance of territorially defined resources are important determinants of the sources, nature, and frequency of conflicts. Ironically, it is on these grounds that there is the most room for optimism. The United States has the deepest and most diverse range of power resources, other democratic leading powers are its close allies, nuclear deterrence inhibits great power conflicts, and territorial aggression is not as tempting as it once was. It is the factors that Liberals focus upon – the domestic structures of states, their values, identities, and cultures, and the international institutions for conflict resolution – that give cause for concern. States unhinged by the collapse of communism or rapid economic change are at risk of internal and external conflicts. Ethnic demagogues have leapt into the breach, using modern communications to incite groups dislocated by rapid economic and political change as a means of gaining power in weakened states.

Most important, international institutions designed around past conflicts have not yet caught up to the changed nature of post–cold war conflicts. The experience of past efforts to prevent conflicts provides ample evidence for the Liberal view that international institutions for conflict management, or their weakness or absence, matter.

In short, the bad news about post–cold war conflicts is that the world is least prepared for the most prevalent type – internal communal conflicts. The good news is that U.S.-led alliance systems and forward-stationed forces are creating a strong structural base for avoiding the most devastating types: regional and great power wars.

Notes

* This article was written while I was Assistant Secretary of Defense. It was originally prepared for the Aspen Institute Conference on Managing Conflict in the Post-Cold War World, Aspen, Colorado, August 2–6, 1995. I am grateful to Andrew Bennett for his assistance.
1 Jack S. Levy, *War in the Modern Great Power System, 1495–1975* (Lexington: University Press of Kentucky, 1983).
2 Joseph S. Nye, Jr., *Understanding International Conflicts* (New York, N.Y.: HarperCollins, 1993), pp. 1–24, 36–41.
3 Paul M. Kennedy, *The Rise and Fall of the Great Powers* (New York, N.Y.: Random House, 1988).
4 Joseph S. Nye, Jr., *Bound to Lead: The Changing Nature of American Power* (New York, N.Y.: Basic Books, 1990).
5 Robert O. Keohane and Joseph S. Nye, Jr., *Power and Interdependence: World Politics in Transition* (Boston: Little, Brown, 1977).
6 Richard N. Rosecrance, *The Rise of the Trading State: Commerce and Conquest in the Modern World* (New York, N.Y.: Basic Books, 1986).
7 Karl W. Deutsch, *Political Community and the North Atlantic Area: International Organization in the Light of Experience* (Princeton, N.J.: Princeton University Press, 1957).
8 Department of Defense, Office of International Security Affairs, *United States Security Strategy for Europe and NATO* (Washington, D.C., June 1995).
9 Department of Defense, Office of International Security Affairs, *United States Security Strategy for the East Asia-Pacific Region* (Washington, D.C., February 1995).
10 Department of Defense, Office of International Security Affairs, *United States Security Strategy for the Middle East* (Washington, D.C., May 1995).
11 Samuel P. Huntington, "The Clash of Civilizations?" *Foreign Affairs* 72 (Summer 1993).

Part 2

America's hard and soft power

5 The changing nature of world power*

Power in international politics is like the weather. Everyone talks about it, but few understand it. Just as farmers and meteorologists try to forecast storms, so do leaders and analysts try to understand the dynamics of major changes in the distribution of power among nations. Power transitions affect the fortunes of individual nations and are often associated with the cataclysmic storms of world war. But before we can examine theories of hegemonic transition – that is, some of the leading efforts to predict big changes in the international political weather – we first need to recognize some basic distinctions among the terms *power, balance of power*, and *hegemony*.

Power

Power, like love, is easier to experience than to define or measure. Power is the ability to achieve one's purposes or goals. The dictionary tells us that it is the ability to do things and to control others. Robert Dahl, a leading political scientist, defines power as the ability to get others to do what they otherwise would not do.[1] But when we measure power in terms of the changed behavior of others, we have to know their preferences. Otherwise, we may be as mistaken about our power as was the fox who thought he was hurting Brer Rabbit when he threw him into the briar patch. Knowing in advance how other people or nations would behave in the absence of our efforts is often difficult.

The behavioral definition of power may be useful to analysts and historians who devote considerable time to reconstructing the past, but to practical politicians and leaders it often seems too ephemeral. Because the ability to control others is often associated with the possession of certain resources, political leaders commonly define power as the possession of resources. These resources include population, territory, natural resources, economic size, military forces, and political stability, among others.[2] The virtue of this definition is that it makes power appear more concrete, measurable, and predictable than does the behavioral definition. Power in this sense means holding the high cards in the international poker game. A basic rule of poker is that if your opponent is showing cards that can beat anything you hold, fold your hand. If you know you will lose a war, don't start it.

Some wars, however, have been started by the eventual losers, which suggests that political leaders sometimes take risks or make mistakes. Often the opponent's cards are not all showing in the game of international politics. As in poker, playing skills, such as bluff and deception, can make a big difference. Even when there is no deception, mistakes can be made about which power resources are most relevant in particular situations (for example, France and Britain had more tanks than Hitler in 1940, but Hitler had greater maneuverability and a better military strategy). On the other hand, in long wars when there is time to mobilize, depth of territory and the size of an economy become more important, as the Soviet Union and the United States demonstrated in World War II.

Power conversion is a basic problem that arises when we think of power in terms of resources. Some countries are better than others at converting their resources into effective influence, just as some skilled card players win despite being dealt weak hands. Power conversion is the capacity to convert potential power, as measured by resources, to realized power, as measured by the changed behavior of others. Thus, one has to know about a country's skill at power conversion as well as its possession of power resources to predict outcomes correctly.

Another problem is determining which resources provide the best basis for power in any particular context. In earlier periods, power resources were easier to judge. According to historian A. J. P. Taylor, traditionally "the test of a Great Power is . . . the test of strength for war."[3] For example, in the agrarian economies of eighteenth-century Europe, population was a critical power resource because it provided a base for taxes and recruitment of infantry. In population, France dominated Western Europe. Thus, at the end of the Napoleonic Wars, Prussia presented its fellow victors at the Congress of Vienna with a precise plan for its own reconstruction in order to maintain the balance of power. Its plan listed the territories and populations it had lost since 1805, and the territories and populations it would need to regain equivalent numbers.[4] In the prenationalist period, it did not much matter that many of the people in those provinces did not speak German or felt themselves to be German. However, within half a century, nationalist sentiments mattered very much. Germany's seizure of Alsace-Lorraine from France in 1870, for example, made hope of any future alliance with France impossible.

Another change that occurred during the nineteenth century was the growing importance of industry and rail systems that made rapid mobilization possible. In the 1860s, Bismarck's Germany pioneered the use of railways to transport armies for quick victories. Although Russia had always had greater population resources than the rest of Europe, they were difficult to mobilize. The growth of the rail system in Western Russia at the beginning of the twentieth century was one of the reasons the Germans feared rising Russian power in 1914. Further, the spread of rail systems on the Continent helped deprive Britain of the luxury of concentrating on naval power. There was no longer time, should it prove necessary, to insert an army to prevent another great power from dominating the Continent.

The application of industrial technology to warfare has long had a powerful impact. Advanced science and technology have been particularly critical power resources since the beginning of the nuclear age in 1945. But the power derived from nuclear weapons has proven to be so awesome and destructive that its actual application is muscle-bound. Nuclear war is simply too costly. More generally, there are many situations where any use of force may be inappropriate or too costly. In 1853, for example, Admiral Matthew C. Perry could threaten to bombard Japan if it did not open its ports for supplies and trade, but it is hard to imagine that the United States could effectively threaten force to open Japanese markets today.

The changing sources of power

Some observers have argued that the sources of power are, in general, moving away from the emphasis on military force and conquest that marked earlier eras. In assessing international power today, factors such as technology, education, and economic growth are becoming more important, whereas geography, population, and raw materials are becoming less important. Kenneth Waltz argues that a 5-percent rate of economic growth in the United States for three years would add more to American strength than does our alliance with Britain.[5] Richard Rosecrance argues that since 1945, the world has been poised between a territorial system composed of states that view power in terms of land mass, and a trading system "based in states which recognize that self-sufficiency is an illusion." In the past, says Rosecrance, "it was cheaper to seize another state's territory by force than to develop the sophisticated economic and trading apparatus needed to derive benefit from commercial exchange with it."[6]

If so, perhaps we are in a "Japanese period" in world politics. Japan has certainly done far better with its strategy as a trading state after 1945 than it did with its military strategy to create a Greater East Asian Co-Prosperity sphere in the 1930s. But Japan's security vis-à-vis its large military neighbors – China and the Soviet Union – depends heavily on U.S. protection. In short, even if we can define power clearly, it still has become more difficult to be clear about the relationship of particular resources to it. Thus, we cannot leap too quickly to the conclusion that all trends favor economic power or countries like Japan.

Like other forms of power, economic power cannot be measured simply in terms of tangible resources. Intangible aspects also matter. For example, outcomes generally depend on bargaining, and bargaining depends on relative costs in particular situations and skill in converting potential power into effects. Relative costs are determined not only by the total amount of measurable economic resources of a country but also by the degree of its interdependence in a relationship. If, for example, the United States and Japan depend on each other but one is less dependent than the other, that asymmetry is a source of power. The United States may be less vulnerable than Japan if the relationship breaks down, and it may use that threat as a source of power.[7] Thus, an assessment of Japanese and American power must look not only at shares of resources but also at the relative vulnerabilities of both countries.

Another consideration is that most large countries today find military force more costly to apply than in previous centuries. This has resulted from the dangers of nuclear escalation, the difficulty of ruling nationalistically awakened populations in otherwise weak states, the danger of rupturing profitable relations on other issues, and the public opposition in Western democracies to prolonged and expensive military conflicts. Even so, the increased cost of military force does not mean that it will be ruled out. To the contrary, in an anarchic system of states where there is no higher government to settle conflicts and where the ultimate recourse is self-help, this could never happen. In some cases, the stakes may justify a costly use of force. And, as recent episodes in Grenada and Libya have shown, not all uses of force by great powers involve high costs.[8]

Even if the direct use of force were banned among a group of countries, military force would still play an important political role. For example, the American military role in deterring threats to allies, or of assuring access to a crucial resource such as oil in the Persian Gulf, means that the provision of protective force can be used in bargaining situations. Sometimes the linkage may be direct; more often it is a factor not mentioned openly but present in the back of statesmen's minds.

In addition, there is the consideration that is sometimes called "the second face of power."[9] Getting other states to change might be called the directive or commanding method of exercising power. Command power can rest on inducements ("carrots") or threats ("sticks"). But there is also an indirect way to exercise power. A country may achieve the outcomes it prefers in world politics because other countries want to follow it or have agreed to a system that produces such effects. In this sense, it is just as important to set the agenda and structure the situations in world politics as it is to get others to change in particular situations. This aspect of power – that is, getting others to want what you want – might be called indirect or co-optive power behavior. It is in contrast to the active command power behavior of getting others to do what you want.[10] Co-optive power can rest on the attraction of one's ideas or on the ability to set the political agenda in a way that shapes the preferences that others express. Parents of teenagers know that if they have structured their children's beliefs and preferences, their power will be greater and will last longer than if they had relied only on active control. Similarly, political leaders and philosophers have long understood the power that comes from setting the agenda and determining the framework of a debate. The ability to establish preferences tends to be associated with intangible power resources such as culture, ideology, and institutions. This dimension can be thought of as soft power, in contrast to the hard command power usually associated with tangible resources like military and economic strength.[11]

Robert Cox argues that the nineteenth-century *Pax Britannica* and the twentieth-century *Pax Americana* were effective because they created liberal international economic orders, in which certain types of economic relations were privileged over others and liberal international rules and institutions were broadly accepted. Following the insights of the Italian thinker Antonio Gramsci, Cox argues that the most critical feature for a dominant country is the ability to obtain a broad measure of consent on general principles – principles that ensure the supremacy of the leading state and dominant social classes – and at the same time to offer some prospect of satisfaction to the less powerful. Cox identifies Britain from 1845 to 1875 and the United States from 1945 to 1967 as such countries.[12] Although we may not agree with his terminology or dates, Cox has touched a major point: soft co-optive power is just as important as hard command power. If a state can make its power legitimate in the eyes of others, it will encounter less resistance to its wishes. If its culture and ideology are attractive, others will more willingly follow. If it can establish international norms that are consistent with its society, it will be less likely to have to change. If it can help support institutions that encourage other states to channel or limit their activities in ways the dominant state prefers, it may not need as many costly exercises of coercive or hard power in bargaining situations. In short, the universalism of a country's culture and its ability to establish a set of favorable rules and institutions that govern areas of international activity are critical sources of power.[13] These soft sources of power are becoming more important in world politics today.

Such considerations question the conclusion that the world is about to enter a Japanese era in world politics. The nature of power is changing and some of the changes will favor Japan, but some of them may favor the United States even more. In command power, Japan's economic strength is increasing, but it remains vulnerable in terms of raw materials and relatively weak in terms of military force. And in co-optive power, Japan's culture is highly insular and it has yet to develop a major voice in international institutions. The United States, on the other hand, has a universalistic popular culture and a major role in international institutions. Although such factors may change in the future, they raise an important question about the present situation: What resources are the most important sources of power today? A look at the five-century-old modern state system shows that different power resources played critical roles in different periods. (See Table 5.1.) The sources of power are never static and they continue to change in today's world.

In an age of information-based economies and transnational interdependence, power is becoming less transferable, less tangible, and less coercive. However, the transformation of power is incomplete. The twenty-first century will certainly see a greater role for informational and institutional power, but military force will remain

Table 5.1 Leading states and major power resources, 1500s–1900s

Period	Leading state	Major resources
Sixteenth century	Spain	Gold bullion, colonial trade, mercenary armies, dynastic ties
Seventeenth century	Netherlands	Trade, capital markets, navy
Eighteenth century	France	Population, rural industry, public administration, army
Nineteenth century	Britain	Industry, political cohesion, finance and credit, navy, liberal norms, island location (easy to defend)
Twentieth century	United States	Economic scale, scientific and technical leadership, universalistic culture, military forces and alliances, liberal international regimes, hub of transnational communication

an important factor. Economic scale, both in markets and in natural resources, will also remain important. As the service sector grows within modern economies, the distinction between services and manufacturing will continue to blur. Information will become more plentiful, and the critical resource will be the organizational capacity for rapid and flexible response. Political cohesion will remain important, as will a universalistic popular culture. On some of these dimensions of power, the United States is well endowed; on others, questions arise. But even larger questions arise for the other major contenders – Europe, Japan, the Soviet Union, and China. But first we need to look at the patterns in the distribution of power – balances and hegemonies, how they have changed over history, and what that implies for the position of the United States.

Balance of power

International relations is far from a precise science. Conditions in various periods always differ in significant details, and human behavior reflects personal choices. Moreover, theorists often suffer from writing in the midst of events, rather than viewing them from a distance. Thus, powerful theories – those that are both simple and accurate – are rare. Yet political leaders (and those who seek to explain behavior) must generalize in order to chart a path through the apparent chaos of changing events. One of the longest-standing and most frequently used concepts is balance of power, which eighteenth-century philosopher David Hume called "a constant rule of prudent politics."[14] For centuries, balance of power has been the starting point for realistic discussions of international politics.

To an extent, balance of power is a useful predictor of how states will behave; that is, states will align in a manner that will prevent any one state from developing a preponderance of power. This is based on two assumptions: that states exist in an anarchic system with no higher government and that political leaders will act first to reduce risks to the independence of their states. The policy of balancing power helps to explain why in modern times a large state cannot grow forever into a world empire. States seek to increase their powers through internal growth and external alliances. Balance of power predicts that if one state appears to grow too strong, others will ally against it so as to avoid threats to their own independence. This behavior, then, will preserve the structure of the system of states.

However, not all balance-of-power predictions are so obvious. For example, this theory implies that professions of ideological faith will be poor predictors of behavior. But despite Britain's criticism of the notorious Stalin-Hitler pact of 1939, it was quick to make an alliance with Stalin's Soviet Union in 1941. As Winston Churchill explained at the time, "If I learned that Hitler had invaded Hell, I would manage to say something good about the Devil in the House of Commons."[15] Further, balance of power does not mean that political leaders must maximize the power of their own states in the short run. Bandwagoning – that is, joining the stronger rather than the weaker side – might produce more immediate spoils. As Mussolini discovered in his ill-fated pact with Hitler, the danger in bandwagoning is that independence may be threatened by the stronger ally in the long term. Thus, to say that states will act to balance power is a strong generalization in international relations, but it is far from being a perfect predictor.

Proximity and perceptions of threat also affect the way in which balancing of power is played out.[16] A small state like Finland, for instance, cannot afford to try to balance Soviet power. Instead, it seeks to preserve its independence through neutrality. Balance of power and the proposition that "the enemy of my enemy is my friend" help to explain the larger contours of current world politics, but only when proximity and perceptions are considered. The United States was by far the strongest power after 1945. A mechanical application of power balance might seem to predict an alliance against the Untied States. In fact, Europe and Japan allied with the United States because the Soviet Union, while weaker in overall power, posed a proximate threat to its neighbors. Geography and psychology are both important factors in geopolitics.

The term *balance of power* is sometimes used not as a prediction of policy but as a description of how power is distributed. In the latter case, it is more accurate to refer to the distribution of power. In other instances, though, the term is used to refer to an evenly balanced distribution of power, like a pair of hanging scales. The problem with this usage is that the ambiguities of measuring power make it difficult to determine when an equal balance exists. In fact, the major concerns in world politics tend to arise from inequalities of power, and particularly from major changes in the unequal distribution of power.

Hegemony in modern history

No matter how power is measured, an equal distribution of power among major states is relatively rare. More often the processes of uneven growth, which realists consider a basic law of international politics, mean that some states will be rising and others declining. These transitions in the distribution of power stimulate statesmen to form alliances, to build armies, and to take risks that balance or check rising powers. But the balancing of power does not always prevent the emergence of a dominant state. Theories of hegemony and power transition try to explain why some states that become preponderant later lose that preponderance.

As far back as ancient Greece, observers attempting to explain the causes of major world wars have cited the uncertainties associated with the transition of power. Shifts in the international distribution of power create the conditions likely to lead to the most important wars.[17] However, while power transitions provide useful warning about periods of heightened risk, there is no iron law of hegemonic war. If there were, Britain and the United States would have gone to war at the beginning of this century, when the Americans surpassed the British in economic and naval power in the Western Hemisphere. Instead, when the United States backed Venezuela in its boundary dispute with British Guyana in 1895, British leaders appeased the rising American power instead of going to war with it.[18]

When power is distributed unevenly, political leaders and theorists use terms such as *empire* and *hegemony*. Although there have been many empires in history, those in the modern world have not encompassed all major countries. Even the

British Empire at the beginning of this century encompassed only a quarter of the world's population and Britain was just one of a half-dozen major powers in the global balance of power. The term *hegemony* is applied to a variety of situations in which one state appears to have considerably more power than others. For example, for years China accused the Soviet Union of seeking hegemony in Asia. When Soviet leader Mikhail Gorbachev and Chinese leader Deng Xiaoping met in 1989, they pledged that "neither side will seek hegemony in any form anywhere in the world."[19]

Although the word comes from the ancient Greek and refers to the dominance of one state over others in the system, it is used in diverse and confused ways. Part of the problem is that unequal distribution of power is a matter of degree, and there is no general agreement on how much inequality and what types of power constitute hegemony. All too often, hegemony is used to refer to different behaviors and degrees of control, which obscures rather than clarifies that analysis. For example, Charles Doran cites aggressive military power, while Robert Keohane looks at preponderance in economic resources. Robert Gilpin sometimes uses the terms *imperial* and *hegemonic* interchangeably to refer to a situation in which "a single powerful state controls or dominates the lesser states in the system."[20] British hegemony in the nineteenth century is commonly cited even though Britain ranked third behind the United States and Russia in GNP and third behind Russia and France in military expenditures at the peak of its relative power around 1870. Britain was first in the more limited domains of manufacturing, trade, finance, and naval power.[21] Yet theorists often contend that "full hegemony requires productive, commercial, and financial as well as political and military power."[22]

Joshua Goldstein usefully defines hegemony as "being able to dictate, or at least dominate, the rules and arrangements by which international relations, political and economic, are conducted. . . . Economic hegemony implies the ability to center the world economy around itself. Political hegemony means being able to dominate the world militarily."[23] However, there are still two important questions to be answered with regard to how the term *hegemony* is used. First, what is the scope of the hegemon's control? In the modern world, a situation in which one country can dictate political and economic arrangements has been extremely rare. Most examples have been regional, such as Soviet power in Eastern Europe, American influence in the Caribbean, and India's control over its small neighbors – Sikkim, Bhutan, and Nepal.[24] In addition, one can find instances in which one country was able to set the rules and arrangements governing specific issues in world politics, such as the American role in money or trade in the early postwar years. But there has been no global, system-wide hegemon during the past two centuries. Contrary to the myths about *Pax Britannica* and *Pax Americana*, British and American hegemonies have been regional and issue-specific rather than general.

Second, we must ask what types of power resources are necessary to produce a hegemonic degree of control. Is military power necessary? Or is it enough to have preponderance in economic resources? How do the two types of power relate to each other? Obviously, the answers to such questions can tell us a great deal about the future world, in which Japan may be an economic giant and a military dwarf while the Soviet Union may fall into the opposite situation. A careful look at the interplay of military and economic power raises doubt about the degree of American hegemony in the postwar period.[25]

Theories of Hegemonic Transition and Stability

General hegemony is the concern of theories and analogies about the instability and dangers supposedly caused by hegemonic transitions. Classical concerns about hegemony among leaders and philosophers focus on military power and "conflicts precipitated by the military effort of one dominant actor to expand well beyond the arbitrary security confines set by tradition, historical accident, or coercive pressures."[26] In this approach, hegemonic preponderance arises out of military expansion, such as the efforts of Louis XIV, Napoleon, or Hitler to dominate world politics. The important point is that, except for brief periods, none of the attempted military hegemonies in modern times has succeeded. (See Table 5.2.) No modern state has been able to develop sufficient military power to transform the balance of power into a long-lived hegemony in which one state could dominate the world militarily.

More recently, many political scientists have focused on economic power as a source of hegemonic control. Some define hegemonic economic power in terms of resources – that is, preponderance in control over raw materials, sources of capital, markets, and production of goods. Others use the behavioral definition in which a hegemon is a state able to set the rules and arrangements for the global economy. Robert Gilpin, a leading theorist of hegemonic transition, sees Britain and America, having created and enforced the rules of a liberal economic order, as the successive hegemons since the Industrial Revolution.[27] Some political economists argue that world economic stability requires a single stabilizer and that periods of such stability have coincided with periods of hegemony. In this view, *Pax Britannica* and *Pax Americana* were the periods when Britain and the United States were strong enough to create and enforce the rules for a liberal international economic order in the nineteenth and twentieth centuries. For example, it is often argued that economic stability "historically has occurred when there has been a sole hegemonic power; Britain from 1815 to World War I and the United States from 1945 to around 1970. ... With a sole hegemonic power, the rules of the game can

Table 5.2 Modern efforts at military hegemony

State attempting hegemony	Ensuing hegemonic war	New order after war
Hapsburg Spain	Thirty Years' War, 1618–1648	Peace of Westphalia, 1648
Louis XIV's France	Wars of Louis XIV	Treaty of Utrecht, 1713
Napoleon's France	1792–1815	Congress of Vienna, 1815
Germany (and Japan)	1914–1945	United Nations, 1945

Source: Charles F. Doran, *The Politics of Assimilation: Hegemony and Its Aftermath* (Baltimore: Johns Hopkins University Press, 1971), 19–20.

be established and enforced. Lesser countries have little choice but to go along. Without a hegemonic power, conflict is the order of the day."[28] Such theories of hegemonic stability and decline are often used to predict that the United States will follow the experience of Great Britain, and that instability will ensue. Goldstein, for example, argues that "we are moving toward the 'weak hegemony' end of the spectrum and . . . this seems to increase the danger of hegemonic war."[29]

I argue, however, that the theory of hegemonic stability and transition will not tell us as much about the future of the United States. Theorists of hegemonic stability generally fail to spell out the causal connections between military and economic power and hegemony. As already noted, nineteenth-century Britain was not militarily dominant nor was it the world's largest economy, and yet Britain is portrayed by Gilpin and others as hegemonic. Did Britain's military weakness at that time allow the United States and Russia, the two larger economies, to remain mostly outside the liberal system of free trade? Or, to take a twentieth-century puzzle, did a liberal international economy depend on postwar American military strength or only its economic power? Are both conditions necessary today, or have modern nations learned to cooperate through international institutions?

One radical school of political economists, the neo-Marxists, has attempted to answer similar questions about the relationship between economic and military hegemony, but their theories are unconvincing. For example, Immanuel Wallerstein defines hegemony as a situation in which power is so unbalanced that

> one power can largely impose its rules and its wishes (at the very least by effective veto power) in the economic, political, military, diplomatic, and even cultural arenas. The material base of such power lies in the ability of enterprises domiciled in that power to operate more efficiently in all three major economic arenas – agro-industrial production, commerce, and finance.[30]

According to Wallerstein, hegemony is rare and "refers to that short interval in which there is simultaneously advantage in all three economic domains." At such times, the other major powers become "*de facto* client states." Wallerstein claims there have been only three modern instances of hegemony – in the Netherlands, 1620–1650; in Britain, 1815–1873; and in the United States, 1945–1967. (See Table 5.3.) He argues that "in each case, the hegemony was secured by a thirty-year-long world war," after which a new order followed – the Peace of Westphalia

Table 5.3 A neo-Marxist view of hegemony

Hegemony	World war securing hegemony	Period of dominance	Decline
Dutch	Thirty Years' War, 1618–1648	1620–1650	1650–1672
British	Napoleonic Wars, 1792–1815	1815–1873	1873–1896
American	World Wars I and II, 1914–1945	1945–1967	1967–

Source: Immanuel Wallerstein, *The Politics of the World Economy* (New York: Cambridge University Press, 1984), 41–42.

after 1648; the Concert of Europe after 1815; and the United Nations–Bretton Woods system after 1945.[31] According to this theory, the United States will follow the Dutch and the British path to decline.

The neo-Marxist view of hegemony is unconvincing and a poor predictor of future events because it superficially links military and economic hegemony and has many loose ends. For example, contrary to Wallerstein's theory, the Thirty Years' War *coincided* with Dutch hegemony, and Dutch decline began with the Peace of Westphalia. The Dutch were not militarily strong enough to stand up to the British on the sea and could barely defend themselves against the French on land, "despite their trade-derived wealth."[32] Further, although Wallerstein argues that British hegemony began after the Napoleonic Wars, he is not clear about how the new order in the balance of power – that is, the nineteenth-century Concert of Europe – related to Britain's supposed ability to impose a global free-trade system. For example, Louis XIV's France, which many historians view as the dominant military power in the second half of the seventeenth century, is excluded from Wallerstein's schema altogether. Thus, the neo-Marxist historical analogies seem forced into a Procrustean ideological bed, while other cases are left out of bed altogether.

Others have attempted to organize past periods of hegemony into century-long cycles. In 1919, British geopolitician Sir Halford Mackinder argued that unequal growth among nations tends to produce a hegemonic world war about every hundred years.[33] More recently, political scientist George Modelski proposed a hundred year cyclical view of changes in world leadership. (See Table 5.4.) In this view, a long cycle begins with a major global war. A single state then emerges as the new world power and legitimizes its preponderance with postwar peace treaties. (Preponderance is defined as having at least half the resources available for global orderkeeping.) The new leader supplies security and order for the international system. In time, though, the leader loses legitimacy, and deconcentration of power leads to another global war. The new leader that emerges from that war may not be the state that challenged the old leader but one of the more innovative allies in the winning coalition (as, not Germany, but the United States replaced Britain). According to Modelski's theory, the United States began its decline in 1973.[34] If his assumptions are correct, it may be Japan and not

Table 5.4 Long cycles of world leadership

Cycle	Global war	Preponderance	Decline
1495–1580	1494–1516	Portugal, 1516–1540	1540–1580
1580–1688	1580–1609	Netherlands, 1609–1640	1640–1688
1688–1792	1688–1713	Britain, 1714–1740	1740–1792
1792–1914	1792–1815	Britain, 1815–1850	1850–1914
1914–	1914–1945	United States, 1945–1973	1973–

Source: George Modelski, *Long Cycles in World Politics* (Seattle: University of Washington Press, 1987), 40, 42, 44, 102, 131, 147.

the Soviet Union that will most effectively challenge the United States in the future.

Modelski and his followers suggest that the processes of decline are associated with long waves in the global economy. They associate a period of rising prices and resource scarcities with loss of power, and concentration of power with falling prices, resource abundance, and economic innovation.[35] However, in linking economic and political cycles, these theorists become enmeshed in the controversy surrounding long-cycle theory. Many economists are skeptical about the empirical evidence for alleged long economic waves and about dating historical waves by those who use the concept.[36]

Further, we cannot rely on the long-cycle theory to predict accurately the American future. Modelski's treatment of political history is at best puzzling. For example, he ranks sixteenth-century Portugal as a hegemon rather than Spain, even though Spain controlled a richer overseas empire and swallowed up Portugal a century later. Likewise, Britain is ranked as a hegemon from 1714 to 1740, even though eighteenth-century France was the larger power. Modelski's categories are odd in part because he uses naval power as the sine qua non of global power, which results in a truncated view of military and diplomatic history. Although naval power was more important for countries that relied on overseas possessions, the balance in Europe depended on the armies on the continent. Britain could not afford to ignore its armies on land and rely solely on its naval power. To preserve the balance of power, Britain had to be heavily involved in land wars on the European continent at the beginning of the eighteenth, nineteenth, and twentieth centuries. More specifically, Modelski underrates the Spanish navy in the sixteenth century as well as the French navy, which outnumbered Britain's, in the late seventeenth century.[37] Some major wars, such as the Thirty Years' War and the Anglo-French wars of the eighteenth century, are excluded altogether from Modelski's organization of history.

Vague definitions and arbitrary schematizations alert us to the inadequacies of such grand theories of hegemony and decline. Most theorists of hegemonic transition tend to shape history to their own theories by focusing on particular power resources and ignoring others. Examples include the poorly explained relationship between military and political power and the unclear link between decline and major war. Since there have been wars among the great powers during 60 percent of the years from 1500 to the present, there are plenty of candidates to associate with any given scheme.[38] Even if we consider only the nine general wars that have involved nearly all the great powers and produced high levels of casualties, some of them, such as the Seven Years' War (1755–1763), are not considered hegemonic in any of the schemes. As sociologist Pitirim Sorokin concludes, "no regular periodicity is noticeable."[39] At best, the various schematizations of hegemony and war are only suggestive. They do not provide a reliable basis for predicting the future of American power or for evaluating the risk of world war as we enter the twenty-first century. Loose historical analogies about decline and falsely deterministic political theories are not merely academic: they may lead to inappropriate policies. The real problems of a post-cold-war world will not be new challenges for hegemony, but the new challenges of transnational interdependence.

Notes

* This article draws from my book *Bound to Lead: The Changing Nature of American Power* (Basic Books, 1990).
1 Robert A. Dahl, *Who Governs? Democracy and Power in an American City* (New Haven, Conn.: Yale University Press, 1961). See also James March, "The Power of Power" in David Easton, ed., *Varieties of Political Theory* (New York: Prentice Hall, 1966), 39–70; Herbert Simon, *Models of Man* (New York: John Wiley, 1957); and David Baldwin, "Power Analysis and World Politics," *World Politics* 31 (January 1979): 161–94.
2 See Ray S. Cline, *World Power Assessment* (Boulder, Colo.: Westview Press, 1977); Hans J. Morgenthau, *Politics among Nations* (New York: Alfred Knopf, 1955), chap. 9; and Klaus Knorr, *The Power of Nations* (New York: Basic Books, 1975), chaps, 3, 4.
3 A. J. P. Taylor, *The Struggle for Mastery in Europe, 1848–1918* (Oxford, Eng.: Oxford University Press, 1954), xxix.
4 Edward V. Gulick, *Europe's Classical Balance of Power* (New York: W. W. Norton, 1955), 248–51.
5 Kenneth N. Waltz, *Theory of International Politics* (Reading, Mass.: Addison-Wesley, 1979), 172.
6 Richard N. Rosecrance, *The Rise of the Trading State* (New York: Basic Books, 1986), 16, 160.
7 Robert O. Keohane and Joseph S. Nye, Jr., *Power and Interdependence* (Boston: Little, Brown, 1977), chap. 1. See also R. Harrison Wagner, "Economic Interdependence, Bargaining Power and Political Influence," *International Organization* 41 (Summer 1988): 461–84.
8 Keohane and Nye, *Power and Interdependence*, 27–29; Robert O. Keohane and Joseph S. Nye, Jr., "Power and Interdependence Revisited," *International Organization* 41 (Autumn 1987): 725–53.
9 Peter Bachrach and Morton S. Baratz, "Decisions and Nondecisions: An Analytical Framework," *American Political Science Review* 57 (September 1963): 632–42. See also Richard Mansbach and John Vasquez, *In Search of Theory: A New Paradigm for Global Politics* (Englewood Cliffs, N.J.: Prentice Hall, 1981).
10 Susan Strange uses the term *structural power*, which she defines as "power to shape and determine the structures of the global political economy" in *States and Markets* (New York: Basil Blackwell, 1988), 24. My term, *co-optive power*, is similar in its focus on preferences but is somewhat broader, encompassing all elements of international politics. The term *structural power*, in contrast, tends to be associated with the neo-realist theories of Kenneth Waltz.
11 The distinction between hard and soft power resources is one of degree, both in the nature of the behavior and in the tangibility of the resources. Both types are aspects of the ability to achieve one's purposes by controlling the behavior of others. Command power – the ability to change what others *do* – can rest on coercion or inducement. Co-optive power – the ability to shape what others *want* – can rest on the attractiveness of one's culture and ideology or the ability to manipulate the agenda of political choices in a manner that makes actors fail to express some preferences because they seem to be too unrealistic. The forms of behavior between command and co-optive power range along this continuum:

| Command power | coercion | inducement | agenda-setting | attraction | Co-optive power |

Further, soft power resources tend to be associated with co-optive power behavior, whereas hard power resources are usually associated with command behavior. But the relationship is imperfect. For example, countries may be attracted to others with command power by myths of invincibility, and command power may sometimes be used to establish institutions that later become regarded as legitimate. But the general association is strong enough to allow the useful shorthand reference to hard and soft power resources.

12 Robert W. Cox, *Production, Power, and World Order* (New York: Columbia University Press, 1987), chaps. 6, 7.
13 See Stephen D. Krasner, *International Regimes* (Ithaca, N.Y.: Cornell University Press, 1983).
14 David Hume, "Of the Balance of Power" in Charles W. Hendel, ed., *David Hume's Political Essays* (1742; reprint, Indianapolis, Ind.: Bobbs-Merrill, 1953), 142–44.
15 Quoted in Waltz, *International Politics*, 166.
16 Stephen M. Walt, "Alliance Formation and the Balance of Power," *International Security* 9 (Spring 985): 3–43. See also by Walt, *The Origins of Alliances* (Ithaca, N.Y.: Cornell University Press, 1987), 3–26, 263–66.
17 A. F. K. Organski and Jack Kugler, *The War Ledger* (Chicago: University of Chicago Press, 1980), chap. 1.
18 Stephen R. Rock, *Why Peace Breaks Out: Great Power Rapprochement in Historical Perspective* (Chapel Hill: University of North Carolina Press, 1989).
19 "New Era Declared as China Visit Ends," *International Herald Tribune*, 19 May 1989.
20 Charles F. Doran, *The Politics of Assimilation: Hegemony and Its Aftermath* (Baltimore: Johns Hopkins University Press, 1971), 70; Robert O. Keohane, *After Hegemony* (Princeton, N.J.: Princeton University Press, 1984), 32; Robert Gilpin, *War and Change in World Politics* (New York: Cambridge University Press, 1981), 29.
21 Bruce M. Russett, "The Mysterious Case of Vanishing Hegemony; or, Is Mark Twain Really Dead?" *International Organization* 39 (Spring 1985): 212.
22 Robert C. North and Julie Strickland, "Power Transition and Hegemonic Succession" (Paper delivered at the meeting of the International Studies Association, Anaheim, Calif., March–April 1986), 5.
23 Joshua S. Goldstein, *Long Cycles: Prosperity and War in the Modern Age* (New Haven, Conn.: Yale University Press, 1988), 281.
24 James R. Kurth, "Economic Change and State Development" in Jan Triska, ed., *Dominant Powers and Subordinate States: The United States in Latin America and the Soviet Union in Eastern Europe* (Durham, N.C.: Duke University Press, 1986), 88.
25 The distinction between definitions in terms of resources or behavior and the importance of indicating scope are indicated in the following table. My usage stresses behavior and broad scope.

Approaches to hegemony

	Power resources	*Power behavior*	*Scope*
Political/military hegemony	Army/navy (Modelski)	Define the military hierarchy (Doran)	Global or regional
Economic hegemony	Raw materials, capital, markets, production (Keohane)	Set rules for economic bargains (Goldstein)	General or issue-specific

26 Doran, *Politics of Assimilation*, 15.
27 Keohane, *After Hegemony*, 32; Gilpin, *War and Change*, 144.

28 Michael Moffitt, "Shocks, Deadlocks and Scorched Earth: Reaganomics and the Decline of U.S. Hegemony," *World Policy Journal* 4 (Fall 1987): 576.

29 Goldstein, *Long Cycles*, 357.

30 Immanuel M. Wallerstein, *The Politics of the World-Economy: The States, the Movements, and the Civilizations: Essays* (New York: Cambridge University Press, 1984), 38, 41.

31 Ibid.

32 Goldstein, *Long Cycles*, 317.

33 Halford J. Mackinder, *Democratic Ideals and Reality: A Study in the Politics of Reconstruction* New York: Henry Holt and Co., 1919), 1–2.

34 George Modelski, "The Long Cycle of Global Politics and the Nation-State," *Comparative Studies in Society and History* 20 (April 1978): 214–35; George Modelski, *Long Cycles in World Politics* (Seattle: University of Washington Press, 1987).

35 William R. Thompson, *On Global War: Historical Structural Approaches to World Politics* (Columbia: University of South Carolina Press, 1988), chaps. 3, 8.

36 Richard N. Rosecrance, "Long Cycle Theory and International Relations," *International Organization* 41 (Spring 1987): 291–95. An interesting but ultimately unconvincing discussion can be found in Goldstein, *Long Cycles*.

37 Paul Kennedy, *The Rise and Fall of the Great Powers: Economic Change and Military Conflict from 1500 to 2000* (New York: Random House, 1987), 99.

38 Jack S. Levy, "Declining Power and the Preventive Motivation for War," *World Politics* 40 (October 1987): 82–107. See also Jack S. Levy, *War in the Modern Great Power System, 1495–1975* (Lexington: University of Kentucky Press, 1983), 97.

39 Pitirim Aleksandrovich Sorokin, *Social and Cultural Dynamics: A Study of Change in Major Systems of Art, Truth, Ethics, Law and Social Relationships* (1957; reprint, Boston: Porter Sargent, 1970), 561.

6   Soft power*

The Cold War is over and Americans are trying to understand their place in a world without a defining Soviet threat. Polls report that nearly half the public believes the country is in decline, and that those who believe in decline tend to favor protectionism and to counsel withdrawal from what they consider "overextended international commitments."

In a world of growing interdependence, such advice is counterproductive and could bring on the decline it is supposed to avert; for if the most powerful country fails to lead, the consequences for international stability could be disastrous. Throughout history, anxiety about decline and shifting balances of power has been accompanied by tension and miscalculation. Now that Soviet power is declining and Japanese power rising, misleading theories of American decline and inappropriate analogies between the United States and Great Britain in the late nineteenth century have diverted our attention away from the real issue – how power is changing in world politics.

The United States is certainly less powerful at the end of the twentieth century than it was in 1945. Even conservative estimates show that the U.S. share of global product has declined from more than a third of the total after World War II to a little more than a fifth in the 1980s. That change, however, reflects the artificial effect of World War II: Unlike the other great powers, the United States was *strengthened* by the war. But that artificial preponderance was bound to erode as other countries regained their economic health. The important fact is that the U.S. economy's share of the global product has been relatively constant for the past decade and a half. The Council on Competitiveness finds that the U.S. share of world product has averaged 23 per cent each year since the mid-1970s. The CIA, using numbers that reflect the purchasing power of different currencies, reports that the American share of world product increased slightly from 25 per cent in 1975 to 26 per cent in 1988.

These studies suggest that the effect of World War II lasted about a quarter century and that most of the decline worked its way through the system by the mid-1970s. In fact, the big adjustment of American commitments occurred with then President Richard Nixon's withdrawal from Vietnam and the end of the convertibility of the dollar into gold.

The dictionary tells us that power means an ability to do things and control others, to get others to do what they otherwise would not. Because the ability to control others is often associated with the possession of certain resources, politicians and diplomats commonly define power as the possession of population, territory, natural resources, economic size, military forces, and political stability. For example, in the agrarian economies of eighteenth-century Europe, population was a critical power resource since it provided a base for taxes and recruitment of infantry.

Traditionally the test of a great power was its strength in war. Today, however, the definition of power is losing its emphasis on military force and conquest that marked earlier eras. The factors of technology, education, and economic growth are becoming more significant in international power, while geography, population, and raw materials are becoming somewhat less important.

If so, are we entering a "Japanese period" in world politics? Japan has certainly done far better with its strategy as a trading state since 1945 than it did with its military strategy to create a Greater East Asian Co-Prosperity Sphere in the 1930s. On the other hand, Japan's security in relation to its large military neighbors, China and the Soviet Union, and the safety of its sea routes depend heavily on U.S. protection. While they may diminish, these problems will not vanish with the end of the Cold War. One should not leap too quickly to the conclusion that all trends favor economic power or countries like Japan.

What can we say about changes in the distribution of power resources in the coming decades? Political leaders often use the term "multipolarity" to imply the return to a balance among a number of states with roughly equal power resources analogous to that of the nineteenth century. But this is not likely to be the situation at the turn of the century, for in terms of power resources, all the potential challengers except the United States are deficient in some respect. The Soviet Union lags economically, China remains a less-developed country, Europe lacks political unity, and Japan is deficient both in military power and in global ideological appeal. If economic reforms reverse Soviet decline, if Japan develops a full-fledged nuclear and conventional military capability, or if Europe becomes dramatically more unified, there may be a return to classical multipolarity in the twenty-first century. But barring such changes, the United States is likely to retain a broader range of power resources – military, economic, scientific, cultural, and ideological – than other countries, and the Soviet Union may lose its superpower status.

The great power shift

The coming century may see continued American preeminence, but the sources of power in world politics are likely to undergo major changes that will create new difficulties for all countries in achieving their goals. Proof of power lies not in resources but in the ability to change the behavior of states. Thus, the critical question for the United States is not whether it will start the next century as the superpower with the largest supply of resources, but to what extent it will be able to control the political environment and get other countries to do what it wants.

Some trends in world politics suggest that it will be more difficult in the future for any great power to control the political environment. The problem for the United States will be less the rising challenge of another major power than a general diffusion of power. Whereas nineteenth-century Britain faced new challengers, the twenty-first century United States will face new challenges.

As world politics becomes more complex, the power of all major states to gain their objectives will be diminished. To understand what is happening to the United States today, the distinction between power over other countries and power over outcomes must be clear. Although the United States still has leverage over particular countries, it has far less leverage over the system as a whole. It is less well-placed to attain its ends unilaterally, but it is not alone in this situation. All major states will have to confront the changing nature of power in world politics.

Such changes, of course, are not entirely new. For example, the rapid growth of private actors operating across international borders, whether large corporations or political groups, was widely recognized in the early 1970s. Even Henry Kissinger, with his deeply rooted belief in classical balance-of-power politics, conceded in a 1975 speech that "we are entering a new era. Old international patterns are crumbling. . . . The world has become interdependent in economics, in communications, in human aspirations."

By the late 1970s, however, the American political mood had shifted. Iran's seizure of the U.S. embassy in Tehran and the Soviet invasion of Afghanistan seemed to reaffirm the role of military force and the primacy of the traditional security agenda. Ronald Reagan's presidency accentuated these trends in the early 1980s. The U.S. defense budget increased in real terms for five straight years, arms control was downgraded, and public opposition to nuclear forces and deterrence grew. Conventional military force was used successfully, albeit against the extremely weak states of Grenada and Libya. The shifting agenda of world politics discredited the 1970s' concern with interdependence and restored the traditional emphasis on military power. But interdependence continued to grow, and the world of the 1980s was not the same as that of the 1950s.

The appropriate response to the changes occurring in world politics today is not to abandon the traditional concern for the military balance of power, but to accept its limitations and to supplement it with insights about interdependence. In the traditional view, states are the only significant actors in world politics and only a few large states really matter. But today other actors are becoming increasingly important. Although they lack military power, transnational corporations have enormous economic resources. Thirty corporations today each have annual sales greater than the gross national products (GNPs) of 90 countries. In the 1980s, the annual profits of IBM and Royal Dutch/Shell Group were each larger than the central government budgets of Colombia, Kenya, or Yugoslavia. Multinational corporations are sometimes more relevant to achieving a country's goals than are other states. The annual overseas production by such corporations exceeds the total value of international trade. In a regional context, a portrait of the Middle East conflict that did not include the superpowers would be woefully inadequate, but so would a description that did not tell of transnational religious groups, oil companies, and terrorist organizations. The issue is not whether state or nonstate actors are more important – states usually are. The point is that in modern times, more complex coalitions affect outcomes.

With changing actors in world politics come changing goals. In the traditional view, states give priority to military security to ensure their survival. Today, however, states must consider new dimensions of security. National security has become more complicated as threats shift from the military (that is, threats against territorial integrity) to the economic and ecological. For example, Canadians today are not afraid that U.S. soldiers will burn Toronto for a second time (as in 1813); rather they fear that Toronto will be programmed into a backwater by a Texas computer. The forms of vulnerability have increased, and trade-offs among policies are designed to deal with different vulnerabilities. The United States, for instance, might enhance its energy security by sending naval forces to the Persian Gulf; but it could accomplish the same goal by enlarging its strategic petroleum reserve, by imposing a gasoline tax to encourage conservation at home, and by improving cooperation in institutions like the International Energy Agency.

While military force remains the ultimate form of power in a self-help system, the use of force has become more costly for modern great powers than it was in earlier centuries. Other instruments such as communications, organizational and institutional skills, and manipulation of interdependence have become important. Contrary to some rhetorical flourishes, interdependence does not mean harmony. Rather, it often means unevenly balanced mutual dependence. Just as the less enamored of two lovers may manipulate the other, the less vulnerable of two states may use subtle threats to their relationship as a source of power. Further, interdependence is often balanced differently in different spheres such as security, trade, and finance. Thus, creating and resisting linkages between issues when a state is either less or more vulnerable than another becomes the art of the power game. Political leaders use international institutions to discourage or promote such linkages; they shop for the forum that defines the scope of an issue in the manner best suiting their interests.

As the instruments of power change, so do strategies. Traditionalists consider the goal of security and the instrument of military force to be linked by a strategy of balancing power. States wishing to preserve their independence from military intimidation follow a balancing strategy to limit the relative power of other states. Today, however, economic and ecological issues involve large elements of mutual advantage that can be achieved only through cooperation. These issues are often critical to the reelection of political leaders. A French president today would not interfere with Germany's increased economic growth because German growth is critical to French economic growth. The French decision to forego an independent economic policy and remain in the European monetary system in the early 1980s is one example of such interdependence.

Traditionalist accounts of world politics often speak of an international system that results from the balancing strategies of states. Although bipolarity and multipolarity are useful terms, today different spheres of world politics have different distributions of power – that is, different power structures. Military power, particularly nuclear, remains largely bipolar in its distribution. But in trade, where the European Community acts as a unit, power is multipolar. Ocean resources, money, space, shipping, and airlines each have somewhat different distributions of power. The power of states varies as well, as does the significance of nonstate actors in different spheres. For example, the politics of international debt cannot be understood without considering the power of private banks.

If military power could be transferred freely into the realms of economics and the environment, the different structures would not matter; and the overall hierarchy determined by military strength would accurately predict outcomes in world politics. But military power is more costly and less transferable today than in earlier times. Thus, the hierarchies that characterize different issues are more diverse. The games of world politics encompass different players at different tables with different piles of chips. They can transfer winnings among tables, but often only at a considerable discount. The military game and the overall structure of the balance of power dominate when the survival of states is clearly at stake, but in much of modern world politics, physical survival is not the most pressing issue.

Converting power

The fragmentation of world politics into many different spheres has made power resources less fungible, that is, less transferable from sphere to sphere. Money is fungible, in that it can be easily converted from one currency to another. Power has always been less fungible than money, but it is even less so today than in earlier periods. In the eighteenth century, a monarch with a full treasury could purchase infantry to conquer new provinces, which, in turn, could enrich the treasury. This was essentially the strategy of Frederick II of Prussia, for example, when in 1740 he seized Austria's province of Silesia.

Today, however, the direct use of force for economic gain is generally too costly and dangerous for modern great powers. Even short of aggression, the translation of economic into military power resources may be very costly. For instance, there is no economic obstacle to Japan's developing a major nuclear or conventional force, but the political cost both at home and in the reaction of other countries would be considerable. Militarization might then reduce rather than increase Japan's ability to achieve its ends.

Because power is a relationship, by definition it implies some context. Diminished fungibility means that specifying the context is increasingly important in estimating the actual power that can be derived from power resources. More than ever, one must ask the question, "Power for what?" Yet at the same time, because world politics has only partly changed and the traditional geopolitical agenda is still relevant, some fungibility of military power remains. The protective role of military force is a relevant asset in bargaining among states. The dependence of conservative oil-producing states on the United States for their security, for example, limited their leverage on the United States during the 1973 oil crisis. The United States is still the ultimate guarantor of the military security of Europe and Japan, and that role is a source of bargaining power in negotiations with its allies.

In general, the allies' need for protection strengthens American influence, and may continue to do so even with a reduced Soviet threat. During the Cold War, the United States often worried about the frailty of its allies and tended to sacrifice some economic interests in its effort to contain the perceived Soviet menace. Despite the waning of that threat, if the United States worries less than its allies do, it may be able to demand more of them.

To evaluate power in a post-Cold War world, it is necessary to recognize instruments and balance-of-power strategies necessary for a successful policy. But new elements in the modern world are diffusing power away from all the great powers. Thus, any successful strategy must incorporate both continuity and change.

The great powers of today are less able to use their traditional power resources to achieve their purposes than in the past. On many issues, private actors and small states have become more powerful. At least five trends have contributed to this diffusion of power: economic interdependence, transnational actors, nationalism in weak states, the spread of technology, and changing political issues.

New forms of communications and transportation have had a revolutionary effect on economic interdependence. A century ago, it took two weeks to cross the Atlantic; in 1927, Charles Lindbergh did it in 33 hours; today, the Concorde flies across in three and a half hours. Modern telecommunications are instantaneous, and satellites and fiber-optic cables have led to a tenfold increase in overseas telephone calls in the last decade. The declining costs of transportation and communication have revolutionized global markets and accelerated the development of transnational corporations that transfer economic activity across borders. World trade has grown more rapidly than world product, becoming more important in all major economies. Trade has more than doubled its role in the U.S. economy over the past two decades. Changes in financial markets are even more dramatic. International monetary flows are some 25 times the world's average daily trade in goods. The rapid expansion of Eurocurrency and Eurobond markets (that is, currencies held outside their home country) has eroded the ability of national authorities to control their capital markets. In 1975, foreign exchange markets handled some $10–15 billion daily; by 1986, they handled $200 billion.

Governments can intervene in such markets; but if they do so with a heavy hand, they will incur enormous costs in their own economic growth and risk unintended effects. For instance, efforts by the U.S. government in the 1960s to slow the export of capital by U.S.-based multinational firms encouraged those firms to keep and borrow dollars outside the United States. The result was the rapid burgeoning of Eurocurrency markets outside U.S. controls.

In addition to constraining the way states pursue their national interests, transnational actors affect the way such interests are initially defined. Transnational investment creates new interests and complicates coalitions in world politics. For example, Honda of America is steadily turning into an American car maker. It plans to export 50,000 cars annually to Japan in the early 1990s. American officials are now pressing Europeans to open their market to Japanese automobiles produced in the United States. In other words, transnational investments have changed an American interest.

The American case is not unique. For years, France restricted Japanese automobiles to 3 per cent of the French market and restricted investment by Japanese companies in France. When Japanese automakers began to establish plants in other European countries that could export to France, the French government dropped its restrictions. Transnational investments changed a long-standing French policy. The diffusion of power to private transnational actors and the resulting complication of national interests is likely to continue even though it is not recognized in many comparisons of the power resources of major states.

Modernization, urbanization, and increased communication in developing countries have also diffused power from government to private actors. Military power is more difficult to apply today than in the past because a social awakening has stirred nationalism in otherwise poor or weak states. This increased social mobilization makes military intervention and external rule more costly. The nineteenth-century great powers carved out and ruled colonial empires with a handful of troops. In 1953, the United States was able to restore the Shah of Iran to his throne through a minor covert action. It is hard to imagine, however, how many troops would have been needed to restore the Shah in the socially mobilized and nationalistic Iran of 1979. The United States and the Soviet Union found the costs of maintaining troops in Vietnam and Afghanistan unsupportable. In each case, the cause was less an increase in the power of a weaker state than the costliness for outsiders of ruling actively antagonistic populations.

Another trend in the diffusion of power is the spread of modern technology, which has enhanced the capabilities of backward states. While the superpowers have kept a large lead in military technology, the forces that many Third World states can deploy in the 1990s make regional intervention more costly than in the 1950s. In addition, at least a dozen Third World states have developed significant arms-export industries. Meanwhile, many arms recipients have sought to diversify their purchases in order to gain leverage over the major or sole supplier. When arms are supplied from outside, the supplier often has leverage through technical assistance, spare parts, and replacements. The growth of indigenous arms industries removes that leverage.

In addition, more countries are acquiring sophisticated weapons capabilities. Today about 20 countries have the capability to make chemical weapons, and by the year 2000 an estimated 15 Third World countries will be producing their own ballistic missiles. Five states had the bomb when the Nuclear Non-Proliferation Treaty was signed in 1968; India, Israel, Pakistan, and South Africa have since developed some nuclear capability. Within the next decade Argentina, Brazil, and several others might also develop military nuclear capability. However, a small nuclear capability will not make these states contenders for global power; in fact, it may increase the risks they face if their neighbors follow suit or if the weapons fall into the hands of rebel or terrorist groups. On the other hand, nuclear capability would add to these states' regional power and increase the potential costs of regional intervention by larger powers. Technology also increases the power of private groups. For instance, handheld antiaircraft missiles helped guerrillas in Afghanistan and new plastic explosives are effective tools for terrorists.

The ability of great powers with impressive traditional power resources to control their environments is also diminished by the changing nature of issues in world politics. Increasingly, the issues today do not pit one state against another; instead, they are issues in which all states try to control nonstate transnational actors. The solutions to many current issues of transnational interdependence will require collective action and international cooperation. These include ecological changes (acid rain and global warming), health epidemics such as AIDS, illicit trade in drugs, and terrorism. Such issues are transnational because they have domestic roots and cross international borders. As the nuclear accident at Chernobyl in the U.S.S.R. demonstrated, even a domestic issue like the safety of nuclear reactors can suddenly become transnational.

Although force may sometimes play a role, traditional instruments of power are rarely sufficient to deal with the new dilemmas of world politics. New power resources, such as the capacity for effective communication and for developing and using multilateral institutions, may prove more relevant. Moreover, cooperation will often be needed from small, weak states that are not fully capable of managing their own domestic drug, health, or ecological problems. For example, the United States cannot use its traditional power resources to force Peru to curtail the production of cocaine if a weak Peruvian government cannot control private gangs of drug dealers. And if the U.S. government cannot control the American demand, a transnational market for cocaine will survive. Although the traditional power resources of economic assistance and military force can assist in coping with terrorism, proliferation, or drugs, the ability of any great power to control its environment and to achieve what it wants is often not as great as traditional hard power indicators would suggest.

The changing nature of international politics has also made intangible forms of power more important. National cohesion, universalistic culture, and international institutions are taking on additional significance. Power is passing from the "capital-rich" to the "information-rich."

Information is becoming more and more plentiful, but the flexibility to act first on new information is rare. Information becomes power, especially before it spreads. Thus a capacity for timely response to new information is a critical power resource. With the rise of an information-based economy, raw materials have become less important and organizational skills and flexibility more important. Product cycles are shortening and technology is moving toward highly flexible production systems, in which the craft-era tradition of custom-tailoring products can be incorporated into modern manufacturing plants. Japan has been particularly adept at such flexible manufacturing processes; the United States and Europe need to do more, and the Soviet Union and China lag seriously behind.

Timely response to information is not only important in manufacturing but also in critical services such as finance, insurance, and transportation. In the past, markets were defined by the limits of transportation and communication between buyers and sellers. Today, however, the new means of communication convey immediate information on market trends to buyers and sellers worldwide. Satellites and fiber-optic cables instantaneously and continuously link people watching little green screens in London, New York, and Tokyo. That China and the Soviet Union do not significantly participate in these transnational credit markets seriously limits their access to intangible aspects of power. In the 1980s, other governments such as Britain and Japan had to follow the United States in the deregulation of money markets and financial operations in order to preserve their positions in these important markets.

Intangible changes in knowledge also affect military power. Traditionally, governments have invested in human espionage. But now major powers like the United States and the Soviet Union employ continuous photographic and electronic surveillance from space, providing quick access to a variety of economic, political, and military information. Other countries, such as France, are beginning to make low-resolution satellite information commercially available, but the United States leads in high-resolution information.

Another intangible aspect of power arises from interdependence. The overt distribution of economic resources poorly describes the balance of power between interdependent states. On the one hand, the influence of the ostensibly stronger state may be limited by the greater organization and concentration of its smaller counterpart. This difference helps to account for Canada's surprising success in bargaining with the United States. On the other hand, if a relationship is beneficial to both parties, the possibility that the weaker side might collapse under pressure limits the leverage of the seemingly stronger partner. The "power of the debtor" has long been known: If a man owes a bank $10,000, the bank has power over him. But if he owes $100 million, he has power over the bank. If Mexico or some Caribbean states became too weak to deal with internal poverty or domestic problems, the United States would face a new foreign policy agenda involving larger influxes of migrants, drugs, or contraband. Similarly, the failure of developing countries to prevent destruction of their forests will affect the global climate; yet those states' very weakness will diminish other countries' power to influence them. The current U.S. neglect of weak Third World countries may reduce its ability to affect their policies on the new transnational issues. The United States will have to devote more attention to the paradoxical power that grows out of political and economic chaos and weakness in poor countries.

The changing face of power

These trends suggest a second, more attractive way of exercising power than traditional means. A state may achieve the outcomes it prefers in world politics because other states want to follow it or have agreed to a situation that produces such effects. In this sense, it is just as important to set the agenda and structure the situations in world politics as to get others to change in particular cases.

This second aspect of power – which occurs when one country gets other countries to *want* what it wants – might be called co-optive or soft power in contrast with the hard or command power of *ordering* others to do what it wants.

Parents of teenagers have long known that if they have shaped their child's beliefs and preferences, their power will be greater and more enduring than if they rely only on active control. Similarly, political leaders and philosophizers have long understood the power of attractive ideas or the ability to set the political agenda and determine the framework of debate in a way that shapes others' preferences. The ability to affect what other countries want tends to be associated with intangible power resources such as culture, ideology, and institutions.

Soft co-optive power is just as important as hard command power. If a state can make its power seem legitimate in the eyes of others, it will encounter less resistance to its wishes. If its culture and ideology are attractive, others will more willingly follow. If it can establish international norms consistent with its society, it is less likely to have to have to change. If it can support institutions that make other states wish to channel or limit their activities in ways the dominant state prefers, it may be spared the costly exercise of coercive or hard power.

In general, power is becoming less transferable, less coercive, and less tangible. Modern trends and changes in political issues are having significant effects on the nature of power and the resources that produce it. Co-optive power – getting others to want what you want – and soft power resources – cultural attraction, ideology, and international institutions – are not new. In the early postwar period, the Soviet Union profited greatly from such soft resources as communist ideology, the myth of inevitability, and transnational communist institutions. Various trends today are making co-optive behavior and soft power resources relatively more important.

Given the changes in world politics, the use of power is becoming less coercive, at least among the major states. The current instruments of power range from diplomatic notes through economic threats to military coercion. In earlier periods, the costs of such coercion were relatively low. Force was acceptable and economies were less interdependent. Early in this century, the United States sent marines and customs agents to collect debts in some Caribbean countries; but under current conditions, the direct use of American troops against small countries like Nicaragua carries greater costs.

Manipulation of interdependence under current conditions is also more costly. Economic interdependence usually carries benefits in both directions; and threats to disrupt a relationship, if carried out, can be very expensive. For example, Japan might want the United States to reduce its budget deficit, but threatening to refuse to buy American Treasury bonds would be likely to disrupt financial markets and to produce enormous costs for Japan as well as for the United States. Because the use of force has become more costly, less threatening forms of power have grown increasingly attractive.

Co-optive power is the ability of a country to structure a situation so that other countries develop preferences or define their interests in ways consistent with its own. This power tends to arise from such resources as cultural and ideological attraction as well as rules and institutions of international regimes. The United States has more co-optive power than other countries. Institutions governing the international economy, such as the International Monetary Fund and the General Agreement on Tariffs and Trade, tend to embody liberal, free-market principles that coincide in large measure with American society and ideology.

Multinational corporations are another source of co-optive power. British author Susan Strange argued in her 1988 book *States and Markets* that U.S. power in the world economy has increased as a result of transnational production:

> Washington may have lost some of its authority over the U.S.-based transnationals, but their managers still carry U.S. passports, can be subpoenaed in U.S. courts, and in war or national emergency would obey Washington first. Meanwhile, the U.S. government has gained new authority over a great many foreign corporations inside the United States. All of them are acutely aware that the U.S. market is the biggest prize.

This power arises in part from the fact that 34 per cent of the largest multinational corporations are headquartered in the United States (compared to 18 per cent in Japan) and in part from the importance of the American market in any global corporate strategy.

American culture is another relatively inexpensive and useful soft power resource. Obviously, certain aspects of American culture are unattractive to other people, and there is always danger of bias in evaluating cultural sources of power. But American popular culture, embodied in products and communications, has widespread appeal. Young Japanese who have never been to the United States wear sports jackets with the names of American colleges. Nicaraguan television broadcast American shows even while the government fought American-backed guerrillas. Similarly, Soviet teenagers wear blue jeans and seek American recordings, and Chinese students used a symbol modeled on the Statue of Liberty during the 1989 uprisings. Despite the Chinese government's protests against U.S. interference, Chinese citizens were as interested as ever in American democracy and culture.

Of course, there, is an element of triviality and fad in popular behavior, but it is also true that a country that stands astride popular channels of communication has more opportunities to get its messages across and to affect the preferences of others. According to past studies by the United Nations Educational, Scientific, and Cultural Organization, the United States has been exporting about seven times as many television shows as the next largest exporter (Britain) and has had the only global network for film distribution. Although American films account for only 6–7 per cent of all films made, they occupy about 50 per cent of world screentime. In 1981, the United States was responsible for 80 per cent of worldwide transmission and processing of data. The American language has become the *lingua franca* of the global economy.

Although Japanese consumer products and cuisine have recently become more fashionable, they seem less associated with an implicit appeal to a broader set of values than American domination of popular communication. The success of Japan's manufacturing sector provides it with an important source of soft power, but Japan is somewhat limited by the inward orientation of its culture. While Japan has been extraordinarily successful in accepting foreign technology, it has been far more reluctant to accept foreigners. Japan's relations with China, for example, have been hampered by cultural insensitivities. Many Japanese are concerned about their lack of "internationalization" and their failure to project a broader message.

While Americans can also be parochial and inward-oriented, the openness of the American culture to various ethnicities and the American values of democracy and human rights exert international influence. West European countries also derive soft power from their democratic institutions, but America's relative openness to immigrants compared to Japan and Europe is an additional source of strength. As European scholar Ralf Dahrendorf has observed, it is "relevant that millions of people all over the world would wish to live in the United States and that indeed people are prepared to risk their lives in order to get there." Maintaining this appeal is important.

In June 1989, after President George Bush criticized the Chinese government for killing student protesters in China, ordinary Chinese seemed more supportive of the United States than ever before. Subsequently, by sending a delegation of too high a level to Beijing to seek reconciliation, Bush squandered some of those soft-power resources. When ideals are an important source of power, the classic distinction between *realpolitik* and liberalism becomes blurred. The realist who focuses only on the balance of hard power will miss the power of transnational ideas.

Americans are rightly concerned about the future shape of a post-Cold War world, but it is a mistake to portray the problem as American decline rather than diffusion of power. Even so, concern about decline might be good for the United States if it cut through complacency and prodded Americans to deal with some of their serious domestic problems. However, pollsters find that excessive anxiety about decline turns American opinion toward nationalistic and protectionist policies that could constrain the U.S. ability to cope with issues created by growing international interdependence. There is no virtue in either overstatement or understatement of American strength. The former leads to failure to adapt, the latter to inappropriate responses such as treating Japan as the new enemy in place of the Soviet Union.

As the world's wealthiest country, the United States should be able to pay for both its international commitments and its domestic investments. America is rich but through its political process acts poor. In real terms, GNP is more than twice what it was in 1960, but Americans today spend much less of their GNP on international leadership. The prevailing view is "we can't afford it," despite the fact that U.S. taxes represent a smaller percentage of gross domestic product than those of other advanced industrial countries. This suggests a problem of domestic political leadership rather than long-term economic decline.

As has happened many times before, the mix of resources that shapes international power is changing. But that does not mean that the world must expect the cycle of hegemonic conflict with its attendant world wars to repeat itself. The United States retains more traditional hard power resources than any other country. It also has the soft ideological and institutional resources to preserve its lead in the new domains of transnational interdependence. In this sense, the situation is quite different from that of Britain at the century's beginning. Loose historical analogies and falsely deterministic political theories are worse than merely academic; they may distract Americans from the true issues confronting them. The problem for U.S. power after the Cold War will be less the new challengers for hegemony than the new challenges of transnational interdependence.

Note

* This article draws from my 1990 book, *Bound to Lead: The Changing Nature of American Power* (New York: Basic Books).

7   The information revolution and American soft power*

The world is still at an early stage of the current information revolution, and its effects on economics and politics are uneven. As with steam in the late eighteenth century and electricity in the late nineteenth, productivity growth lagged as society had to learn to fully utilize the new technologies.[1] Social institutions change more slowly than technology. For example, the electric motor was invented in 1881, but it was nearly four decades before Henry Ford pioneered the reorganization of factories to take full advantage of electric power. Computers today account for 2 percent of America's total capital stock, but "add in all the equipment used for gathering, processing and transmitting information, and the total accounts for 12 percent of America's capital stock, exactly the same as the railways at the peak of their development in the late nineteenth century. Three-quarters of all computers are used in the service sector such as finance and health where output is notoriously hard to measure."[2] The increase in productivity of the US economy began to show up only as recently as the mid-1990s.[3]

The advent of truly mass communications and broadcasting a century ago, which was facilitated by newly cheap electricity, provides some lessons about possible social and political effects today. It ushered in the age of mass popular culture.[4] The effects of mass communication and broadcasting, though not the telephone, tended to have a centralizing political effect. While information was more widespread, it was more centrally influenced even in democratic countries than in the age of the local press. President Roosevelt's use of radio in the 1930s worked a dramatic shift in American politics. These effects were particularly pronounced in countries where they were combined with the rise of totalitarian governments, which were able to suppress competing sources of information. Indeed, some scholars believe that totalitarianism could not have been possible without the mass communications that accompanied the second industrial revolution.[5]

In the middle of the twentieth century, people feared that the computers and communications of the current information revolution would create the central governmental control dramatized in George Orwell's vision of *1984*. Mainframe computers seemed set to enhance central planning and increase the surveillance powers of those at the top of a pyramid of control. Government television would dominate the news. Through central databases, computers can make government identification and surveillance easier, and commercialization has already altered the early libertarian culture and code of the Internet.[6] Nonetheless, the technology of encryption is evolving, and programs such as Gnutella and Freenet enable users to trade digital information anonymously.[7] They promise greater space for individuals than the early pessimists envisioned, and the Internet is more difficult for governments to control than the technology of the second information revolution was. On balance, the communication theorist Ithiel de Sola Pool was correct in his characterization of "technologies of freedom."[8]

As computing power has decreased in cost and computers have shrunk in size and become more widely distributed, their decentralizing effects have outweighed their centralizing effects. The Internet creates a system in which power over information is much more widely distributed. Compared with radio, television, and newspapers, controlled by editors and broadcasters, the Internet creates unlimited communication one-to-one (via e-mail), one-to-many (via a personal home page or electronic conference), many-to-one (via electronic broadcast), and, perhaps most important, many-to-many (online chat room). "Internet messages have the capacity to flow farther, faster, and with fewer intermediaries."[9] Central surveillance is possible, but governments that aspire to control information flows through control of the Internet face high costs and ultimate frustration. Rather than reinforcing centralization and bureaucracy, the new information technologies have tended to foster network organizations, new types of community, and demands for different roles for government.[10]

What this means is that foreign policy will not be the sole province of governments. Both individuals and private organizations, here and abroad, will be empowered to play direct roles in world politics. The spread of information will mean that power will be more widely distributed and informal networks will undercut the monopoly of traditional bureaucracy. The speed of Internet time means that all governments, both here and overseas, will have less control of their agendas. Political leaders will enjoy fewer degrees of freedom before they must respond to events, and then will have to share the stage with more actors. Privatization and public-private partnerships will increase. As the United States shapes its foreign policy in the information age, it will have to avoid being mesmerized by terms such as *unipolarity* or *hegemony* and by measures of strength that compare only the hard power of states run by centralized governments. The old images of sovereign states balancing and bouncing off each other like billiard balls will blind us to the new complexity of world politics.

A new world politics

The effects on central governments of the third industrial revolution are still in their early stages. Management expert Peter Drucker and the futurists Heidi Toffler and Alvin Toffler argue that the information revolution is bringing an end to the hierarchical bureaucratic organizations that typified the age of the first two industrial revolutions.[11] In civil societies, as decentralized organizations and virtual communities develop on the Internet, they cut across territorial jurisdictions and develop their own patterns of governance. Internet guru Esther Dyson refers to the "disintermediation of government" and portrays a global society of the connected being overlaid on traditional local geographical communities.[12]

If these prophets are right, the result would be a new cyber-feudalism, with overlapping communities and jurisdictions laying claims to multiple layers of citizens' identities and loyalties. In short, these transformations suggest the reversal of the modern centralized state that has dominated world politics for the past three and a half centuries. A medieval European might have owed equal loyalty to a local lord, a duke, a king, and the Pope. A future European might owe loyalty to Brittany, Paris, and Brussels, as well as to several cyber-communities concerned with religion, work, and various hobbies.

While the system of sovereign states is still the dominant pattern in international relations, one can begin to discern a pattern of crosscutting communities and governance that bears some resemblance to the situation before the Peace of Westphalia formalized the state system in 1648. Transnational contacts across political borders were typical in the feudal era but gradually became constrained by the rise of centralized nation-states. Now sovereignty is changing. Three decades ago, transnational contacts were already growing, but they involved relatively small numbers of élites involved in multinational corporations, scientific groups, and academic institutions.[13] Now the Internet, because of its low costs, is opening transnational communications to many millions of people.

The issue of sovereignty is hotly contested in American foreign policy today. The sovereigntists, closely allied with the new unilateralists, resist anything that seems to diminish American autonomy.[14] They worry about the political role of the United Nations in limiting the use of force, the economic decisions handed down by the World Trade Organization, and efforts to develop environmental institutions and treaties. In their eyes, the notion of an international community of opinion is illusory.

Even excluding the fringe groups that believe the United Nations has black helicopters ready to swoop into American territory, the debate over the fate of the sovereign state has been poorly framed. As a former UN official put it, "There is an extraordinarily impoverished mind-set at work here, one that is able to visualize long-term challenges to the system of states only in terms of entities that are institutionally substitutable for the state."[15] A better historical analogy is the development of markets and town life in the early feudal period. Medieval trade fairs were not substitutes for the institutions of feudal authority. They did not tear down the castle walls or remove the local lord, but they did bring new wealth, new coalitions, and new attitudes summarized by the maxim "Town air brings freedom."

Medieval merchants developed the *lex mercatoria*, which governed their relations, largely as a private set of rules for conducting business.[16] Similarly today, a range of individuals and entities, from hackers to large corporations, are developing the code and norms of the Internet partly outside the control of formal political institutions. The development of transnational corporate intranets behind firewalls and encryption "represent private appropriations of a public space."[17] Private systems, such as corporate intranets or worldwide newsgroups devoted to specific issues like the environment, do not frontally challenge the governments of sovereign states; they simply add a layer of relations that sovereign states do not effectively control. Americans will participate in transnational Internet communities without ceasing to be loyal Americans, but their perspectives will be broader than those of typical, loyal Americans before the Internet came into existence.

Or consider the shape of the world economy, in which a nation's strength is usually measured by its imports and exports from other sovereign nations. Such trade flows and balances still matter, but the decisions on what to produce and whether to produce it at home or overseas are increasingly made within the domains of transnational corporations. Some American companies, such as Nike, produce virtually none of their products inside the US, although intangible (and valuable) design and marketing work is completed there. In the 1990s, declining information and telecommunications costs allowed firms to broaden the geographic dispersion of their operations. Thus, imports and exports provide a very incomplete picture of global economic linkages. For example, overseas production by American transnational corporations was more than twice the value of American exports; sales by foreign-owned companies inside the United States were nearly twice the value of imports.[18] Microeconomic links "have created a non-territorial 'region' in the world economy – a decentered yet integrated space-of-flows, operating in real time, which exists alongside the spaces-of-places that we call national economies."[19] If we restrict our images to billiard ball states, we miss this layer of reality.

Even in the age of the Internet, the changing role of political institutions is likely to be a gradual process. After the rise of the territorial state, other successors to medieval rule such as the Italian city-states and the Hanseatic League persisted as viable alternatives, able to tax and fight for nearly two centuries.[20] Today, the Internet rests on servers located in specific nations, and various governments' laws affect access providers. The real issue is not the continued existence of the sovereign state, but how its centrality and functions are being altered. "The reach of the state has increased in some areas but contracted in others. Rulers have recognized that their effective control can be enhanced by walking away from some issues they cannot resolve."[21] All countries, including the United States, are facing a growing list of problems that are difficult to control within sovereign boundaries – financial flows, drug trade, climate change, AIDS, refugees, terrorism, cultural intrusions – to name a few. Complicating the task of national governance is not the same as undermining sovereignty. Governments adapt. In the process of adaptation, however, they change the meaning of sovereign jurisdiction, control, and the role of private actors.

Take, for example, the problems of controlling US borders. In one year, 475 million people, 125 million vehicles, and 21 million import shipments come into the country at 3700 terminals in 301 ports of entry. It takes five hours to inspect a fully loaded forty-foot shipping container, and more than 5 million enter each year. In addition, more than 2.7 million undocumented immigrants have simply walked or ridden across the Mexican and Canadian borders in recent years. A terrorist could easily slip in, and it is easier to bring in a few pounds of a deadly biological or chemical agent than to smuggle in the tons of illegal heroin and cocaine that arrive annually. The only way for the Customs Service and the Immigration and Naturalization Service to cope with such flows is to reach beyond the national borders through intelligence and cooperation inside the jurisdiction of other states, and to rely on private corporations to develop transparent systems for tracking international commercial flows so that enforcement officials can conduct virtual audits of inbound shipments before they arrive. Thus, customs officers work throughout Latin America to assist businesses in the implementation of security programs that reduce the risk of being exploited by drug smugglers, and cooperative international mechanisms are being developed for policing trade flows.[22] The sovereign state adapts, but in doing so it transforms the meaning and exclusivity of governmental jurisdiction. Legal borders do not change, but they blur in practice.

National security – the absence of threat to a country's major values – is changing. Damage done by climate change or imported viruses can be larger in terms of money or lives lost than the effects of some wars. Even if one frames the definition of national security more narrowly, the nature of military security is changing. As the US Commission on National Security in the Twenty-first Century pointed out, the country has not been invaded by foreign armies since 1814, and the military is designed to project force and fight wars far from our shores. But the military is not well equipped to protect us against an attack on our homeland by terrorists wielding weapons of mass destruction or mass disruption or even hijacked civil aircraft.[23] Thus in July 2001, the secretary of defense, Donald Rumsfeld, dropped from the Pentagon's planning priorities the ability to fight two major regional conflicts and elevated homeland defense to a higher priority. As the US discovered only a few months later, however, military measures are not a sufficient solution to its vulnerabilities.

Today, attackers may be governments, groups, individuals, or some combination. They may be anonymous and not even come near the country. In 1998, when Washington complained about seven Moscow Internet addresses involved in the theft of Pentagon and NASA secrets, the Russian government replied that phone numbers from which the attacks originated were inoperative. The US had no way of knowing whether the government had been involved or not. More than 30 nations have developed aggressive computer-warfare programs, but as anyone with a computer knows, any individual can also enter the game. With a few keystrokes, an anonymous source anywhere in the world might break into and disrupt the (private) power grids of American cities or the (public) emergency response systems.[24] US government firewalls are not enough. Every night American software companies send work electronically to India, where software engineers can work while Americans sleep and send it back the next morning. Someone outside our borders could also embed trapdoors deep in computer code for use at a later date. Nuclear deterrence, border patrols, and stationing troops overseas to shape regional power balances will continue to matter in the information age, but they will not be sufficient to provide national security.

Competing interpretations of sovereignty arise even in the domain of law. Since 1945, human rights provisions have coexisted in the charter of the United Nations alongside provisions that protect the sovereignty of states. Article 2.7 says that nothing shall authorize the United Nations to intervene in matters within domestic jurisdictions. Yet the development of a global norm of antiracism and repugnance at the South African practice of apartheid led large majorities at the UN to abridge this principle. More recently, the NATO intervention in Kosovo was the subject of hot debate among international lawyers, with some claiming it was illegal because it was not explicitly authorized by the UN Security Council and others arguing that it was legal under the evolving body of international humanitarian law.[25] The 1998 detention of General Augusto Pinochet in the United Kingdom in response to a Spanish request for extradition based on human rights violations and crimes committed while he was president of Chile is another example of this complexity. In 2001, a magistrate in Paris tried to summon former US secretary of state Henry Kissinger to testify in a trial related to Chile.

Information technology, particularly the Internet, has eased the tasks of coordination and strengthened the hand of human rights activists, but political leaders, particularly in formerly colonized countries, cling to the protections that legal sovereignty provides against outside interventions. The world is likely to see these two partly contradictory bodies of international law continue to coexist for years to come, and Americans will have to wrestle with these contradictions as we decide how to promote human rights and when to intervene in conflicts for humanitarian reasons.

For many people, the national state provides a source of political identity that is important to them. People are capable of multiple identities – family, village, ethnic group, religion, nationality, cosmopolitan – and which predominates often depends on the context.[26] In many preindustrial countries, subnational identities (tribe or clan) prevail. In some postindustrial countries, including the United States, cosmopolitan identities such as "global citizen" or "custodian of planet Earth" are beginning to emerge. Since large identities (such as nationalism) are not directly experienced, they are "imagined communities" that depend very much on the effects of communication.[27] It is still too early to understand the full effects of the Internet, but the shaping of identities can move in contradictory directions at the same time – up to Brussels, down to Brittany, or fixed on Paris – as circumstances dictate.

The result may be greater volatility rather than consistent movement in any one direction. The many-to-many and one-to-many characteristics of the Internet seem "highly conducive to the irreverent, egalitarian, and libertarian character of the cyber-culture." One effect is "flash movements" – sudden surges of protest – triggered by particular issues or events, such as antiglobalization protests or the sudden rise of the anti-fuel tax coalition that captured European politics in the autumn of 2000.[28] Politics becomes more theatrical and aimed at global audiences. The Zapatista rebels in Mexico's Chiapas state relied less on bullets than on transnational publicity, much of it coordinated on the Internet, to pressure the Mexican government. The political scientist James Rosenau has tried to summarize such trends by inventing a new word, *fragmegration*, to express the idea that both integration toward larger identities and fragmentation into smaller communities can occur at the same time. One does not need to alter the English language to realize that apparently contradictory movements can occur simultaneously. They do not spell the end of the sovereign state, but they do make its politics more volatile and less self-contained within national shells.

Private organizations also increasingly cross national boundaries. Transnational religious organizations opposed to slavery date back to 1775, and the nineteenth century saw the founding of the Socialist International, the Red Cross, peace movements, women's suffrage organizations, and the International Law Association, among others. Before World War I, there were 176 international nongovernmental organizations (NGOs). In 1956, they numbered nearly a thousand; in 1970, nearly two thousand. More recently, there has been an explosion in the number of NGOs, increasing to approximately 26,000 during the 1990s alone. Furthermore, the numbers do not tell the full story, because they represent only formally constituted organizations.[29] Many claim to act as a "global conscience" representing broad public interests beyond the purview of individual states, or interests that states are wont to ignore. They develop new norms by directly pressing governments and business leaders to change policies, and indirectly by altering public perceptions of what governments and firms should be doing. In terms of power resources, these new groups rarely possess much hard coercive power, but the information revolution has greatly enhanced their *soft power* – the power of attraction that is associated with ideas, cultures, and policies.

Not only is there a great increase in the number of transnational and governmental contacts, but there has also been a change in type. Earlier transnational flows were heavily controlled by large bureaucratic organizations such as multinational corporations or the Catholic Church that could profit from economies of scale. Such organizations remain important, but the lower costs of communication in the Internet era have opened the field to loosely structured network organizations with little headquarters staff, and even individuals. These nongovernmental organizations and networks are particularly effective in penetrating states without regard to borders. Because they often involve citizens who are well placed in the domestic politics of several countries, they are able to focus the attention of the media and governments on their preferred issues. The treaty banning land mines was the result of an interesting coalition of Internet-based organizations working with middle-power governments, such as Canada, and some individual politicians and celebrities, including the late Princess Diana. Environmental issues are another example. The role of NGOs was important as a channel of communication across delegations in the global warming discussions at Kyoto in 1997. Industry, unions, and NGOs competed in Kyoto for the attention of media from major countries in a transnational struggle over the agenda of world politics. Sometimes, NGOs compete with each other for media attention. The World Economic Forum, an NGO that invites top government and business leaders to Davos, Switzerland, each winter, included some NGOs in its 2001 programs, but that did not prevent other NGOs from staging local demonstrations and yet others from holding a counterforum in Porto Alegre, Brazil, designed to garner global attention.

A different type of transnational community, the scientific community of like-minded experts, is also becoming more prominent. By framing issues such as ozone depletion or global climate change, where scientific information is important, such "epistemic communities" create knowledge and consensus that provide the basis for effective cooperation.[30] The Montreal Convention on ozone was in part the product of such work. While not entirely new, these scientific communities have also grown as a result of the lowered costs of communications.

Geographical communities and sovereign states will continue to play a major role in world politics for a long time to come, but they will be less self-contained and more porous. They will have to share the stage with actors who can use information to enhance their soft power and press governments directly, or indirectly by mobilizing their publics. Governments that want to see rapid development will find that they have to give up some of the barriers to information flow that historically protected officials from outside scrutiny. No longer will governments that want high levels of development be able to afford the comfort of keeping their financial and political situations inside a black box, as Burma and North Korea have done. That form of sovereignty proves too expensive. Even large countries with hard power, such as the US, find themselves sharing the stage with new actors and having more trouble controlling their borders. Cyberspace will not replace geographical space and will not abolish state sovereignty, but like the town markets in feudal times, it will coexist with them and greatly complicate what it means to be a sovereign state or a powerful country. Americans shaping foreign policy in the global information age will have to become more aware of the importance of the ways that the Internet creates new communications, empowers individuals and non-state actors, and increases the role of soft power.

Three dimensions of information

In understanding the relation of information to power in world politics, it helps if one distinguishes three different dimensions of information that are sometimes lumped together.[31] The first dimension is flows of data such as news or statistics. There has been a tremendous and measurable increase in the amount of information flowing across international borders. The average cost of that information has been declining, and the points of access have been increasing. Declining costs and added points of access help small states and non-state actors. On the other hand, the vast scale of the flows puts a premium on the capacities of editors and systems integrators, which is a benefit to the large and powerful.

A second dimension is information that is used for advantage in competitive situations. With competitive information, the most important effects are often at the margin. In this instance going first matters most, and that usually favors the more powerful. Much competitive information is associated with commerce, but, the effect of information on military power can also be thought of as a subset of competitive information.

The third dimension is strategic information – knowledge of your competitor's game plan. There is nothing new about strategic information. It is as old as espionage. Any country or group can hire spies, and to the extent that commercial technologies and market research provide technical capabilities that were previously available only at the cost of large investment, there is an equalizing effect. But to the extent that large investments in intelligence gathering produce more and better strategic information, the large and powerful will benefit. While it is true that fewer of the interesting intelligence questions in a post-Cold War world are secrets (which can be stolen) than mysteries (to which no one knows the answer), large intelligence collection capabilities still provide important strategic advantages.

One of the most interesting aspects of power in relation to increasing flows of information is the "paradox of plenty."[32] A plenitude of information leads to a poverty of attention. When we are overwhelmed with the volume of information confronting us, it is hard to know what to focus on. Attention rather than information becomes the scarce resource, and those who can distinguish valuable signals from white noise gain power. Editors, filters, and cue givers become more in demand, and this is a source of power for those who can tell us where to focus our attention. Power does not necessarily flow to those who can produce or withhold information. Unlike asymmetrical interdependence in trade, where power goes to those who can afford to hold back or break trade ties, power in information flows goes to those who can edit and authoritatively validate information, sorting out what is both correct and important. Because of its free press, this generally benefits the United States.

Among editors and cue givers, credibility is the crucial resource and an important source of soft power. Reputation becomes even more important than in the past, and political struggles occur over the creation and destruction of credibility. Communities tend to cluster around credible cue givers, and, in turn, perceived credibility tends to reinforce communities. Internet users tend to frequent Web sites that provide information they find both interesting and credible. Governments compete for credibility not only with other governments but with a broad range of alternatives including news media, corporations, NGOs, intergovernmental organizations, and networks of scientific communities.

Thinking counterfactually, Iraq might have found it easier to have won acceptance for its view of the invasion of Kuwait as a postcolonial vindication, analogous to India's 1975 capture of Goa, if CNN had framed the issue from Baghdad rather than from Atlanta (from which Saddam was portrayed as analogous to Hitler in the

1930s). Soft power allowed the United States to frame the issue. Nongovernmental organizations can mount public relations campaigns that impose significant costs and alter the decisions of large corporations, as Greenpeace did in the case of Royal Dutch Shell's disposal of its Brentspar drilling rig. The sequel is equally illustrative, for Greenpeace lost credibility when it later had to admit that some of its factual statements had been inaccurate.

Politics then becomes a contest of competitive credibility. Governments compete with each other and with other organizations to enhance their own credibility and weaken that of their opponents – witness the struggle between Serbia and NATO to frame the interpretation of events in Kosovo in 1999. Reputation has always mattered in world politics, but the role of credibility becomes an even more important power resource because of the deluge of free information and the "paradox of plenty" in an information age. The BBC, for example, was an important soft power resource for the UK in Eastern Europe during the Cold War. Now it (and other government broadcasts) has more competitors, but to the extent that it maintains credibility in an era of white noise, its value as a power resource may increase.

Soft power in the global information age

One implication of the increasing importance of editors and cue givers in this global information age is that the relative importance of soft power – cultural and ideological appeal – will also increase, because soft power rests on credibility. Countries that are well placed in terms of soft power do better.[33] The countries that are likely to gain soft power in an information age are:

1   Those whose dominant culture and ideas are closer to prevailing global norms (which now emphasize liberalism, pluralism, and autonomy);
2   Those with the most access to multiple channels of communication and thus more influence over how issues are framed; and
3   Those whose credibility is enhanced by their domestic and international performance. These dimensions of power in an information age suggest the growing importance of soft power in the mix of power resources, and a strong advantage to the United States.

Of course, soft power is not brand new, nor was the US the first government to try to utilize its culture to create soft power. After its defeat in the Franco-Prussian War, the French government sought to repair the nation's shattered prestige by promoting its language and literature through the Alliance Française, created in 1883. "The projection of French culture abroad thus became a significant component of French diplomacy."[34] Italy, Germany, and others soon followed suit. The advent of radio in the 1920s led many governments into the area of foreign language broadcasting, and in the 1930s, Nazi Germany perfected the propaganda film. The US government was a latecomer to the idea of using American culture for the purposes of diplomacy. It established a Committee on Public Information during World War I but abolished it with the return of peace. By the late 1930s, the

Roosevelt administration became convinced that "America's security depended on its ability to speak to and to win the support of people in other countries." With World War II and the Cold War, the government became more active, with official efforts such as the United States Information Agency, the Voice of America, the Fulbright program, American libraries, lectures, and other programs. But much soft power arises from societal forces outside government control. Even before the Cold War, "American corporate and advertising executives, as well as the heads of Hollywood studios, were selling not only their products but also America's culture and values, the secrets of its success, to the rest of the world."[35] Soft power is created partly by governments and partly in spite of them.

A decade ago some observers thought the close collaboration of government and industry in Japan would give it a lead in soft power in the information age. Japan could develop an ability to manipulate perceptions worldwide instantaneously and "destroy those that impede Japanese economic prosperity and cultural acceptance."[36] When Matsushita purchased MCA, its president said that movies critical of Japan would not be produced.[37] Japanese media tried to break into world markets, and the government-owned NHK network began satellite broadcasts in English. The venture failed, however, as NHK's reports seemed to lag behind those of commercial news organizations, and the network had to rely on CNN and ABC.[38] This does not mean that Japan lacks soft power. On the contrary, its pop culture has great appeal to teenagers in Asia.[39] But Japan's culture remains much more inward-oriented than that of the United States, and its government's unwillingness to deal frankly with the history of the 1930s undercuts its soft power.

To be sure, there are areas, such as the Middle East, where ambivalence about American culture limits its soft power. All television in the Arab world used to be state-run until tiny Qatar allowed a new station, Al-Jazeera, to broadcast freely, and it proved wildly popular in the Middle East.[40] Its uncensored images have had a powerful political influence, for example, on American efforts to mediate the Arab-Israeli conflict and the US campaign in Afghanistan. As an Arab journalist described the situation in November 2000, "Al-Jazeera has been for this intifada what CNN was to the Gulf War."[41] Even in Iran, where the government outlawed a video trade it saw as "the means by which America is trying to kill our revolution," pirated videos were widely available, and the ban "has only enhanced the lure of both the best and the worst of Western secular culture."[42]

There are, of course, tensions even within Western secular culture that limit American soft power. In the mid-1990s, 61 percent of French, 45 percent of Germans, and 32 percent of Italians perceived American culture as a threat to their own. Majorities in Spain, France, Germany, and Italy thought there were too many American-made films and television programs on national TV.[43] Both Canada and the European Union place restrictions on the amount of American content that can be shown.

In reality, such attitudes reflect ambivalence rather than rejection. In the 1920s, the Germans were the pacesetters of cinematography, as were the French and the Italians in the 1950s and 1960s. India produces many more films than does Hollywood, but all the distribution channels in the world couldn't turn Indian movies into global blockbusters. In the eyes of German journalist Josef Joffe, the explanation is obvious: "America has the world's most open culture, and therefore the world is most open to it."[44] Or as a perceptive French critic notes, "Nothing symbolizes more the triumph of American culture than the quintessential art form of the twentieth century: the cinema . . . This triumph of the individual motivated by compassion or a noble ambition is universal . . . the message is based on the openness of America and the continuing success of its multicultural society." But he also notes that "the more the French embrace America, the more they resent it."[45] Or as a Norwegian observed, "American culture is becoming everyone's *second* culture. It doesn't necessarily supplant local traditions, but it does activate a certain cultural bilingualism."[46] Like many second languages, it is spoken with imperfections and different meanings. The wonder, however, is that it is spoken at all.

Of course, Serbs wearing Levi's and eating at McDonald's not only supported repression in Kosovo, but also used a Hollywood film, *Wag the Dog*, to mock the United States during the war. Child soldiers in Sierra Leone committed atrocities such as lopping off the hands of civilians while wearing American sports team T-shirts. Nevertheless, as cultural historian Neal Rosendorf has argued, throughout the twentieth century popular culture has made the United States seem to others "exciting, exotic, rich, powerful, trend-setting – the cutting edge of modernity and innovation."[47] Despite the vulgarity, sex, and violence, "our pictures and music exalt icons of freedom, celebrating a society conducive to upward mobility, informality, egalitarian irreverence, and vital life-force. This exaltation has its appeals in an age when people want to partake of the good life American style, even if as political citizens, they are aware of the downside for ecology, community, and equality."[48] For example, in explaining a new movement toward using lawsuits to assert rights in China, a young Chinese activist explained, "We've seen a lot of Hollywood movies – they feature weddings, funerals and going to court. So now we think it's only natural to go to court a few times in your life."[49] At the same time, such images of a liberal society can create a backlash among conservative fundamentalists.

Ambivalence sets limits on popular culture as a source of American soft power, and marketing by US corporations can create both attraction and resistance. As historian Walter LaFeber puts it, transnational corporations "not only change buying habits in a society, but modify the composition of the society itself. For the society that receives it, soft power can have hard effects."[50] Protest is often directed at McDonald's and Coca-Cola. For better or worse, there is not much the US government can do about these negative effects of American cultural exports. Efforts to balance the scene by supporting exports of American high culture – libraries and art exhibits – are at best a useful palliative. Many aspects of soft power are more a by-product of American society than of deliberate government actions, and they may increase or decrease government power. The background attraction (and repulsion) of American popular culture in different regions and among different groups may make it easier or more difficult for American officials to promote their policies. In some cases, such as Iran, American culture may produce rejection (at least for ruling élites); in others, including China, the attraction and rejection among different groups may cancel each other. In still other cases, such as Argentina, American human rights policies that were rejected by the military government of the 1970s produced considerable soft power for the United States two decades later when those who were earlier imprisoned subsequently came to power.

The Argentine example reminds us not to exaggerate the role of popular culture and that soft power is more than just cultural power. Soft power rests on agenda setting as well as attraction, and popular culture is only one aspect of attraction (and not always that). The high cultural ideas that the United States exports in the minds of the half a million foreign students who study every year in American universities, or in the minds of the Asian entrepreneurs who return home after succeeding in Silicon Valley, are more closely related to élites with power. Most of China's leaders have a son or daughter educated in the United States who portray a realistic view of the US that is often at odds with the caricatures in official Chinese propaganda.

Government polices at home and abroad can enhance or curtail soft power. For example, in the 1950s, racial segregation at home undercut American soft power in Africa, and today, capital punishment and weak gun control laws undercut our soft power in Europe. Similarly, foreign policies strongly affect US soft power. Jimmy Carter's human rights policies are a case in point, but so also are government efforts to promote democracy in the Reagan and Clinton administrations. Conversely, foreign policies that appear arrogant and unilateral in the eyes of others diminish American soft power.

The soft power that is becoming more important in the information age is in part a social and economic by-product rather than solely a result of official government action. NGOs with soft power of their own can complicate and obstruct government efforts to obtain the outcomes it wants, and purveyors of popular culture sometimes hinder government agents in achieving their objectives. But the larger long-term trends are in America's favor. To the extent that official policies at home and abroad are consistent with democracy, human rights, openness, and respect for the opinions of others, the United States will benefit from the trends of this global information age, even though pockets of reaction and fundamentalism will persist and resist in some countries. There is a danger, however, that the US may obscure the deeper message of its values through arrogance and unilateralism. US culture, high and popular, helps produce soft power in an information age, but government actions also matter – not only through programs such as the Voice of America and Fulbright scholarships but, even more important, when American policies avoid arrogance and stand for values that others admire. The trends of the information age are in America's favor, but only if it avoids stepping on its own message.

Notes

* This article draws upon my book *The Paradox of American Power: why the world's only superpower can't go it alone* (Oxford: Oxford University Press, 2002).

1 Douglass North, *Structure and Change in Economic History* (New York: W. W. Norton), pp. 163–64. See also Paul A. David, "Understanding Digital Technology's Evolution and the Path of Measured Productivity Growth: Present and Future in the Mirror of the Past," in Erik Brynjolfsson and Brian Kahin, eds., *Understanding the Digital Economy* (Cambridge, MA: MIT Press, 2000), pp. 50–92.
2 "Productivity: Lost in Cyberspace," *The Economist*, 13 September 1997, p. 72.
3 US Department of Commerce, "Digital Economy 2000," <http://www.esa.doc.gov/de2000.pdf>.
4 Peter F. Drucker, "The Next Information Revolution," *Forbes*, 24 August 1998, pp. 46–58.
5 Carl J. Friedrich and Zbigniew K. Brzezinski, *Totalitarian Dictatorship and Autocracy* (New York: Praeger, 1965). On the other hand, as films, cassettes, and faxes spread, the later technologies of the second information revolution helped to undermine governmental efforts at information autarky – witness the Soviet Union and Eastern Europe. The overall effects were not always democratizing. In some cases, such as Iran, the technologies of the second information revolution merely changed the nature of the autocracy.
6 Lawrence Lessig, *Code and Other Laws of Cyberspace* (New York: Basic Books, 2000).
7 For example, Ian Clarke, the youthful Irish inventor of Freenet, says he is a freespeech absolutist who makes no exception for child pornography or terrorism. "My point of view is not held by most people, but the technology has given me the ability to do what I think is right without having to convince anyone." "Entertainment Industry Vows to Fight Against Online Piracy," *Boston Globe*, 31 May 2000, p. 1.
8 Ithiel de Sola Pool, *Technologies of Freedom* (Cambridge, MA: Belknap, 1983).
9 Pippa Norris, *The Digital Divide: Civic Engagement, Information Poverty and, the Internet Worldwide* (New York: Cambridge University Press, 2001), p. 232.
10 For speculation on how the Internet will affect government, see Elaine Kamarck and Joseph S. Nye Jr., eds., *Democracy.com?* (Hollis,NH: Hollis Publishing, 1999), Chapter 1.
11 See Alvin Toffler and Heidi Toffler, *Creating a New Civilization: The Politics of the Third Wave* (Kansas City, Mo.: Turner Publishing, 1995); Drucker, "The Next Information Revolution."
12 Esther Dyson, *Release 2.1: A Design for Living in the Digital Age* (New York: Broadway Books, 1998).
13 Robert O. Keohane and Joseph S. Nye Jr., *Transnational Relations and World Politics* (Cambridge, MA: Harvard University Press, 1997).
14 Peter Spiro, "The New Sovereigntists," *Foreign Affairs*, Vol. 79, No. 6 (November/December 2000), pp. 9–15.
15 John G. Ruggie, "Territoriality and Beyond: Problematizing Modernity in International Relations," *International Organization*, Vol. 47, No. 1 (Winter 1993), p. 143 and p. 155.
16 Henry H. Perritt Jr., "The Internet as a Threat to Sovereignty?" *Indiana Journal of Global Legal Studies* (Spring 1998), p. 426.
17 Saskia Sassen, "On the Internet and Sovereignty," *Indiana Journal of Global Legal Studies* (Spring 1998), p. 551.
18 Joseph Quinlan and Marc Chandler, "The US Trade Deficit: A Dangerous Illusion," *Foreign Affairs*, Vol. 80, No. 3 (May/June 2001), p. 92 and p. 95.
19 Ruggie, "Territoriality and Beyond," p. 172.
20 Hendryk Spruyt, *The Sovereign State and Its Competitors* (Princeton: Princeton University Press, 1994).
21 Stephen Krasner, "Sovereignty," *Foreign Policy* (January/February 2001), p. 24; see also Linda Weiss, *The Myth of the Powerless State* (Ithaca, NY: Cornell University

Press, 1998). See also "Geography and the Net," *The Economist*, 11 August 2001, pp. 18–20.

22 Stephen E. Flynn, "Beyond Border Control," *Foreign Affairs*, Vol. 79, No. 6 (November/December 2000), pp. 57–68.

23 U.S. Commission on National Security in the Twenty-first Century, *Road Map for National Security: Imperative for Change* (http://www.nssg.gov/PhaseIIIFR.pdf), Chapter 1.

24 James Adams, "Virtual Defense," *Foreign Affairs*, Vol. 80, No. 3 (May/June 2001), pp. 98–112.

25 Adam Roberts, "The So-called 'Right' of Humanitarian Intervention," *Yearbook of International Humanitarian Law* (Summer 2001).

26 Harold Guetzkow, *Multiple Loyalties: Theoretical Approach to a Problem in International Organization* (Princeton: Princeton University Press, 1955).

27 Benedict Anderson, *Imagined Communities: Reflections on the Origin and Spread of Nationalism* (New York: Verso, 1991).

28 Norris, *The Digital Divide*, p. 191.

29 Ann Florini ed., *The Third Force: The Rise of Transnational Civil Society* (Washington, D. C.: Carnegie Endowment for International Peace, 2000), Chapter 1; Margaret E. Keck and Kathryn Sikkink, *Activists Beyond Borders: Advocacy Networks in International Politics* (Ithaca, NY: Cornell University Press, 1998), Chapter 2; James N. Rosenau, *Turbulence in World Politics* (Princeton: Princeton University Press, 1990), p. 409; "The Non-Governmental Order," *The Economist*, 11 December 1999.

30 Peter M. Haas, "Introduction: Epistemic Communities and International Policy Coordination," *International Organization*, Vol. 46, No. 1 (Winter 1992).

31 I owe these distinctions to Robert O. Keohane. See Robert O. Keohane and Joseph S. Nye Jr., "Power and Interdependence in the Information Age," *Foreign Affairs*, Vol. 77, No. 5 (September/October 1998), pp. 81–94.

32 Herbert A. Simon, "Information 101: It's Not What You Know, It's How You Know It," *The Journal for Quality and Participation* (July/August 1998), pp. 30–33.

33 Of course, as I argued above, soft power varies with the targeted audience. Thus American individualism may be popular in Latin America at the same time that it appears offensively libertine in some Middle Eastern countries. Moreover, governments can gain and lose soft power depending on their performance at home.

34 Richard Pells, *Not Like Us* (New York: Basic Books, 1997), pp. 31–32.

35 Ibid., Chapter xiii, p. 33.

36 Jerome C. Glenn, "Japan: Cultural Power of the Future," *Nikkei Weekly*, 7 December 1992, p. 7.

37 "Multinational Movies: Questions on Politics," *New York Times*, 27 November 1990, D7.

38 "Japanese News Media Join Export Drive," *International Herald Tribune*, 10 May 1991; David Sanger, "NHK of Japan Ends Plan for Global News Service," *New York Times*, 9 December 1991.

39 Calvin Sims, "Japan Beckons and East Asia's Youth Fall in Love," *New York Times*, 5 December 1999, A3; "Advance of the Amazonesu," *The Economist*, 22 July 2000, p. 61.

40 Mark Huband, "Egypt Tries to Tempt Back Broadcasters," *Financial Times* (London), 7 March 2000, p. 14.

41 John Kifner, "Tale of Two Uprisings," *New York Times*, 18 November 2000, A6.

42 Chris Hedges, "Iran Is Unable to Stem the West's Cultural Invasion," *New York Times*, 28 March 1992, A11.

43 United States Information Agency Office of Research, "European Opinion Alert," 16 March 1994 and 27 May 1994.

44 Josef Joffe, "America the Inescapable," *New York Times* [Sunday] *Magazine*, 8 June 1997, p. 38.
45 Dominique Moisi, "America the Triumphant," *Financial Times* (London), 9 February 1998, p. 12; Moisi, "The Right Argument at the Wrong Time," *Financial Times* (London), 22 November 1999, p. 13.
46 Quoted in Todd Gitlin, "World Leaders: Mickey, *et al*.," *New York Times*, 3 May 1992, Arts and Leisure section, p. 1.
47 Neal M. Rosendorf, "Social and Cultural Globalization: Concepts, History, and America's Role," in Nye and Donahue, eds., *Governance in a Globalizing World* (Washington, D. C.: Brookings Institution Press, 2000).
48 Todd Gitlin, "Taking the World by (Cultural) Force," *The Straits Times* (Singapore), 11 January 1999, p. 2.
49 Elisabeth Rosenthal, "Chinese Test New Weapon From West: Lawsuits," *New York Times*, 16 June 2001.
50 Walter LaFeber, *Michael Jordan and the New Global Capitalism* (New York: Norton, 1999), p. 157.

8 The new Rome meets the new barbarians

Shortly after September 11 President Bush's father observed that

> just as Pearl Harbor awakened this country from the notion that we could somehow avoid the call of duty to defend freedom in Europe and Asia in World War Two, so, too, should this most recent surprise attack erase the concept in some quarters that America can somehow go it alone in the fight against terrorism or in anything else for that matter.

But America's allies have begun to wonder whether that is the lesson that has been learned – or whether the Afghanistan campaign's apparent success shows that unilateralism works just fine. The United States, that argument goes, is so dominant that it can largely afford to go it alone.

It is true that no nation since Rome has loomed so large above the others, but even Rome eventually collapsed. Only a decade ago, the conventional wisdom lamented an America in decline. Bestseller lists featured books that described America's fall. Japan would soon become "Number One". That view was wrong at the time, and when I wrote "Bound to Lead" in 1989, I, like others, predicted the continuing rise of American power. But the new conventional wisdom that America is invincible is equally dangerous if it leads to a foreign policy that combines unilateralism, arrogance and parochialism.

A number of adherents of "realist" international-relations theory have also expressed concern about America's staying-power. Throughout history, coalitions of countries have arisen to balance dominant powers, and the search for traditional shifts in the balance of power and new state challengers is well under way. Some see China as the new enemy; others envisage a Russia–China–India coalition as the threat. But even if China maintains high growth rates of 6% while the United States achieves only 2%, it will not equal the United States in income per head (measured in purchasing-power parity) until the last half of the century.

Still others see a uniting Europe as a potential federation that will challenge the United States for primacy. But this forecast depends on a high degree of European political unity, and a low state of transatlantic relations. Although realists raise an important point about the levelling of power in the international arena, their quest for new cold-war-style challengers is largely barking up the wrong tree.

They are ignoring deeper changes in the distribution and nature of power in the contemporary world.

Three kinds of power

At first glance, the disparity between American power and that of the rest of the world looks overwhelming. In terms of military power, the United States is the only country with both nuclear weapons and conventional forces with global reach. American military expenditures are greater than those of the next eight countries combined, and it leads in the information-based "revolution in military affairs". In economic size, America's 31% share of world product (at market prices) is equal to the next four countries combined (Japan, Germany, Britain and France). In terms of cultural prominence, the United States is far and away the number-one film and television exporter in the world. It also attracts the most foreign students each year to its colleges and universities.

After the collapse of the Soviet Union, some analysts described the resulting world as uni-polar, others as multi-polar. Both are wrong, because each refers to a different dimension of power that can no longer be assumed to be homogenised by military dominance. Uni-polarity exaggerates the degree to which the United States is able to get the results it wants in some dimensions of world politics, but multi-polarity implies, wrongly, several roughly equal countries.

Instead, power in a global information age is distributed among countries in a pattern that resembles a complex three-dimensional chess game. On the top chessboard, military power is largely uni-polar. To repeat, the United States is the only country with both intercontinental nuclear weapons and large state-of-the-art air, naval and ground forces capable of global deployment. But on the middle chessboard, economic power is multi-polar, with the United States, Europe and Japan representing two-thirds of world product, and with China's dramatic growth likely to make it the fourth big player. On this economic board, the United States is not a hegemon, and must often bargain as an equal with Europe.

The bottom chessboard is the realm of transnational relations that cross borders outside government control. This realm includes actors as diverse as bankers electronically transferring sums larger than most national budgets at one extreme, and terrorists transferring weapons or hackers disrupting Internet operations at the other. On this bottom board, power is widely dispersed, and it makes no sense to speak of uni-polarity, multi-polarity or hegemony. Those who recommend a hegemonic American foreign policy based on such traditional descriptions of American power are relying on woefully inadequate analysis. When you are in a three-dimensional game, you will lose if you focus only on the top board and fail to notice the other boards and the vertical connections among them.

A shrinking and merging world

Because of its leading position in the information revolution and its past investment in traditional power resources, the United States will probably remain the world's most powerful single country well into this new century. While potential coalitions to check American power could be created, it is unlikely that they would become firm alliances unless the United States handles its hard coercive power in an overbearing unilateral manner that undermines its soft or attractive power – the important ability to get others to want what you want.

As Josef Joffe, editor of *Die Zeit*, has written, "Unlike centuries past, when war was the great arbiter, today the most interesting types of power do not come out of the barrel of a gun." Today there is a much bigger payoff in "getting others to want what you want", and that has to do with cultural attraction and ideology, along with agenda-setting and economic incentives for co-operation. Soft power is particularly important in dealing with issues arising from the bottom chessboard of transnational relations.

The real challenges to American power are not coming from other states, however, and the temptation to unilateralism may ultimately weaken the United States. The contemporary information revolution and the globalisation that goes with it are transforming and shrinking the world. At the beginning of this new century, these two forces have combined to increase American power. But, with time, technology will spread to other countries and peoples, and America's relative pre-eminence will diminish.

For example, at the start of the century the American twentieth of the global population represents more than half the Internet. In a decade or two, Chinese will probably be the dominant language of the Internet. It will not dethrone English as a *lingua franca*, but at some point in the future the Asian cyber-community and economy will loom larger than the American.

Even more important, the information revolution is creating virtual communities and networks that cut across national borders. Transnational corporations and non-governmental actors, such as terrorist networks, will play larger roles. Many of these organisations will have soft power of their own as they attract citizens into coalitions that cut across national boundaries. It is worth noting that, in the 1990s, a coalition based on NGOs created a landmines treaty against the opposition of the strongest bureaucracy in the strongest country.

September 11th was a terrible symptom of the deeper changes that were already occurring in the world. Technology has been diffusing power away from governments, and empowering individuals and groups to play roles in world politics – including wreaking massive destruction – which were once reserved to governments. Privatisation has been increasing, and terrorism is the privatisation of war. Globalisation is shrinking distance, and events in faraway places, like Afghanistan, can have a great impact on American lives.

At the end of the cold war, many observers were haunted by the spectre of the return of American isolationism. But in addition to the historic debate between isolationists and internationalists, there was a split within the internationalist camp between unilateralists and multilateralists. Some, like the columnist Charles Krauthammer, urge a "new unilateralism" whereby the United States refuses to play the role of "docile international citizen" and unashamedly pursues its own ends. They speak of a uni-polar world because of America's unequalled military power. But military power alone cannot produce the outcomes Americans want on many of the issues that matter to their safety and prosperity.

As an assistant secretary of defence in 1994–95, I would be the last to deny the importance of military security. It is like oxygen. Without it, all else pales. America's military power is essential to global stability and an essential part of the response to terrorism. But the metaphor of war should not blind us to the fact that suppressing terrorism will take years of patient, unspectacular civilian co-operation with other countries. The military success in Afghanistan dealt with the easiest part of the problem, and al-Qaeda retains cells in some 50 countries. Rather than proving the unilateralists' point, the partial nature of the success in Afghanistan illustrates the continuing need for co-operation.

The perils of going alone

The problem for Americans in the twenty-first century is that more and more things fall outside the control of even the most powerful state. Although the United States does well on the traditional measures, there is increasingly more going on in the world that those measures fail to capture. Under the influence of the information revolution and globalisation, world politics is changing in a way that means Americans cannot achieve all their international goals by acting alone. For example, international financial stability is vital to the prosperity of Americans, but the United States needs the co-operation of others to ensure it. Global climate change too will affect Americans' quality of life, but the United States cannot manage the problem alone. And in a world where borders are becoming more porous to everything from drugs to infectious diseases to terrorism, America must mobilise international coalitions to address shared threats and challenges.

The barbarian threat

In light of these new circumstances, how should the only superpower guide its foreign policy in a global information age? Some Americans are tempted to believe that the United States could reduce its vulnerability if it withdrew troops, curtailed alliances and followed a more isolationist foreign policy. But isolationism would not remove the vulnerability. The terrorists who struck on September 11th were not only dedicated to reducing American power, but wanted to break down what America stands for. Even if the United States had a weaker foreign policy, such groups would resent the power of the American economy which would still reach well beyond its shores. American corporations and citizens represent global capitalism, which some see as anathema.

Moreover, American popular culture has a global reach regardless of what the government does. There is no escaping the influence of Hollywood, CNN and the Internet. American films and television express freedom, individualism and change, but also sex and violence. Generally, the global reach of American culture helps to enhance America's soft power. But not, of course, with everyone. Individualism and liberties are attractive to many people but repulsive to some, particularly fundamentalists. American feminism, open sexuality and individual choices are profoundly subversive of patriarchal societies. But those hard nuggets of opposition are unlikely to catalyse broad hatred unless the United States abandons its values and pursues arrogant and overbearing policies that let the extremists appeal to the majority in the middle.

On the other hand, those who look at the American preponderance, see an empire, and urge unilateralism, risk an arrogance that alienates America's friends. Granted, there are few pure multilateralists in practice, and multilateralism can be used by smaller states to tie the United States down like Gulliver among the Lilliputians, but this does not mean that a multilateral approach is not generally in America's interests. By embedding its policies in a multilateral framework, the United States can make its disproportionate power more legitimate and acceptable to others. No large power can afford to be purely multilateralist, but that should be the starting point for policy. And when that great power defines its national interests broadly to include global interests, some degree of unilateralism is more likely to be acceptable. Such an approach will be crucial to the longevity of American power.

At the moment, the United States is unlikely to face a challenge to its preeminence from other states unless it acts so arrogantly that it helps the others to overcome their built-in limitations. The greater challenge for the United States will be to learn how to work with other countries to control more effectively the non-state actors that will increasingly share the stage with nation-states. How to control the bottom chessboard in a three-dimensional game, and how to make hard and soft power reinforce each other are the key foreign policy challenges. As Henry Kissinger has argued, the test of history for this generation of American leaders will be whether they can turn the current predominant power into an international consensus and widely-accepted norms that will be consistent with American values and interests as America's dominance ebbs later in the century. And that cannot be done unilaterally.

Rome succumbed not to the rise of a new empire, but to internal decay and a death of a thousand cuts from various barbarian groups. While internal decay is always possible, none of the commonly cited trends seem to point strongly in that direction at this time. Moreover, to the extent it pays attention, the American public is often realistic about the limits of their country's power. Nearly two-thirds of those polled oppose, in principle, the United States acting alone overseas without the support of other countries. The American public seems to have an intuitive sense for soft power, even if the term is unfamiliar.

On the other hand, it is harder to exclude the barbarians. The dramatically decreased cost of communication, the rise of transnational domains (including the Internet) that cut across borders, and the "democratisation" of technology that puts massive destructive power into the hands of groups and individuals, all suggest dimensions that are historically new. In the last century, Hitler, Stalin and Mao needed the power of the state to wreak great evil. As the Hart-Rudman Commission on National Security observed last year, "Such men and women in the twenty-first century will be less bound than those of the twentieth by the limits of the state, and less obliged to gain industrial capabilities in order to wreak havoc . . . Clearly the threshold for small groups or even individuals to inflict massive damage on those they take to be their enemies is falling dramatically."

Since this is so, homeland defence takes on a new importance and a new meaning. If such groups were to obtain nuclear materials and produce a series of events involving great destruction or great disruption of society, American attitudes might change dramatically, though the direction of the change is difficult to predict. Faced with such a threat, a certain degree of unilateral action, such as the war in Afghanistan, is justified if it brings global benefits. After all, the British navy reduced the scourge of piracy well before international conventions were signed in the middle of the nineteenth century.

Number one, but . . .

The United States is well placed to remain the leading power in world politics well into the twenty-first century. This prognosis depends upon assumptions that can be spelled out. For example, it assumes that the American economy and society will remain robust and not decay; that the United States will maintain its military strength, but not become over-militarised; that Americans will not become so unilateral and arrogant in their strength that they squander the nation's considerable fund of soft power; that there will not be some catastrophic series of events that profoundly transforms American attitudes in an isolationist direction; and that Americans will define their national interest in a broad and far-sighted way that incorporates global interests. Each of these assumptions can be questioned, but they currently seem more plausible than their alternatives.

If the assumptions hold, America will remain number one. But number one "ain't gonna be what it used to be." The information revolution, technological change and globalisation will not replace the nation-state but will continue to complicate the actors and issues in world politics. The paradox of American power in the twenty-first century is that the largest power since Rome cannot achieve its objectives unilaterally in a global information age.

Part 3
Ideas and morality

9 Nationalism, statesmen, and the size of African states*

> To determine the size of the polis – to settle how large it can properly be, and whether it ought to consist of the members of one people or several – is a duty incumbent on the statesman.
>
> Aristotle

Nineteen hundred and sixty was the year of triumph of African nationalism. Yet as the coups of 1966 soon underlined, the independent states were not yet nations. A conclusion drawn from this, and one that is reinforced by the prevalent academic theories of political development, is that African leaders should forego their concern with their neighbors and focus their attention solely on the internal tasks of nation building.

But such a conclusion is too simple. It is one thing to turn inward to internal development in Nigeria or Congo-Kinshasa, but it is open to question whether any degree of concentration on internal problems would bring about significant economic or political development in Togo, Upper Volta, or Chad. Two-thirds of the independent African states have only a few million inhabitants and per capita incomes of under a hundred dollars a year – a small market for industrialization and a thin base over which to spread the overhead of services that go along with sovereign status.[1] Several states, for instance Malawi, Gambia, and Dahomey, are dependent on the former colonial power for support of their recurrent budgets as well as for capital expenditure. It is doubtful whether African microstates can achieve a level of economic development on the basis of their present size which will allow them to develop governmental institutions capable of providing sufficient and effective rewards and punishments necessary for rapid nation building. In other words, some sort of external arrangements with other African states may be a necessary condition for internal nation building. Otherwise, military interventions which periodically focus attention on internal order will merely be part of a dreary cycle.

Why then has there been so little progress on improving the external conditions of development in Africa? Why have African leaders accepted the boundaries arbitrarily determined on the drawing boards of nineteenth century European chancelleries? In the eyes of some younger African elites, the explanation lies in the selfishness of the current generation of African leaders. In the eyes of some outside observers, the explanation lies in the intensity of African nationalism. The purpose of this chapter is not to provide solutions but to demonstrate the inadequacy of the above explanations and to interpret the dilemma of African nationalist leaders who are concerned about the development of their small states.

One thing to make clear at the outset is that I am not arguing that large size is good for states and small size always bad. Nor does small size necessarily mean, as is frequently said, that African states are "unviable." Viability is in the living, and in an age when a combination of nuclear bipolarity and international organization tend to dampen violent conflict and put a safety net below small states, many so-called "unviable" states will go right on vying for external support. But life can be lived at a variety of levels, and viability says nothing about the level at which equilibrium is finally achieved. After all, some Caribbean countries have limped along for more than a century.

One must also beware of too simple assumptions about the relation of size to development. Highly developed countries like Switzerland, Norway, and New Zealand have populations little larger than those of the small African states. But it is argued that the small developed nations began their economic growth in a period of more liberal international trade and thus were better able to specialize in manufactures for the world market rather than have to rely on small internal markets.[2] While this argument tends to underrate the possibility of developing countries producing manufactures for the world market today, one can still feel uneasy about alleged lessons from small developed countries.[3]

On the political side as well, one must avoid overly simple statements about the relation of size to development. The two Latin American states consistently judged by scholars as having the most highly developed stable democratic institutions are Uruguay and Costa Rica – two of the smaller republics, with populations of 2.8 and 1.2 million respectively. Other small states, however, tend to be ranked at the bottom of the list by Latin Americanists.[4] In short, the key variable seems to be the homogeneity of the populations – neither Uruguay nor Costa Rica had large unassimilated Indian populations. Recognizing this variable, an economist suggests that small states may have better prospects for growth because they may tend to be more homogeneous.[5] But whatever the merits of the propositions in general, they seem inaccurate in Africa. Gambia, one of the smallest sovereign states, has the same ethnic divisions as its larger neighbor Senegal. The politics of Dahomey, to take another of the smallest states, has been plagued by ethnic heterogeneity.

In summary, although we cannot come to simple conclusions about the relation of the size of states to their economic and political development, we *can* say that most African states are severely restricted in terms of their internal markets and in the services of sovereignty that they can afford to provide – and further that under African conditions there is no reason to believe that small size indicates a homogeneity that might be a mitigating factor.

A frequently suggested solution to the problem is to consolidate African states into larger units – whether federations or various more limited forms of functional arrangements such as common markets or common service organizations. Given the general verbal commitment to overcoming "balkanization" on the part of African leaders, one might expect that the prospects for such a solution are good. Some observers have concluded that "Africans really have an advantage over every other attempt . . . to bring about regional cooperation," and that pan-Africanism has shown a trend away from "amorphous protest to the fashioning of organized cooperation." Many younger Africans believe that they will some day break out of the small state "cages" inherited from colonialism.[6]

Thus far the evidence suggests the contrary. If anything, African leaders have strengthened the bars of the inherited cages. One case where ideology led to amalgamation – the Mali Federation – was a case of "premature" union in which the coercive, utilitarian, and ideological powers of the union were not sufficient to maintain it for more than a few months of independence. Other putative amalgamations, such as the Ghana–Guinea–Mali Union, remained at the purely verbal level – even though all three states had constitutions providing for sacrifice of sovereignty on the altar of African unity; two (Guinea and Mali) were contiguous and shared a similar colonial background and ideological outlook, and the third (Ghana) invested some $22.4 million in the project.[7] Efforts on the part of East African leaders to consolidate the high degree of economic and functional cooperation inherited from colonial rule by forming a federation in 1963 proved abortive. Indeed, with one exception, the few successful amalgamations of territories in Africa occurred before independence and more often than not involved United Nations action. The one exception, the union between Tanganyika and Zanzibar in 1964 involved the absorption of two little islands with the same linguistic background as the country 360 times their size and off whose coast they lay – an exception, but one from which it is difficult to generalize for more than the smallest enclaves.

More limited functional arrangements such as customs unions and shared services appear to be an attractive solution in Africa because they allow simultaneous pursuit of the three values of independence, development and unity without forcing a choice among them.[8] But functional arrangements and "technocratic federations" depend on a certain degree of at least short-run separability of economic or technical problems from political ones. Such separability is rare in Africa. The location of industry in a customs union, for instance, is not a simple problem of welfare benefits to be calculated, compromised, and redistributed. Industry is a key symbol of modernity and sovereignty is a game in which the ultimate stakes are racial dignity. Thus pan-Africanist Guinea was unable to accept a United Nations plan for the establishment of a West African steel industry. Pan-Africanist Tanzania was unable to tolerate an East African common market in which a disproportionate amount of industry tended to locate in neighboring Kenya,[9] and Chad, unhappy with the distribution of benefits, withdrew from the hopeful new Union Douanière et Economique de l'Afrique Centrale, which commenced in Equatorial Africa in 1966.

Even the most limited technical arrangements are frequently plagued by politics. When Senegal failed to break relations with Britain over the Rhodesia issue in 1965, Guinea related the question to cooperation in the Senegal River Committee. Despite its subsequent return, the scheme remained highly politicized. Common services shared by Niger and Dahomey broke down over a minor dispute in 1963. When Somali irrendentism led to armed clashes with Ethiopia in 1963, the latter bombed the base of the joint Desert Locust Survey for fear that the light aircraft of the organization might be used by the Somalis for military purposes.[10] At the continental level, the technical commissions of the Organization of African Unity, such as the Health, Sanitation and Nutrition Commission and the Commission of Jurists, have failed even to attain quorums, while the former colonial Commission for Technical Cooperation in Africa (CCTA) has atrophied since incorporation by the OAU. Indeed, in general the OAU found personnel and budgetary assessments difficult to obtain from member states. The Secretary-General reported a $2.5 million debt and serious understaffing to the October 1965 meeting and in 1966 the member states decided to reduce the budget by two thirds.[11]

The obstacles to African unity whether in the form of amalgamation or functional arrangements are sometimes attributed to evil men or to outside interference. Yet if Africa were governed by angels in a vacuum, the problems would remain because of the postcolonial situation in which such leaders would find themselves. Similarly, it is inadequate to attribute the problems of common markets in Africa to "profound feelings of nationalism."[12] The problem in Africa is quite the contrary – the lack of profundity of the feeling of nationalism. To see the present problem in perspective, it is necessary to go back to the colonial period.

With the establishment of colonial rule, Africans gained a new racial identity. Even illiterate Africans were aware of the racial difference of their colonial rulers and of their disruptive influence on traditional communities. The result was a wide variety of diffuse reactions ranging from reformism to millennial escapism which Hodgkin called African nationalism and Lord Hailey labeled "Africanism."[13] Educated elites tended to reject the traditional community as the basis for political action at least in part because it could not provide the power necessary to achieve racial dignity on the world scene. Thus the elites expressed the sense of racial identity in continental terms and labeled politics based on traditional communities as "tribalism."[14] In Julius Nyerere's words, "Once the tribal unit had been rejected as not being sensible in Africa, then there can be no stopping short of Africa itself as the political grouping. For what else is there? 'Nations' in any real sense of the word do not at present exist in Africa."[15]

Nyerere's formulation was a statement of preference as much as fact. Nations might not exist, but states did. The newness of the *inter*state system obscures a longer period of impact of state structure on African identities. African states did not spring full grown from the head of the United Nations; rather they developed in the womb of colonial rule. Political development does not begin with independence.

By constant use of the terms "nation" and "nationalism" we do ourselves a disservice. The "rising tide of African nationalism" suggests analogies with nineteenth-century Europe when a new formula of political community and legitimacy was used to destroy institutions and restructure the international order. Indeed, this may have been what educated African elites and sympathetic Western observers, perhaps unconsciously, wished the terms to suggest, since by using Western slogans of national self-determination, particularly in the period after the Atlantic Charter, they were able to shake the colonial sense of moral legitimacy. But seeing the change in Africa as "African nationalism" or "pan-African nationalism" as the elites sometimes phrase it, leaves us unable to explain the weakness of Africa-wide institutions.

The inadequacy of the analogy implied in the slogan was illustrated by the isolated position of the Somali, a linguistic, ethnic, and religious group trying to reshape state boundaries to their sense of community. "Somali nationalism began as an exclusive movement aimed at the amalgamation of the Somali territories in the Horn of Africa ... There was no need in this situation ... to appeal to a wider identity as 'Africans.' "[16] The uniqueness of the Somali case was dramatized by the July 1964 resolution of the O.A.U. recognizing that the colonial borders so often described as meaningless, "constitute a tangible reality," and pledging "to respect the borders existing on their achievement of national independence."[17] This caused a heated debate in Somalia's National Assembly and a resolution denying that the O.A.U. resolution was binding on the Somali Republic.[18] The Somalis continued to speak of "self-determination" in the postcolonial period. Kenya, which is more typical of the rest of Africa and within whose borders a large number of Somalis reside, insisted that "seeking to create new African nations on the basis of tribal or religious identities is a sin against pan-Africa and a most dangerous weapon for destroying African solidarity."[19] Indeed, one of the remarkable features of the new African state system has been the comparative rarity of irrendentism. Paradoxically, the arbitrariness of African borders has enhanced rather than decreased their significance.

We can gain a somewhat different perspective if we switch temporarily from words which bear an implicit analogy to the nineteenth century, to words which imply an analogy with Europe of the sixteenth and seventeenth centuries. Unlike the slogans of nationalism which assumed the existence of a community, the slogan of "sovereignty" was used to subordinate both internal and external feudal loyalties to the monarchy.[20] That this centralization frequently proceeded under monarchs who denied any intention of reducing external loyalties and swore fealty to the Pope, suggests interesting comparisons with African leaders who wish to subordinate tribal loyalties to the state while simultaneously swearing fealty to pan-Africa.

We cannot understand the dilemma of the pan-Africanist leaders unless we see that the origins of the "sovereign revolution" lie in the colonial period. Not only was colonial rule a source of modernization, but it created the political *infrastructure* – budgets, bureaucracies, armies, police, propaganda devices – around which mobilized groups tended to cluster.[21] Loyalties tend to shift to the source of rewards. Thus even though the colonial state never became fully legitimate because it was colonial, the identities and attention of the educated and other mobilized groups became focused on it in order to influence rewards and to cope with the problems of the new way of life that it fostered. Clan and "tribal" associations were formed in such a way that they often enlarged identities to include peripheral groups to better compete or fulfill their new functions much as caste and associations have in India.[22] What was crudely called "tribalism" often concealed important social changes.

Because African "nationalism" was an ideology held by an elite wishing to call a nation into being rather than a widespread sentiment of community, organization was crucial in its propagation.[23] Before independence the critical organization for this purpose was the nationalist party, which in nearly all cases was constructed at the territorial level.[24] It was there that the mobilized groups clustered and the important institutions existed. Both had to be captured to make the "self-determination" which had been expressed in broad terms a narrower but more tangible reality.

Ironically the approach of independence heightened general awareness of identity at several levels, including ethnic "micro-nationalism" or "tribalism" in the pejorative language of the pan-Africanist. At the same time, independence increased the importance of national loyalties as citizens become better placed to affect government rewards. For instance, in the Ivory Coast, where nearly a quarter of the population were alien Africans, increased governmental autonomy was marked by riots and expulsions of non-indigenous Africans.[25] Similar though less violent experiences occurred in Niger, Congo, and Uganda.

In short, the internal consolidation of "sovereignty" began with the foundation of the colonial state and was reinforced by the formation of territorial "nationalist" organizations. When independence and Africanization removed the colonial stigma which hindered legitimization of the state, it would have been remarkable if internal consolidation had not increased regardless of the "good" or "bad" intentions of the leaders, or the differences in the nature of the new regimes.

Observers have been prone to dichotomize the new political systems first by the numbers of parties; later, when the single party became the dominant institution, by the elite versus mass-mobilization nature or pragmatic versus revolutionary style of the major party and now, perhaps, as military versus civilian.[26] After independence, with a few exceptions and for a variety of reasons including personalist leadership in some cases (Ghana, Malawi) and governmental competition for the scarce resource of middle-level bureaucrats (Tanzania, Zambia), the more impressive party bureaucracies were weakened leaving the inherited colonial state the key institution.[27] Close identification of party and state tended to legitimize the state rather than strengthen the party.

Whether one distinguished African regimes by the nature of their dominant institutions or differentiates them according to the degree of their tolerance of traditional pluralism, they are all faced with a similar set of problems which tend to enhance the importance of the state – though not necessarily increasing its capacity. Rapid economic development is desired to assert racial dignity as well as for welfare, thus diminishing the time available to wait for payoffs from supranational schemes which might better enhance long-run effectiveness. Ethnic malintegration has been another common problem, and the state machinery – used both for punishment and reward – has been a vital instrument in strengthening the elite's ability to cope with it.[28] Insecurity has been another problem. The persistence of independence legitimacy which one might have expected to limit the violence and social effects of most revolts and mutinies was suprisingly brief. Even before the spectacular coups of 1965–66, the previous two years had seen seven heads of state or government forcibly deposed and plots discovered in a dozen other states, including all types of regimes.[29] Even where it does not lead to increasing centralization, build-up of security forces and military coups, the threat of instability diverts leaders' attention to internal affairs. In terms of Karl Deutsch's communications analogy, statesmen are less likely to hear and respond to each others' messages if their ears are continually full of the noise of internal problems.

Levels of social mobilization are low in African countries compared with economically more developed areas, but in terms of African institutional capacity, they are high. In general, the colonial education pyramid had a very narrow top and a comparatively broad base. The result was mobilization of considerable number of school leavers who are attracted to urban areas, creating urban unemployment rates of 20 percent or higher in some places. At the same time, the colonial education systems produced only a handful of university and secondary school graduates to staff governmental bureaucracies which were denuded of experienced personnel because of pressures for Africanization.[30] In addition, and in contrast to European history, most African states had universal suffrage and an egalitarian ideology before they proceeded far in capital formation. The single-party tendency can be seen as a partial retraction of the substance of universal suffrage – an interesting example of the notion that political development can be advanced by reducing the burdens of mobilization on institutions.[31] But in general Deutsch is probably correct in stating that in the race between rates of mobilization and institutional capability, the "only variable with which policy makers usually can work is capability."[32]

Cooperative arrangements can increase capability for economic development, but the payoffs are often long run, and such arrangements cannot solve the other problems of insecurity and party reintegration. Moreover, such arrangements run counter to the growing use of state loyalties to affect governmental rewards, and to the statist political culture within which most African elites have developed their ideas. Whatever else "African socialism" may mean, it generally implies a distrust of the private sector and reliance on state planning.[33] A pre-condition of planning is some degree of certainty about the boundaries within which resources are to be allocated. It is understandable in origin but rather ironic in practice that the strongest pan-Africanists are also the strongest African socialists.

A recent work on political integration suggests that international integration differs from other kinds because it means "integrating the integrated." The units involved are "sovereign." In a legal sense this means they have "the ultimate right to make decisions." In a realistic political sense, it means they have a "general competence to make decisions."[34] African states are not highly integrated and have little sovereignty in the latter sense. Thus international integration in Africa is "integrating the integrat*ing*." It seems less difficult to integrate the integrat*ed* or the unintegrated than the integrat*ing* – those *with* a high degree of realistic sovereignty than those with less, but an intense concern with getting more.[35]

In summary, the majority of African states are hindered in their prospects for economic and political development by their small size and internal heterogeneity. The roots of the problem lie deep in the colonial experience and the postcolonial situation rather than depending simply on (removable) bad leaders. Similarly, the problem lies not in the intensity of African nationalism (in the sense of a widespread national consciousness) but in the weakness of African nationalism. It is one of the tragic ironies of African development, that in spite of intensive pre-independence talk of rejecting artificial colonial boundaries on the part of African statesmen, it has been the despised colonial statesmen who so completely determined the size of the polis.

Notes

* This essay draws upon my early work on regional economic integration.
1 There is no absolute line for distinguishing "small" states. S. Kuznets sets the dividing line in the modern world at roughly 10 million population in "Economic Growth of Small Nations," in Austin Robinson, ed., *The Economic Consequences of the Size of Nations* (London, Macmillan, 1960), p. 14.
2 Sidney Dell, *Trade Blocs and Common Markets* (London, Oxford University Press, 1963).
3 On neglected possibilities, see Raymond Vernon, "Prospects and Problems in the Export of Manufactured Products from Less-Developed Countries," *Contributed Paper No. 2* (Geneva, UNCTAD, 1964).
4 Russell Fitzgibbon and Kenneth Johnson, "Measurement of Latin American Political Change," in John Martz, ed., *The Dynamics of Change in Latin American Politics* (Englewood Cliffs. Prentice-Hall, 1965), pp. 113–129.
5 Kuznets, "Economic Growth," pp. 28–31.
6 Herbert Spiro, "Political Stability in the New African States," *The Annals*, 354 (July 1964), 106–107; Norman Padelford, "The Organization of African Unity," *International Organization*, 18 (Summer 1964), 546.
7 See I. William Zartman, *International Relations in the New Africa* (Englewood Cliffs, Prentice-Hall, 1966), p. 127.
8 Ibid., p. 150.
9 J. S. Nye, *Pan-Africanism and East African Integration* (Cambridge, Harvard University Press, 1965), chap. 5.
10 *West Africa*, January 1, 1966; Zartman, *International Relations in the New Africa*, p. 158.
11 *New York Times*, October 25, 1965; *West Africa*, October 16, 1965.
12 Dell cites this as an obstacle to common markets in developing areas, *Trade Blocs and Common Markets*, p. 172.
13 *Nationalism in Colonial Africa* (New York, New York University Press, 1957); *An African Survey: Revised 1956* (London, Oxford University Press, 1957).
14 French elites were more explicit about race in their concern with negritude. The role of Western Hemisphere Negroes in shaping this identity was considerable. For an introduction to pan-Africanism, see Colin Legum, *PanAfricanism: A Short Political Guide* (New York, Praeger, 1962).
15 *An Address to the Norwegian Students Association in Oslo* (Dar es Salaam, Government Printing Office, 1963), p. 4. This simplification avoids the problem of

defining "tribe." In reality many traditional African systems involved several levels of community. See Paul Bohanan, *Africa and Africans* (New York, Natural History Press, 1964), chap. 8 and 12.

16 I. M. Lewis, "Pan-Africanism and Pan-Somalism," *Journal of Modern African Studies*, 1.2 (1963), 159,148.

17 "General Record of the First Assembly of Heads of State and Government: Resolution 16" (mimeo, July 1964).

18 Jeane Contini, "The Somali Republic: Politics with a Difference," *Africa Report* (November 1964), p. 8.

19 "Pan-African Unity and the N.F.D. Question in Kenya," unpub. ms., Addis Ababa, 1963. For the wider context, see Rupert Emerson, *Self-Determination Revisited in the Era of Decolonization* (Cambridge, Harvard University Press, 1964).

20 Even the analogy of the monarch may not be too farfetched in some cases. See David Apter, "Ghana," in James Coleman and Carl Rosberg, eds., *Political Parties and National Integration in Tropical Africa* (Berkeley, University of California Press, 1964), p. 311; and Immanuel Wallerstein, *Africa: The Politics of Independence* (New York, Random House, 1961).

21 See Martin Kilson, "African Political Change and the Modernization Process," *Journal of Modern African Studies*, 1 (December 1963), 427.

22 Compare Immanuel Wallerstein, "Ethnicity and National Integration in West Africa," *Cahiers d'Études Africaines*, no. 3 (1960), 129–139; and Lloyd and Susanne Rudolph, "The Political Role of India's Case Associations," *Pacific Affairs*, 33 (March 1960), 5–22.

23 Ernst Haas makes this distinction. *Beyond the Nation-State* (Stanford, Stanford University Press, 1964), p. 465.

24 Aristide Zolberg shows that even in the case of the major exception, the Rassemblement Démocratique Africain in the former French African federations, the important unit in the late colonial period was the territorial party. *One-Party Government in the Ivory Coast* (Princeton, Princeton University Press, 1964), p. 95.

25 Ibid., p. 245.

26 Ruth Schachter, "Single-Party Systems in West Africa," *American Political Science Review*, 55 (June 1961); Thomas Hodgkin, *African Political Parties;* Martin Kilson, "Authoritarian and Single Party Tendencies in African Politics," *World Politics*, 15 (January 1964); Coleman and Rosberg, *Political Parties.*

27 Conversely, weak parties often gained strength from association with government. Also, the decline of party bureaucracies is only relative, and their role in legitimacy should not be ignored. See J. S. Nye, "The Impact of Independence on Two African Nationalist Parties," in A. Castagno and J. Butler, eds., *Boston University Papers on Africa* (Boston, Boston University Press, 1967).

28 Zolberg, *One-Party Government in the Ivory Coast*, p. 194; Nye, "The Impact of Independence."

29 Robert Good, "Changing Patterns of African International Relations," *American Political Science Review*, 58 (September 1964), 637; *The Economist*, London, April 27, 1963.

30 For instance, Zambia came to independence in 1964 with approximately 100 (African) university graduates and 1,500 secondary school graduates but 50,000 youths seeking jobs in addition to 74,000 adult unemployed. *East Africa and Rhodesia* (October 22, 1964), p. 109. The extreme case of the colonial education pyramid was, of course, the Belgian Congo.

31 Samuel Huntington, "Political Development and Political Decay," *World Politics*, 17 (April 1965), 419. In waggish form this becomes "African democracy: one man, one vote – once." Tanzania which held meaningful elections in 1965, is an exception.

32 "Communication Theory and Political Integration," in Philip Jacob and James Toscano, eds., *The Integration of Political Communities* (Philadelphia, Lippincott, 1964), p. 71.

33 See W. H. Friedland and Carl Rosberg, eds., *African Socialism* (Stanford, Stanford University Press, 1964); Elliot Berg, "Socialism and Economic Development in Tropical Africa," *Quarterly Journal of Economics*, 78 (November 1964), 549–573.

34 Jacob and Toscano, *Integration of Political Communities*, pp. 9, 72.

35 For instance, the Indian half of the Guatemala population is largely unintegrated and this has not prevented Guatemala from playing a major role in the Central American Common Market. See J. S. Nye, "Central American Regional Integration," *International Conciliation*, 562 (March 1967).

10 The ethics of foreign policy*

The difficult domain of international politics

The task of moral reasoning about international politics is not a simple one. The Realists deserved to win the debate with the shallow moralizing Idealists of the interwar years. There are good reasons why ethical behavior is more difficult to define and carry out in international than in domestic politics, and why the simple use of personal moral maxims in the international domain can have immoral consequences. The structure of moral language stresses universality and impartiality among individuals – "do unto others as you would have them do unto you." But international politics occurs among individuals organized into states. We practice our daily moral habits in a sheltered space. Sovereign states provide enough domestic order to allow us to follow moral intentions, but many of our normal moral institutions are "off balance" in international politics. A simple-minded transposition of individual moral maxims to relations *among states* can lead to immoral consequences. A statesman who chooses to turn the other cheek may put his people's lives in peril. When there are such gaps between our moral intuitions and the consequences of following them, it is easier to moralize than to act morally. The Oxford students who in 1933 vowed never to fight may well have encouraged Hitler in his belief that Britain would not resist his aggression.

A second problem rising from the existence of states is the prospect of ethical egoism. Many moral philosophers admit the logical possibility of a totally amoral egoistic life, but believe it is extremely difficult for individuals to practice.[1] On the other hand, amoral behavior may be more feasible for sovereign states. This is a point that Thomas Hobbes recognized three centuries ago when he argued that the roughly equal insecurity of individuals draws them out of the state of nature into government, but that once people are organized into states they feel safe enough in their daily lives that they would rather tolerate the state of nature than submit to the leviathan of a world government.

Another problem growing out of the existence of states is the relationship between order and justice. Both values are important. As Paul Ramsey points out, "order is a means to justice, but also justice is a means of serving order." A well ordered domestic polity can concentrate its political debate and efforts on improving justice. But if efforts to promote justice internationally ignore the power of states, they may promote disorder, which makes justice unachievable. As an instrumental value, some degree of order is necessary though not sufficient for justice. In Ramsey's words, "there is an asymmetry between these values . . . we must attend to the preservation of an ordered polity and an orderly interstate system so that there can be the conditions for improving the justice actualized among men and between states."[2]

The absence of international institutions means there are only weak legislative or adjudicative means of balancing the conflicting claims of order and justice. At best there is prudence, custom, and the weak institutions of international law and organization. A lack of substantive consensus on values among widely disparate cultures exacerbates the problem. Simply consider the different premises of American moralizing about the rights of individuals; Soviet moralizing about advancing the right class through history, and Khomeini's moralizing about the revealed truths of Shiite Islam. It is not surprising that the reciprocity and trust which help to sustain impartiality are difficult to develop internationally. Finally, there is the additional difficulty of assessing the consequences of actions when one must consider a third level of effects on the system of states as well as upon individual states and persons. International politics is just that much more complicated.

Inadequacy of total skepticism

Considering the nature of the international milieu, it is not surprising that serious students of international politics have tended to be cautious about the role of ethics in foreign policy and have warned about the possibly disastrous consequences of well-intentioned moral crusades in a domain as difficult as that of international politics. At the same time there is a difference between healthy realism and total skepticism. It does not follow from the difficulty of applying ethical considerations that they have no role at all. The cynic or total skeptic who argues that there is no role for ethics in international politics tends to smuggle his preferred values into foreign policy, often in the form of narrow nationalism. When faced with moral choices, to pretend not to choose is merely a disguised form of choice.

Philosophers say that "ought" implies "can." When something is impossible, we have no moral obligation to do it. But situations of absolute necessity where impossibility precludes obligation are relatively rare. "Do or die" situations are the exception, and even they raise moral choices. For example, the acute security dilemma that Israel faced in June 1967 may have allowed few choices other than pre-emptive attack, but there were many choices before and after June 1967.[3] And most day-to-day relations among states do not involve acute security situations. Obviously, there is less leeway for moral consideration in wartime conditions or when survival is at stake. But one cannot legitimately banish ethics by arguing that international politics is a "state of war" or that we are engaged in a Cold War with an amoral adversary. As Arnold Wolfers has pointed out, much of international politics allows choices about the definition of indefinite concepts like "national interest," "survival," and "prudence."[4] The statesman who says, "I had no choice," usually did have, albeit unpleasant ones!

The fact that international politics is a difficult domain for ethics means that one must be cautious about too simple a transposition of moral maxims from the domain of individuals to the domain of states. But it does not release the statesman from the duty of moral reasoning; it merely complicates his task. One must examine the arguments given for why there is "no choice" or why normal moral rules are alleged to be inapplicable in particular cases. The burden of proof rests on those who wish to depart from normal personal morality. While that burden may often be met, the quality of the argument and conclusions deserves close examination. Some arguments for disregarding normal moral rules may be fallacious. For example, it does not follow from the fact that idealists have often made foolish decisions in the past, that skeptics are justified in banning all moral reasoning from the domain of international politics.

There are at least three arguments used by total skeptics to exclude ethics from international politics that simply do not carry the weight which is attributed to them. For example, it is sometimes argued that ethical behavior requires self-sacrifice, and that nations cannot sacrifice themselves.[5] But this rests on the false juxtaposition of sacrificial love versus egoism, whereas the proper comparison is impartial justice versus egoism. Love may be a higher virtue in personal relations, but from the point of view of ethical language, it is a supererogatory virtue. Justice does not require sacrifice of one's interest; it only requires impartial treatment of competing interests. To act with justice may be difficult in international politics, but it is not impossible.

Similarly, the fact that states must act to defend their interests if they wish to survive in international politics in the long run does not mean that only selfish acts are possible. It does mean that most international acts will involve mixed motives. But some degree of altruism or consideration of others can often safely be included in the motives for foreign policy. Nor does the existence of different national moral standards make our own moral choices impossible. The sociological fact of normative relativism alerts us to the danger of conflicting moral views and may engender caution about the potentially immoral consequences of blindly trying to impose our moral standards on other cultures. But it does not excuse us from making moral choices about our own actions. Just because some others may execute prisoners of war or assassinate opponents does not make it right for us to do so. Two wrongs don't make us right.

It is sometimes questioned whether the United States can afford to act ethically when it is locked in a bipolar rivalry with an adversary whose doctrine rejects "bourgeois morality" and sees the goal of proletarian victory as justifying the means. The difference in moral views should alert us not to expect the Soviet Union necessarily to behave as we do, but it does not justify our behaving as they do. We may choose to act morally because of our desire to preserve our integrity as a society. To ignore Soviet behavior would be foolish, but to imitate it would be a particularly insidious way of losing the political competition.

Some skeptics question the application of moral concepts to individuals who live beyond our borders because of the absence of a common community that defines rights and obligations. Where political processes and communities are separate, why should we be concerned about justice beyond our borders? One answer is that we are concerned to the extent that our interactions and interdependence (economic, political, security) have effects on the conditions for justice in other countries. Another answer is the fact that many of our citizens do feel at least some sense of community – whether it be ethnic, religious, or cosmopolitan – beyond our borders. They define their welfare to include a sense of virtue in relation to such transnational communities.

In short, no domain of human activity can be categorized a priori as amoral when choices exist. But the particular characteristics of international politics make it a domain in which it is much more difficult to apply ethics than it is in a well-ordered domestic polity. The fact that shallow or superficial moral reasoning often neglects this distinction is grounds for cautionary warnings. It is not grounds for maintaining that ethics should play no role in international politics and foreign policy. The danger of shallow moral reasoning must be met by better moral reasoning that takes into account the difficulty of the domain, not by futilely pretending to ban moral reasoning from foreign policy. The dangers of shallow moral reasoning – whether the soft moralizing of the sentimental idealists or the spurious a priori exclusion of ethics by the total skeptics – can only be cured by more rigorous moral reasoning.

Judging moral arguments

How should one judge moral reasoning? Obviously I must start with certain normative assumptions. Since I am writing about American foreign policy. I assume the traditions of Western moral and political philosophy, and the values and procedures of American liberal democracy. This still leaves wide room for moral disagreements over how to express our values in foreign policy. Moreover, some people merely state their moral views and refuse to reason about them. My interest is with arguments about morality and foreign policy that go beyond primitive assertion.

Relativists and emotivists sometimes deny the prospect of judging moral arguments and assert that moral statements are mere expressions of taste. Ultimate ends are not susceptible to proof, but it is not senseless to discuss them. People do it every day, even if they sometimes fail to convince each other. Much of moral reasoning occurs in the area of argument that is beyond mere assertion but short of proving ultimate values. Moreover, much of ethical reasoning is not about ultimate ends, but about means, consequences, and the balancing of competing moral claims. Sometimes one encounters a primitive intuitionist or a believer in revealed truth who refuses to provide any reasons, but this is rare and their case is rarely compelling to those who do not already share their assumptions. In practice, we find ourselves constantly examining the clarity, logic and consistency of moral reasoning in many domains, including international politics. And the formal structure of ethical language – prescription, overridingness, and universalizability – differentiate it from mere expressions of taste.[6]

Nonetheless, even within Western ethical traditions, significant differences still exist, particularly over the role of rules and personal virtue versus the weighing of consequences. The consequentialist tradition – which includes but is broader than utilitarianism – places its emphasis on outcomes. The deontological or Kantian tradition stresses following rules and having the right motives as sufficient for judging the morality of actions. The aretaic approach stresses an ethics of virtue rather than an ethics of consequences. It can be described as the difference between an emphasis on the integrity of "who I am," versus an emphasis versus an ethics of doing.[7]

The significance of these differences can be captured by an adaptation of a hypothetical case used by Bernard Williams in his attack upon utilitarianism.[8] Imagine that you are visiting El Salvador and you happen upon a village square where an army captain is about to order his men to shoot two peasants lined up against a wall. When asked the reason, you are told someone in this village shot at his men last night. When you object to the killing of possibly innocent people, you are told that civil wars do not permit moral niceties. Just to prove the point that we all have dirty hands in such situations, the captain hands you a rifle and tells you that if you will shoot one peasant, he will free the other. Otherwise both die. He warns you not to try any tricks because his men have their guns trained on you. Will you shoot one person with the consequences of saving one, or will you allow both to die but preserve your moral integrity by refusing to play his dirty game?

Integrity is clearly an important value. But at what point does the principle of not taking an innocent life collapse before the consequentialist burden? Would it matter if there were twenty or 1000 peasants to be saved? What if killing or torturing one innocent person could save a city of ten million persons from a terrorist's nuclear device? At some point, does not integrity become the ultimate egoism of fastidious self-righteousness in which the purity of the self is more important than the lives of countless others? Is it not better to follow a consequentialist approach, admit remorse or regret over the immoral means, but justify the action by the ends?[9] And in the domain of international politics where issues of survival sometimes arise, will not an absolute ethics of being rather than doing run the additional risk that you will not survive to be?

On the other hand, the dangers of too simple an application of consequentialism are well known. Once the ends justify the means, the dangers of slipping into a morality of convenience greatly increase. The "act-utilitarian" who tries to judge each case without the benefit of rules may find the task impossible to accomplish except with a shallowness which makes a travesty of moral judgment. And given human proclivities to weight choices in their own favor, and the difficulties of being sure of consequences of complex activities, impartiality may be easily lost in the absence of rules. Moreover, when it becomes known that integrity plays no role and one will always choose the lesser of evils in terms of immediate consequences, one opens oneself to blackmail by those who play dirty games. When it becomes known that one will always choose the lesser evil in any situation, there may develop a Gresham's law of bad moral choices driving out the prospect of good ones. Once one allows departure from rules and integrity, is one not on a slippery slope to rationalizing anything? Particularly in complex organizations like governments, a widespread permission to waive rules and think only of consequences can lead to a rapid erosion of moral standards.

It is clear that we need both rules and the weighing of consequences in moral reasoning and the sophisticated consequentialist will consider the broader and longer term consequences of valuing both integrity of motives and rules that constrain means. He will also realize the critical role of rules in maintaining moral standards in complex institutions. In short, a sophisticated consequentialist analysis must take the view of an "institutional utilitarian" – asking the question "if I override normal moral rules because it will lead to better consequences in this case, will I be damaging the institution by eroding moral rules in a manner which will lead to worse consequences in future cases?"[10]

But if we need both rules and consideration of consequences, how do we reconcile them in practice? One way is to treat rules as prima facie moral duties, and appeal to a consequentialist critical level of moral reasoning to judge competing moral claims. But if every rule has its exception, how do we protect against too easy a collapse into consequentialism? How does one introduce hand holds or stopping points on the "slippery slope?" Two devices help. The first is always to start with a strong presumption in favor of rules and place a substantial burden of proof upon those who wish to turn to consequentialist arguments. This burden must include a test of proportionality which weighs the consequences of departure from normal rules not only in the immediate case but also in terms of the probable longrun effects on the system of rules. For particularly heinous practices such as torture, the presumption may be near absolute, and the burden of proof be "beyond reasonable doubt."

The second device is to develop procedures which protect the impartiality which is at the core of moral reasoning and that is so vulnerable in the transition from the deontic to the consequentialist approach. For example, structuring justification from the perspective of the victim or the deceived, and developing ways to consult or inform third parties in order to protect against selfish assumptions are useful approaches. In the case of lying, Sissela Bok argues that such procedures may involve publicity.[11] The practice of consulting courts, Congressional committees, allies and other countries can all serve as means to protect impartiality. In other words, while there is no perfect procedure for incorporating rules in a sophisticated consequentialist approach, the presumptivist and procedural approach is less self-serving and more impartial than others.

One of the most common pitfalls in moral reasoning might be called "one-dimensional ethics." An action is said to be justified because it has good motives or because it has good consequences. But in common practice, people tend to make ethical judgments along three dimensions of motives, means and consequences, and this introduces additional complexity and degree into ethical judgments.

It is easy to agree on the moral quality of actions which are good or bad on all three scores: bad motives, bad means and bad consequences. And we might agree to rank low those acts which have good consequences but which inadvertently grew out of bad motives. But there is less agreement about the ranking of two acts which both rest on good motives, but one uses good means and produces bad consequences while the other uses bad means but produces good consequences. In practice, we judge particular means in terms of auxiliary principles such as double effect (having unintended but foreseeable consequences); omissions being (sometimes) less culpable than acts; and a general sense of proportionality. None of these principles is without pitfalls which are spelled out in the literature of moral philosophy, but used carefully, they allow us to introduce some order into our moral dilemmas.[12] No formula can solve moral problems, but some can aid us in the unavoidable task of weighing competing moral claims.

A good example of one dimensional moral reasoning is the case of those who equated the American intervention in Grenada with the Soviet intervention in Afghanistan. Along the dimension of motives – to maintain a sphere of influence – the two actions were similar, but the bloodiness of the means and the probable consequences (in terms of restoring local autonomy) were quite different. Similarly, on a one-dimensional approach, the American intervention in the Dominican Republic in 1965 and the Soviet intervention in Czechoslovakia were similarly flawed, but the American action was partially redeemed by the eventual consequences of creating a more autonomous and democratic Dominican society. But good consequences alone are not sufficient to make an action good. If a murderer is trying to kill me and I am saved because a second murderer kills my would-be assailant first, the consequences are good, but the action is not. An invasion that has fortuitous consequences is better than one with disastrous consequences, but a three dimensional judgement might still judge it as a morally flawed action.

This was part of the problem with the American intervention in Vietnam. Norman Podhoretz has argued that our involvement was moral because we were trying to save the South Vietnamese from totalitarianism.[13] The people who led us were those who had learned from the Munich experience that totalitarian aggression must be resisted even if it is costly. But if American idealism was part of the cause of our role in the Vietnam war, that same idealism tended to blind leaders to the facts of polycentric communism and local nationalism as alternative means to America's less idealist end of preserving a balance of power in Asia. It also blinded them to the inappropriateness of involvement in a guerrilla war in an alien culture and the immoral consequences that would follow from the disproportion between our goals and our means.

In a sense, American policy in the Vietnam war might be compared to a well-intentioned friend trying to bring your child home on time on an icy evening. He speeds, the car skids off the road and your child is killed. His motives were good, but the consequences horrible because of his inattention to means and facts. It is not murder, but it may be negligent homicide. His good intent reduces the charge, but it does not exonerate him. Our moral judgment is one of degree, not a binary choice of completely wrong or completely right.

Ends, means, and consequences are all important. Careful appraisal of facts and weighing of uncertainties along all three dimensions are critical to good moral reasoning. Right versus wrong is often less difficult to handle than right versus right and degrees of wrong. And this is particularly complicated in international politics where there is less agreement about what is right and where the consequences of actions are often more difficult to estimate than in well-ordered domestic polities. But once again, the difficulty of moral reasoning in foreign policy does not justify our avoiding it; rather we must work harder to do it better.

Citizens and statesmen[14]

Another complication in thinking about ethics and foreign policy is being clear about the different levels of analysis and relationships involved. We often speak of a state acting morally or immorally when we refer to its behavior toward the citizens of other states. That assumes that states have moral obligations to other states and their citizens – a question that is examined in the next section. But what do we mean when we speak of a state acting – all the citizens or just the top leaders? Do the citizens and the statesmen have the same moral duties to foreigners? And what are the obligations that citizens and statesmen owe to each other?

When we speak of states, we are referring to collectivities, and collective responsibility is a difficult concept. Different people have different degrees of responsibility for state actions and deserve different degrees of blame or approbation. Moreover, institutions such as governments develop standard operating procedures which take on a life of their own. For example, in assigning moral responsibility for the Soviet Union's shooting down of a Korean civil aircraft with the loss of 269 lives, was the interceptor pilot to blame for firing? or were his immediate supervisors to blame for giving orders? or were the top leaders to blame for permitting procedures to exist that failed to allow adequately for uncertainty and mistakes? Whatever one's views about the allocation of blame, we are not prevented from making the moral judgment that the Soviet action was wrong.

It is perfectly appropriate to make moral judgments about the consequences of actions by institutions.[15] Our awareness of the complexities of collective responsibility draws our attention to questions of structural factors that constrain moral choices in particular cases, and it may allow us to partly exonerate a person who is acting in a state role in a manner that we would not accept if he were acting simply as an individual. For example, if the Director of the CIA went to Managua as a tourist and shot three civilians on the street, we would judge him guilty of murder. If he followed presidential orders and consulted with Congress before approving a covert action in which three Nicaraguan civilians were killed, we would face a more complex moral judgment in which he would share only a portion of any blame (if we decided the action to be blameworthy at all). In short, we judge people acting in institutional roles somewhat differently than when they are acting as individuals.

On the other hand, while the standards of judgment are more complex, the standards for statesmen are not completely different. Filling an institutional role does not exonerate a person from all observance of normal moral standards. The burden of proof still rests on the individual who claims exemption, and the quality of the arguments he uses must be carefully judged in terms of motives, alternative means, and probable long-run consequences. Just as we found it was not enough for a statesman to say that anything is acceptable "because international politics is an amoral realm," so also is it unacceptable to justify any action simply on the grounds that one is acting as political leader rather than as an individual. In fact, some role-based defenses ("I was only following orders, only carrying out policy") have been judged inadmissible for individuals since Hitler's atrocities and the Nuremberg trials focused new attention on issues of collective responsibility. The statesman, bureaucrat or soldier may claim to be judged by a different standard at the critical consequentialist level rather than by the same rules that the individual is, but he is not excused from asking moral questions about whether the action, the procedure, the policy, the role, and the institution are justifiable before he acts in a manner that deviates from normal moral rules. Institutional roles complicate our moral choices. Careful moral reasoning about foreign policy must pay particular attention to arguments given for any transition from the normal moral rules that govern individual behavior to a different behavior allegedly (and possibly) justified by institutional and collective reasons.

The perspective of the citizen

What levels of moral behavior should citizens expect of their leaders? Some citizens may demand a higher or lower than normal moral standard. Sometimes a leader must act in one or the other manner for important long-run consequentialist reasons. What the citizen can expect of his leader is good procedures and reasons in making the case for going from normal rules to consequentialism.

What then are the obligations that citizens owe each other when they introduce their ethical concerns into foreign policy preferences? One can argue that there should be few restrictions except the obligation to think through the consequences and weigh the effects on their fellow citizens. These might be called rules of reason.

To have a constructive influence on foreign policy an individual's moral views should be well thought out. Too often actions based on normal moral rules and good intentions have morally offensive consequences in the complex arena of world politics. The full consequences of actions usually cannot be predicted with certainty; but neither are we totally ignorant about the future results of a certain course of action. Citizens can ask each other to consider the full range of likely consequences. The responsible citizen in a democracy should be aware of the costly and sometimes dangerous effects if all citizens press for their personal moral solutions to all issues.

What norms and procedures can protect against such problems? Democratic theory is a start, but alone is not sufficient. If citizens wish to express a moral preference in foreign policy, there should be a presumption in favor of expression. But given the danger of mass hysteria (or indifference), long-run interests may be neglected. And the practice of building majorities by log-rolling may undercut the common interest. Simple pursuit of pressure groups' interests can lead to lowest common denominator solutions which may risk long-run prudential interests as well as lead to immoral consequences. For example, legislated curtailment of aid to Turkey as punishment for genocide against Armenians in World War I could greatly reduce our defense and deterrence capabilities vis-a-vis the Persian Gulf.

Arthur Schlesinger has suggested a rule that as many issues as possible be disposed of on prudential grounds.[16] This would help to reduce the amount of heated moral debate in a democracy. But Schlesinger's suggestion still begs the question of strong moral preferences and the definition of prudence. We need to go further and qualify moral debate and pressure by a Rawlsian-type rule of reason. A citizen should press a moral concern upon his government's foreign policy so long as he would agree on incorporating that concern if he did not know his position in society. Under such an approach, the obligations that citizens owe each other when introducing their moral preferences into foreign policy are prudential attention to the realities of international life and a restraint of universalizability when they urge actions which may jeopardize common interests.

The perspective of the statesman

If individuals will and should apply their moral views to foreign policy, qualified only by democratic practice and a Rawlsian rule of reason, what of the statesman? How are officials limited in what they may do for moral reasons by their obligations to their constituents? The obligation of a statesman is to maintain and improve the well-being of the people he represents, in all of the dimensions that are relevant to them. His objectives would thus normally encompass their physical security and economic well-being; but they also include their psychological security and well-being. He or she must, insofar as possible, consider *all* the consequences of the actions he directs, now and in the future. He should act as a trustee for the interests of those he represents.

As Niebuhr and others have pointed out, a trustee is not entitled to sacrifice the interests of others.[17] He must act prudentially on their behalf. And a prudent statesman approaching his task with utter realism must take moral views of citizens into account in weighing his actions. There are three major reasons why this is so.

First, the realistic statesman must consider the influence of his current actions on the ability of his successors to exercise a degree of discretion appropriate for management of foreign policy. To ignore systematically the moral sentiments of his citizenry will undermine trust not only in him, but in his office. It will lead to loss of public support for foreign policy, so necessary especially in a democracy, but also in other forms of government. Second, since the psychological well-being of his citizenry is part of the statesman's responsibility, he must take the self-respect of his citizens as citizens directly into account, quite apart from the possible ultimate loss of their support.

Third, an important element in the ability of any country to carry out its foreign policy objectives is its reputation abroad. This reputation rests in part on consistency and reliability in behavior. Underlying this is the confidence of other nations that a nation will carry out its commitments. The ability to make credible commitments can aid the statesman enormously in pursuit of his current and future objectives. Confidence and credibility depend upon a number of factors, by no means only on morality, but the establishment of trust among nations is immeasurably easier if they share common moral values, and if those moral values are seen to inform foreign policy actions. With trust based on shared moral sentiment, certain commitments become credible that would not otherwise be possible (e.g. placement of tactical nuclear weapons in densely populated friendly nations).

Does this prudential approach exhaust the statesman's use of morality in foreign policy? Is there room for the statesman to interject his own moral standards, higher or lower, into his decisions and actions in foreign policy? If two courses of action are assessed to be completely equivalent in their net benefit to the nation, taking into account all expected future as well as present consequences, the choice between them from the trustee's role is a matter of indifference, and he might as well decide between them on the basis of his personal moral code as on any other criterion. On the other hand, once one allows the trustee to interject his personal moral code into his decisions (when it differs from the public's) it could involve the trustee in sacrificing the well-being of his citizenry.

Statesmen as trustees must sometimes violate their individual moral code for long-range consequentialist reasons such as protecting the public order that makes it possible for citizens to adhere to normal moral rules.[18] A statesman who was perfectly consistent by individual moral standards might often find himself in conflict with his consequentialist responsibilities as trustee. For example. Henry Stimson held the noble personal moral view that "gentlemen do not read one another's mail."[19] Simplistic moral consistency might have required Stimson to oppose the creation of the National Security Agency and its predecessors. Yet breaking diplomatic and naval codes in the 1930s probably altered the outcome of the Second World War, and in any case greatly shortened it.

It does not follow from this discussion of the trustee's role that the statesman's personal moral views have no role in foreign policy. For one thing, the statesman is a moral educator as well as a trustee. Part of his role is to help the community shape its moral preferences and understanding of issues. The educator helps the citizenry to define and evaluate particular situations. In the simple terms used by Theodore Roosevelt, the presidency is a "bully" pulpit. Public views of morality are not indelibly fixed. The statesman can seize opportunities to raise the moral level as well as warn against dangers of moralism. By "educating his electorate," the statesman may reduce the tension between his personal moral views and his obligations as a trustee. For example, a leader may view institutionalized racial injustice in South Africa as morally repugnant. He may also see prudential reasons (e.g., Soviet influence, security of sea routes, non-proliferation) for not breaking relations with the white South African government. But he may believe it right to expend some of his country's political influence on the racial issue rather than husbanding it all for use on the security issues. He may use a combination of moral and prudential arguments to persuade the public to see the trade-offs in the same manner that he does.

Should he fail, however, his trustee role limits the extent of his personal moral intervention. Just how constraining the trustees' role should be is a debatable point. On an overly simple plebiscitary model of direct democracy, if the statesman finds a situation morally repugnant (and assuming that his efforts at public education have failed), he can only resign as trustee and have full freedom to press for his individual moral preferences in the definition of the national interest. But as Edmund Burke pointed out two centuries ago, the trustee in representative government must consider the long-term interests of his people, not merely their current preferences, even if he thus risks electoral defeat. Such long-term interest may include the prospect of evolution of their moral views – such as the prospect that a decade hence, the public may regret a failure to have taken a moral stance on South Africa. In retrospect, many Americans wish their trustees in the 1930s had taken greater electoral risks to rescue more Jews from Hitler's genocide. Nonetheless, while there is some flexibility in the Burkean conception, the notion of trusteeship constrains the statesman. If his educational efforts fail despite ample time and information, the democratic presumption in favor of the public's considered views must ultimately limit the statesman.

Second, the exception allowed above – where two courses of action are equivalent in benefit – is defined narrowly, but in practice encompasses a relatively wide range of situations because of uncertainty in calculating consequences in the complex international system. Many situations arise where prudential considerations could go either way. For example, in deciding whether to give asylum to a prominent refugee from China, the statesman must consider the effects on relations with China and the balance of power in East Asia. But he must also consider the effects on America's reputation as a country that defends the rights of individuals, and the long-run effects of opening one's country to blackmail once it departs from a standard of integrity. Since the uncertainty about consequences and net benefit is likely to be large, the actual leeway to decide the issue on a personal moral proclivity toward the rights of individuals may be quite large in practice.

Finally, the statesman's moral roles are not fully exhausted by the obligations to those for whom he acts as trustee. His primary obligations are to his own people, but as I shall argue in the next section, he has a residual cosmopolitan obligation to respect the rights of other peoples in situations where there are choices among means to promote his own people's interests. This residual obligation may shrink almost to zero in the realm of survival and necessity – for example in a situation of impending enemy attack. (Even in such a situation there are moral questions about the future of humanity if the statesman chose to respond with a pre-emptive nuclear strike.) But as Wolfers has pointed out, much of international politics is not the realm of necessity, and even in the definition of security interests, the statesman can make moral choices among means.[20] In Just War Theory, his obligations to respect the rights of those beyond his borders include just cause, reasonable chance of success, proportionality and discrimination between combatants and civilians. He may follow such an approach for prudential reasons or in reflection of the moral preferences of his citizenry. But even faced with an indifferent citizenry, he might accept a moral obligation to choose means which reduce the loss of rights or life imposed on other human beings.

There are certain risks to admitting exceptions to the trustee theory. Insofar as public opinion in the statesman's country admits some obligation to foreigners (such as just war theory), there is no problem. But if the trustee role is weakened to allow the statesman to follow his personal moral code, whether higher or lower, how can we be sure that his actions will have good consequences? Suppose the statesman is a cosmopolitan religious fundamentalist, who places no value on the souls or lives of atheists. Would we still wish to weaken the trustee theory to admit idiosyncratic moral preferences? One view would restrict the statesman to the role of trustee, albeit with a Burkean degree of flexibility. Another would rely upon the protections of constitutional checks and balances. There may be no way to use procedural principles to tie the hands of the reckless fundamentalist that would not also tie the hands of a statesman trying to rescue Jews in the 1930s. Thus some flexibility and open moral debate is bound to remain.

Even taking these qualifications into account, the statesman's exercise of *personal* moral choice, whether by a higher or lower standard in terms of normal rules, will be more constrained in foreign policy than that of the citizen because of his institutional role. This is not to say that morality plays no role for the statesman. As we have seen, his or her transition from normal rules to consequentialism requires careful moral reasoning. Nor does it mean morality plays no role in foreign policy. The citizen is not so constrained, and citizens may demand that their trustees express widely held moral values in national policy. But the statesman must temper this popular preference by introducing prudential considerations.

Obligations to foreigners

Thus far, although I have alluded to cosmopolitan values, I have concentrated on the obligations that citizens owe each other and that statesmen owe to citizens when introducing the ethical considerations into the difficult domain of international politics.

There are four basic views about the moral obligations that we owe to people who are not our fellow citizens. I have already argued that one view, that of the total skeptic who denies any duties beyond borders, rests on premises that do not stand up to careful scrutiny. When we turn to those who admit obligations owed to foreigners, we encounter three quite different schools of thought: the realist, the state moralist, and the cosmopolitan approaches.[21] The realist and the state moralist tend to stress the value of order; the cosmopolitan values individual justice more highly.

In contrast with the total skeptic, the Realist accepts some moral obligations to foreigners, but only of a minimal sort related to the immoral consequences of disorder. More extensive obligations exist only where there is community which defines and recognizes rights and duties. Such communities exist only in weak forms at the international level, and this sets strict bounds on international morality. Moreover, the world of sovereign states is a world of selfhelp without the moderating effects of a common executive, legislature, or judiciary. In such a domain, chaos is the greatest danger. The range of moral choices is severely constricted, because the government which attempts to indulge a broad range of moral preferences may fail in its primary duty of preserving order. As Hans Morgenthau has written, "The state has no right to let its moral disapprobation . . . get in the way of successful political action, itself inspired by the moral principle of national survival . . . Realism, then, considers prudence . . . to be the supreme virtue in politics."[22]

This form of realism can be distinguished from the position of the radical skeptic discussed earlier. The Realist places the greatest stress on national survival and on the instrumental value of order. The most significant means of preserving international order is the balance of power. International politics is characterized by such inequality and so little structure, that on consequentialist grounds, maintaining the balance of power deserves a strong priority over both interstate and individual justice. Prudent pursuit of self-interest will at least produce order and avert disastrously immoral consequences which the unbridled pursuit of justice might produce in a world of unequal states. This is accentuated by the existence of nuclear weapons. We owe foreigners the minimal obligation of order that avoids chaos leading to nuclear war. As Henry Kissinger replied to critics who accused him of an amoral policy because of his lack of zeal in pursuit of human rights, "peace is a moral priority." There are no rights among the incinerated!

The Realist has a strong argument in reminding us that justice depends upon a degree of order, and that international moral crusades can lead to disorder, injustice, and immoral consequences. But while it is true that the problem of order makes international politics less hospitable ground for moral arguments about justice than is domestic politics, it does not follow that justice is totally excluded in the international realm. Order may deserve priority, but it need not be treated as an absolute value in a lexicographic ranking. One can assign a high value to order and still admit degrees of trade-offs between order and justice. Both statesmen and citizens constantly weigh such tradeoffs in international affairs. As we saw earlier, survival may come first, but much of international politics is not about survival. Choices among alternative courses of action must be made on many other issues, large and small, and these choices can be (and are) informed by many moral values. Moreover, while the balance of power is the primary means of preserving order in international politics, it is not the only means nor a totally unambiguous means. There are not strong institutions to enforce norms; but weak international institutions of law and diplomacy do supplement the balance of power in preserving some degree of order.

The second approach stresses morality among states and the significance of state sovereignty and self-determination. One variant of the state-moralist viewpoint stresses a just order among a society of states. For example, John Rawls asks what rules the states would choose or would have chosen for just relations among themselves if they did not know in advance how strong or wealthy they would be.[23] The principles that Rawls derives: self-determination, nonintervention, and obligation to keep treaties, are analogous to existing principles of international law. The Realist would object that in addition to the ambiguities in the concepts, justice among states does not always contribute to order in a world of radical inequality. On the contrary, some degree of hierarchy and balance of power based on force may be necessary to keep order in a world lacking effective institutions to enforce the principles of international law.

The cosmopolitan, on the other hand, would object that justice among states would not necessarily produce justice for individuals. Michael Walzer seeks to alleviate this moral problem by portraying the rights of states as a collective form of their citizen's individual rights to life and liberty. The nation-state may be seen as a pooled expression of individual rights. It represents "the rights of contemporary men and women to live as members of a historic community and to express their inherited culture through political forms worked out among themselves . . ."[24] Thus, there is a strong presumption against outside intervention. However, this presumption is not absolute. Foreigners have an obligation to refrain from intervention unless the lack of fit between a government and the community that it represents is radically apparent. Thus, for example, Walzer would allow intervention to prevent massacre and enslavement; to balance a prior intervention in a civil war; or to assist secession movements that have demonstrated their representative character. In such circumstances, it would be contradictory to regard the state as representing the pooled rights of its individual citizens. This presumption and its exceptions are again analogous to many of the existing rules of international law. But again, it does not guarantee either realist order or cosmopolitan individual justice.

The virtues of Walzer's refined state-moralist approach is that it bases the rights of states on the rights of individuals, while taking account of the reality of the way that international politics is structured, and conforming quite closely to existing principles of international law. A weakness in the approach is the ambiguity of the concept of self-determination.[25] Who is the self that determines? How do we know when there is a radical lack of fit between government and people? Must an oppressed group fight and prevail to demonstrate its claim to speak as a people worthy of international recognition? If so, is not might making right? Or as a critic asks, "In Walzer's world, are there not self-identified political, economic, ethnic, or religious groups (for example, capitalists, democrats, communists, Moslems, the desperately poor) who would favor foreign intervention over Walzer's brand of national autonomy (and individual rights) if it would advance the set of rights, values, or interests at the core of their understanding of justice? . . . Why should Walzer's individual right to national autonomy be more basic than other human rights, such as freedom from terror, torture, material deprivation, illiteracy, and suppressed speech . . . Walzer's ideal is but one normative, philosophical conception among others, no more grounded and often less grounded in peoples' actual moral attitudes (and social identities) than other conceptions."[26] In short, the state moralist approach is particularly weak when it treats self-determination and national sovereignty as absolute principles which must come first in a lexical ordering. In practice, peoples do want self-determination and autonomy, but they want other values as well. There is a constant problem of trade-off and balancing competing moral claims.

The third, cosmopolitan, approach stresses the common nature of humanity. States and boundaries exist, but this does not endow them with moral significance. Ought does not follow from is. As David Luban has written, "The rights of security and subsistence . . . are necessary for the enjoyment of any other rights at all. No one can do without them. Basic rights, therefore, are universal. They are not respectors of political boundaries, and require a universalist politics to implement them; even when this means breaching the wall of state sovereignty."[27] Many citizens hold multiple loyalties to several communities at the same time. They may wish their governments to follow policies which give expression to the rights and duties engendered by other communities in addition to those structured at the national level.

While the cosmopolitan approach has the virtue of accepting transnational realities and avoids the sanctification of the nation-state, an unsophisticated cosmopolitanism also has serious drawbacks. First, if morality is about choice, then to underestimate the significance of states and boundaries is to fail to take into account the main features of the milieu in which choices must be made. To pursue individual justice at the cost of survival, or to launch human rights crusades that cannot hope to be fulfilled, yet interfere with prudential concerns about order may lead to immoral consequences. Applying ethics to foreign policy is more than merely constructing philosophical arguments; it must be relevant to the domain in which moral choice is to be exercised.

The other problem with an unsophisticated cosmopolitan approach is ethical; it discards the moral dimension of national politics. As Hoffmann has written, "States may be no more than collections of individuals and borders may be mere facts. But a moral significance is attached to them . . ."[28] There are rights of people to live in historic communities and autonomously to express their own political choices. A pure cosmopolitan view which ignores these rights of self-determination fails to do justice to the difficult job of balancing rights in the international realm.

The difference between Realists, cosmopolitans and state moralists is a difference over how to balance transnational and national values. Different people may approach the balancing of such values in different ways, but the statesman's trusteeship role requires that he give priority (though not exclusive attention) to interstate order and national interests. Since sophisticated Realists admit that justice affects the legitimacy of order; sophisticated cosmopolitans admit the political significance of boundaries, and sophisticated state moralists admit the possibility of duties beyond borders, the three positions often tend to converge in practice. Each has a part of the wisdom that must be considered in balancing competing moral claims in hard cases. But they start with different presumptions, and thus specify different conditions for qualifying or over-riding their presumptions as they are applied to particular cases.

For example, the three approaches could lead to quite different conclusions regarding the obligations to foreign citizens involved in any American intervention against the Sandinista government of Nicaragua, other (prudential) things being equal. The Realist might try to justify intervention on the grounds of the hierarchical order of spheres of influence which he sees as critical to maintaining nuclear peace. The state-moralist would prohibit intervention unless conditions in Nicaragua approached genocide. The left-wing cosmopolitan might justify intervention from Costa Rica that had a reasonable prospect of producing better human rights conditions than exist now, but might oppose intervention by forces in Honduras that would restore a repressive Somoza style regime. (The right-wing cosmopolitan might argue that the consequences of totalitarianism justify either intervention.) In practice, of course, prudential and national interest considerations might lead all three to a common policy position. But to the extent that the argument involves ethics, the three approaches are still distinctive. Each must be subjected to the standards of good moral reasoning described earlier, and no one seems fully adequate. It may be possible, however, to construct a composite position.

The minimal obligations of common humanity

If one wishes to avoid metaphysical arguments about natural law, it is safer to ground arguments about rights and obligations in the existence of a sense of community. Where a sense of community exists, it is possible to define rights and obligations. There are multiple senses of community in world politics today, but those which transcend national boundaries in universal form are relatively weak. Nonetheless, many people, including Realists, acknowledge a weak form of community symbolized by the notion of "common humanity." Defining another being as part of the human community entails restraints on how we treat him or her. For example, we do not kill them for food or pleasure (as is done with animals by those who do not define community in terms of all sentient beings).[29] Nor do we allow them to starve if we are in a position to help.

It is still debatable what rights and obligations follow from such a weak form of community as the notion of "common humanity." Rights and their correlative obligations can involve modest claims (being left free from interference) or strong claims (being provided something one does not have). A weak sense of community may give rise not only to weak forms of rights and obligations. Walzer argues, for example, that "the idea of distributive justice presupposes a bounded world, a community within which distributions take place, a group of people committed to dividing, exchanging, and sharing, first of all among themselves. It is possible to imagine such a group extended to include the entire human race, but no such extension has yet been achieved. For the present, we live in smaller distributive communities."[30]

Some cosmopolitans would reply that the fact that the current sense of community is bounded does not mean that it is right to draw conclusions about limited obligations.[31] "Ought does not follow from is." The sense of community in world politics was more limited at times in the past and may be more expansive at times in the future. Rather than derive norms from current facts, one should derive them from an ideal sense of human community. This would be more consistent with the criteria of impartiality and universalizability that are essential characteristics of moral reasoning. If one were to engage in Rawls' mental experiment of imagining what principles of justice all people might agree to if they were behind a "veil of ignorance" regarding their actual advantages, one would not allow enormous inequalities of wealth based on nationality. From this point of view, the burden of proof rests with those who depart from the cosmopolitan ideal. They must justify any preference to compatriots.

Although "ought does not follow from is," the facts about what exists severely shape and constrain normative judgments. If "ought implies can" then is and ought are logically distinct but empirically intertwined. To apply Rawls' concepts of justice without regard to boundaries (which Rawls himself eschews) is a debatable procedure. If communal identity is one of the essential attributes of a person, assuming the disembodied "selves" implied in Rawls' "veil of ignorance" thought experiment may be a poor way of approaching the issue of impartiality and universalizability.[32]

Impartiality is not the same as egalitarianism. It does not mean "each one equals one." Universalizability means similar actions in similar situations. It prohibits moral justification based simply on the egoism of the actor. It does not exclude considerations of the interests of the actor if similar interests would be allowed weight for similar actors. It is not moral to justify an action "because it is me." It may sometimes be moral to justify an action "because the object is mine." For example, if you could save only one of two drowning children, one of which is your own, you may be morally justified in saving your own. Your child has a right to expect such a duty from you on the basis of the roles of parent and child in the family community relationship. Of course, one would have to admit the same justification for any parent similarly placed, even if one were the absent parent of the child not saved.

Social roles create and carry rights and duties, regardless of whether they are voluntarily assumed; whether the roles be those of family or citizenship. But given the existence of multiple levels of community and multiple roles, the preference for one's own child or compatriot cannot morally be admitted as absolute. If one assumed the role of lifeguard and then noticed the drowning children, one would have an additional obligation to save the child where there was a higher probability of success. And at some point, a consequentialist would object to a preference for saving one's own child that did not consider the relative probabilities or the numbers of other children involved. In short, some preference for family or compatriots may be justified on grounds of impartiality and universalizability, but it would not be possible to reconcile an absolute preference with these criteria.

What obligations do we owe to foreigners in the world as it now exists? Imagine a thought experiment in which rational people were trying to answer that question before the deck of national cards were dealt and one did not know if one would be dealt a high (rich nation) or low (poor nation) card. Assume we (1) accept a sense of common humanity, but (2) have a preference for autonomous national community (or assume that it is the only feasible form of organization at this time), and (3) realize the dangers and difficulties of preserving order in a world organized into states. (4) We lack a common ideal or vision of the good, and our concern for order must often have priority over justice. But even in this imperfect world, we would wish to set some limits on national exclusivity and preference to compatriots. If we knew that we all had this dangerous preference for (or accepted the existence of) national communal identity at this point in history, but did not know whether we would belong to a rich strong nation or a poor weak one, what limitations would we want all nations to follow on preference to compatriots and what obligations would we wish all nations to accept toward foreigners? The result might produce at least four clusters of obligations.

First, because we recognize each other as part of common humanity despite national differences, one would admit negative duties not to kill, enslave, or destroy the autonomy of other peoples. While community generally implies reciprocal awareness of obligation, reciprocity may not be necessary to justify adherence to these duties. Even if another people lacks a sense of common humanity at this time, our definition of them as human and a thought experiment about universalizability would produce such restraints. We do unto others as we *would have* them do unto us. Thus even in wartime, a cosmopolitan Realist could accept the morality of limits on killing of innocent civilians (and other restraints of just war theory), despite the failure of the enemy to observe such restraints. Whether he would live up to this moral standard or succumb to psychological pressures to respond in kind is another question. But the moral standard is clear.

These negative duties include a prima facie obligation not to intervene in other states on Walzer's grounds that such intervention destroys the autonomy of the common life of another community. We could disregard these prohibitions on intervention in situations where genocide, enslavement or egregious deprivation of human rights made a mockery of the prima facie assumption that the autonomous political process in that state represented the pooled rights of the individual citizens. Deciding whether such conditions exist will be debated in the light of the facts in particular instances. But while agreeing that such conditions would release us from the negative duty of non-intervention, it would not necessarily create a positive duty of intervention, particularly if such intervention would be costly or dangerous in a world of states. Positive duties exist, but they are limited.

A second obligation to foreigners (and limit on our preference for compatriots) is the generally accepted consequentialist principle of taking responsibility for the consequences of our actions. It may be that "the great majority of actions that occur within the boundaries of a nation-state are not either the direct or indirect results of the actions of those who are outside its national borders."[33] But as the literature on interdependence shows, many actions and conditions that affect the prospects for justice within a nation are affected by actions of others outside the nation.[34] Such interdependence is a matter of degree and effects are often difficult to ascertain. Moreover, there are thorny questions about time and a moral "statute of limitations."[35] Nonetheless, according to the principle of responsibility for the consequences of our actions, we have obligations to foreigners in some proportion to the strength of the effects that we are able to ascertain as ours.

A third obligation to foreigners is Samaritanism – the obligation to provide readily available assistance to another who is in dire need. "It is commonly said of such cases that positive assistance is required if (1) it is needed or urgently needed by one of the parties, and (2) if the risks and costs of giving it are relatively low for the other party ... But the limit on risks and costs is sharply drawn."[36] The Samaritan need not comb "the bushes along the roadsides to insure that there are no needy sufferers" lurking there.[37] The Samaritan obligation differs from the first category in being a positive rather than a negative duty, but its rationale is similarly related to the definitions involved in a weak sense of common humanity. It refers to situations where the distinction between acting to take life and omitting to save a life are so fine, that the distinction between acts and omissions seems wholly arbitrary.

Samaritanism creates an obligation to help other foreigners achieve their basic rights of subsistence and autonomy, where we are able to do so at relatively low cost and risk. But it does not require us to give our wealth to the poor up to some point of imagined common utility. And while there are ambiguities in defining the extent of the principle in particular cases, it will not sustain obligations to promote extended definitions of basic human rights, nor justify interventions to advance justice that simultaneously run great risks in terms of disorder. It would lead to obligations to respond to particularly horrendous behavior such as genocide, but the nature of the response would be limited where costs and risks were very high. In short, Samaritanism establishes minimal positive obligations whose extent will be debated in light of the facts of particular cases. It still leaves a large area of foreign need which individuals and groups may wish to fill, but which would not be a national obligation derived from the assumptions above.

A fourth obligation to foreigners is to practice beneficence or charity in situations where they can be made better off without making compatriots significantly worse off. This obligation extends more broadly than Samaritanism but remains a modest limit on preference to compatriots since it does not make them significantly worse off. Situations do arise where we can make foreigners better off at virtually no cost to ourselves, for example by maintaining fair trade or by proffering food aid at a time of large domestic surpluses. It would seem morally arbitrary to fail to act simply because the beneficiaries were foreigners. Again the difference between an omission and an action would be too close to sustain scrutiny. A thought experiment about impartiality in an imperfect world of nations would quickly include such a rule among the obligations that all would wish to observe even if they did not know their eventual nationality or social advantages.

Finding pure Pareto-optimal situations is often difficult in practice. Some costs exist, if not to the nation, then to some groups of compatriots. But if the obligation of beneficence is to have any meaning, minimal costs to the nation must be ignored, and particular groups which do incur costs should be compensated. This is the argument, if not always the practice, for providing adjustment assistance to small groups which suffer while larger groups (at home and abroad) benefit from expanded trade. In short, the beneficence principle creates a modest (but nontrivial) positive obligation to foreigners.

Cosmopolitans would go further and adduce a fifth cluster of obligations to assist others in achieving basic rights even at high costs. Given the assumptions in our thought experiment, would our rational people want an obligation to assist others in the achievement of their rights at any cost? If others were suffering severe deprivations such as genocide, enslavement, or invasion, would not a sense of common humanity make us accept an obligation to help them even at costs not admitted by the Samaritan or beneficence principles? Not necessarily. Such an obligation would be severely constrained both by the realist and state moralist assumptions about order which we allowed in our original thought experiment. Given the widespread practice of minor deprivations of human rights, and the power of some states (such as the USSR) involved in major deprivations, the costs of becoming a global moral policeman would be unacceptably high. To prevent an Amin from massacring Ugandans, a South Africa from practicing apartheid, a Lebanon from practicing religious fratricide, and a Soviet Union from incarcerating dissidents – all at the same time – would involve an extremely high, if not impossible, level of costs for American foreign policy. It seems unlikely that the participants in our thought experiment would demand such actions as obligations. On the other hand, they might hope that states would stretch the Samaritan and beneficence principles and occasionally incur certain costs on a voluntary or charitable, if not obligatory basis. The realist and state moralist concerns about order imply limits on the fifth sort of obligation, but they do not prohibit supererogatory actions where they can be prudently reconciled with interstate order. And they do not prevent individuals from taking supererogatory personal charitable actions which their state might have to eschew for reasons of interstate order. Nor do they prevent citizens from encouraging the evolution of a stronger sense of community beyond the nation state for the future. In short, a realistic thought experiment about the limited obligations beyond borders in the imperfect world which we now inhabit does not preclude more idealistic thought experiments about worlds that might evolve in the future.

Problems of intervention and autonomy

I will exemplify these approaches by considering problems of intervention, but first it is important to clarify the concept of intervention. An important aspect of competing moral claims in a world of nation states, is national autonomy and self-determination. For example, if the government of a country needing land reform were so weak that the only way to effect reform would be for an outside government to administer land reform through a colonial administration, most people today would argue that such outside involvement would not be justified.

Part of what we owe to others in recognition of their special status as humans is respect for their autonomy. Autonomy cannot be absolute, but as Jonathan Glover has written, a concern for basic human rights includes a presumption in favor of autonomy.[38] Even if one argues that moral obligation is owed only among individuals, nation states can be seen as communities of pooled individual rights. At the same time, national autonomy may sometimes conflict with the autonomy of individuals and groups within a nation. Moreover, unlike the legal concept of sovereignty, national autonomy is often highly qualified in practice.

Thus moral proscriptions against outside involvement cannot be absolute. Walzer argues that the state is the arena where self-determination is worked out and from which foreign armies have to be excluded. He says there should be a presumption of legitimacy of internal processes unless there is a radical lack of fit between government and community. But the rules allowing foreigners to disregard the presumption against outside involvement are as important as the presumption itself. These rules are rightly restrictive when one focuses, as Walzer does, on extreme forms of intervention associated with large scale use of lethal force. But these rules for war do not give much guidance when one is dealing with an issue like human rights or economic assistance.

When we consider outside involvement in the socio-economic realm, it is important to remember that national autonomy is not absolute. Sovereign nations do not fully control their destinies. First, the workings of the international economy typically have important effects across the national boundaries even in the absence of any overt governmental intervention. And in some cases, these transnational economic effects may have life and death consequences for impoverished people in poor countries that are just as significant and even more likely than military action.

Second, nation states are not like billiard balls, hard and closed unto themselves and merely ricocheting off each other. As argued earlier, many citizens in many states have multiple loyalties both below and above the national level which give rise to various senses of community. Citizens may welcome outside involvement in their national affairs – up to a certain point.

Third, few countries are fully self-sufficient, and outside assistance and involvement can help to turn a theoretical autonomy in the current period into a greater real autonomy in the future. Some outside involvement now may strengthen a national capacity to influence its own destiny in the future. If this strengthens a state, it may reduce the chances of future outside interventions.

Finally, self-determination is not a precise concept. It is one thing to say that every group has the right to choose its own sovereignty, but how is such a choice to be decided? A democratic principle is not enough because the decision of where (within what boundaries) and when (now or later) and on what agenda (what is excluded?) one votes will often lead to radically different outcomes. In other words, there is always a certain degree of moral arbitrariness in the decisions about which rights of national self-determination are observed and which are not. We can think of degrees of self-determination in proportion to the extent to which sectors of a society are able to participate in determining national views. Self-determination can be seen as an attribute of societies, while sovereignty is an attribute of states. When a small and unrepresentative elite sets national policies which are against the interests of large parts of the population, national autonomy may conflict with self-determination. Thus the respect for autonomy of the state cannot be absolute.

Not only is there a porousness and relativism about the concept of national autonomy, but the concept of outside involvement must also be seen as complex. One can imagine a variety of dimensions with respect to method, scope, purpose, and duration. One can also envisage a variety of actors inside and outside a country having intended and unintended effects. One can also imagine a variety of degrees of outside involvement.

From a moral point of view, the degree of coercion involved in outside involvement is very important. Governments have coercive powers. One can imagine a range of actions by outsiders extending from declarations or speeches aimed at the citizenry in the other country at one end of the spectrum, and full-scale military invasion at the other end. In between one would find such actions as economic assistance, military assistance, providing funding or arms to opposition groups (usually covertly), and small scale military intervention.

The term "intervention" is sometimes used broadly to refer to the entire spectrum of deliberate outside involvements in another country's domestic affairs. More commonly in international law and diplomacy, it is used more narrowly to refer to the upper half of the scale – where an outsider "interferes coercively in the domestic affairs of another state."[39]

We might judge some outside involvement to be immoral, regardless of degree of coercion, if the intentions were malevolent; for example, if the purpose were to exercise domination or if the consequences were bad. But if we judged the intentions and consequences to be good, then we would focus on the means of outside involvement, particularly the degree of coercion because of its costs in terms of autonomy and its inconsistency with established rules of international law. Whether one is looking at a broad or narrow definition of intervention, one would look at questions of "proportionality" – the costs of outside involvement in relation to the danger being averted or the severity of the wrong being righted. In assessing proportionality, one must look both at the direct consequences as well as the unintended ones. And assessment of proportionality in highly coercive cases, i.e., in relation to the narrow definition of intervention – are doubly complex because they must include the long-run consequences for an existing system of international rules if one violates them in a particular case.

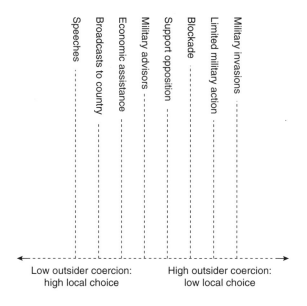

Figure 10.1 Intervention.

Military intervention

Consequentialist arguments about proportionality are easily abused, and once one departs from an absolute prohibition against military intervention, it is essential that good moral reasoning protect against such abuse. It is not adequate moral reasoning, for a statesman to justify violation of international law against intervention by invoking a low probability hypothetical future ("they might have gone Communist and that might have tipped the balance of power"). Nor is it adequate to justify intervention on the moral imperative of preventing an abstraction like "totalitarian rule," if the conditions for totalitarianism are unlikely. Even if there is some danger, consistent moral reasoning requires an explanation of why one does not intervene in other equally egregious cases of present or potential injustice.

In terms of the arguments developed earlier, one can protect against spurious consequentialist reasoning by starting with a strong presumption in favor of rules; by requiring broad and careful causal analysis in the calculation of consequences; by preferring to observe rules where the calculation of consequences involves large uncertainties; and by developing procedures to ensure impartiality when one concludes that a departure from normal rules is justified.

Among the negative duties that we owe to foreigners is not to kill them or take away their autonomy. The prohibitions against military intervention in international law help to reinforce these negative duties. Thus it makes sense to start with a state moralist position with its presumption in favor of nonintervention unless Walzer's rules of disregard apply (e.g., genocide, counter-intervention etc.). The cosmopolitan who contemplates military intervention because of the severity of the injustices being suffered must consider both the competing moral claims of autonomy and of the interstate legal order. Similarly, the Realist contemplating military intervention must weigh the degree of threat to our interests from a change in the balance of power against the same competing moral claims. The consequences considered must include the long-term effect on the institutional framework of international law which not only contributes to interstate order, but reinforces important negative moral duties to foreigners.

Even if the severity of the security threat is real or the deprivation of rights is egregious, careful causal analysis is needed to calculate consequences. The prospects of success at reasonable costs in terms of lives and local autonomy must be weighed. Unintended consequences must be estimated. Will it be possible to withdraw quickly? Is it reasonable to believe that proportionality can be maintained once intervention has begun? If the purpose is to replace a government, what is the probability that the successor government will be better? And if the only way to ensure the improvement is to maintain a presence that approaches imperial rule, will not the costs to local autonomy be disproportionate to the ends sought? Such considerations are analogous to those required by traditional just war theory.[40]

Another consideration is the assessment of probable consequences of not intervening. Are there alternatives? What are their risks and costs? What about responsibility for our past actions? Should we intervene to counter the effects of past interventions, particularly if the net effect is to increase local autonomy over the long run? Similarly, in some instances where a high degree of outside intervention by others exists, to refuse to counterintervene means, in Talleyrand's phrase, that intervention and nonintervention may amount to the same thing. The distinction between acts and omissions may vanish in such instances.

The probability of success is another important consideration derived from just war theory. This is not because success makes everything all right. Quite the contrary. Had Hitler won, he would still have been wrong. But a reasonable prospect of success protects against a disproportion between goals and means leading to immoral unintended consequences. Vietnam is a case in point. Ironically, in the area of military intervention, too limited a use of force may contribute to immoral consequences. On the other hand, the converse is not true unless one can be sure that an overwhelming force is able to discriminate between civilian and military targets.

All such assessments of consequences are highly problematic. We can never know the full consequences of our actions. The more tenuous or uncertain the causal reasoning about consequences, the more cautious one should be about departing from the rules against intervention. The costs to the system of rules, local autonomy, and human lives from a military intervention is likely to be more immediate and certain than the hypothesized benefits and dangers averted. There should be a "clear and present danger" test. When the uncertainties are large and the dangers lie at the end of a long hypothetical causal chain, the presumption in favor of the rules is reinforced.

If, despite such careful analysis, it seems that military intervention is still justified, it is essential to take steps to assure the preservation of impartiality. The higher one goes on the scale of coercion, the greater the presumption should be in favor of multilateral efforts in order to limit the tearing of the fabric of international legal order, and to ensure against the dangers of national hubris and egoism when calculations of proportionality are invoked. Multilateral actions, consultation with allies, and public diplomacy in international organizations are all cumbersome, but they help to protect against too easy a disregard of impartiality when judging consequences. One can admit that the prohibitions against military intervention are not absolute, but still insist that special care must be taken to protect the quality of moral reasoning about competing moral claims once one departs from the rules.

Non-military intervention

The same considerations are true of less coercive degrees of outside involvement in the domestic affairs of other countries. Even when they are not so clearly proscribed by legal rules, there are still difficult tasks to be undertaken in weighing competing moral claims. The presumption in favor of local autonomy still stands, but we may choose to override it when our relatively non-coercive actions are commanded by obligations of Samaritanism, beneficence, responsibility for the effects of our past actions, or by a supererogatory desire to promote justice. We still must consider proportionality and the severity of the situation. For example, in terms of the subsistence rights, are people starving? If so, higher degrees of involvement would be justified than if conditions were not so severe. Similar arguments can be made in relation to arguments based upon political liberty, and order. Are the prospects for enhancing political liberty particularly promising? In the absence of outside intervention is violent disorder highly likely? If so, a higher degree of international involvement may be justified.

A second factor to be considered is the degree of existing transnational interdependence. When there is a high degree of transnational interdependence, we may need to be involved in order to be responsible for the effects of our actions. A new involvement may counter other forms of involvement. In addition, where there is a high degree of interdependence, there is also likely to be a higher degree of leverage and capability to affect a situation. In short, where it is not possible to be uninvolved, as for example in the United States' historical relationship to Central America, some deliberate outside involvement may be justified to redress the negative effects of other forms of involvement. Indeed, they may not lead to a net reduction in overall autonomy.

One can also assess the justifiable degree of relatively non-coercive international involvement in terms of the effects on individual and local autonomy within another country. Some communities may be structured in such a way that large portions of the population that are strongly affected by these decisions are not able to participate in the process or even significantly to affect it. In such instances, a degree of outside involvement which tends to strengthen the weaker parties by promoting devolution, decentralization, or otherwise providing them with resources, may actually increase the capability of an indigenous political process to make autonomous trade-offs in a fashion which reflects the wishes of a large portion of the population. Conversely, however, the outside involvement cannot extend to the point that it is the outsider rather than the indigenous peoples who have the strongest effect on these decisions.

Finally, one must consider procedures to ensure impartiality in balancing competing moral claims even in relatively non-coercive outside involvement. It is all too easy for humans unconsciously to weigh their own interests more heavily when balancing competing moral claims. This is particularly true for outside governments where power politics and idealism often create a complex mix of motives. Thus, it is important that a procedure for making such judgments include the perspective of the country in which the intervention occurs. This argues for both a high degree of local involvement in decision-making, and for an explanation of policy judgments which is accessible and acceptable to local audiences. It also suggests the value of involvement of international agencies as a means of protecting against cultural imperialism, conscious or unconscious, in processes of implementation. As with military intervention, while the rules are not absolute, the presumption should be in favor of the negative obligation to respect the autonomy of others, and special care must be taken to preserve impartiality in the consequentialist moral reasoning used to justify outside involvement.

Conclusions

Ethics and foreign policy are inextricably intertwined for Americans. To deplore this fact as did the mainstream conventional wisdom of post-World War II Realism, is to abdicate responsibility for disciplining moral reasoning in this domain. We do not need a new debate between Realism and Idealism. Quite the contrary, we need to marry Realist insights about the dangerous consequences of too simple an application of the rules of individual moral behavior in the complex domain of international politics, with insights about the limited but real moral obligations to foreigners that arise from the effects of interdependence and the admission of a (weak) sense of common humanity.

I have argued that one must give balanced consideration to various kinds of moral claims about obligations to foreigners and the duties of citizens and statesmen because no simple moral theory is adequate in the domain of international politics. Politics among nations without a common sovereign is different from life in a well ordered domestic polity. In the absence of strong institutions and the absence of a common culture upon which such institutions could be built at this point in history, international politics remains a domain of self-help in which force is the ultimate arbiter. In a world where force plays a significant role, balancing power to maintain order must often take priority over questions of justice. Failure to preserve order can lead to disastrously immoral consequences.

But I have shown than the fact that international politics is a difficult domain for moral reasoning does not preclude all considerations of justice. Even in the morally imperfect world we currently inhabit, a primitive sense of common humanity and the concern for universalizability built into the structure of ethical language give rise to some obligations to foreigners. What we need are not thought experiments based on assumptions about our obligations in an imaginary ideal world of disem-bodied individuals, but efforts to specify our obligations in our imperfect world of states, as well as thoughts about how to develop attitudes and institutions that may permit the evolution of a broader scope for justice in some future international politics. In short, the best answer to the question of what obligation we owe to foreigners must combine the insights of the Realist and Cosmopolitan approaches.

Similarly, in answering the question about the moral duties of statesmen, we need to avoid the complete double standards of behavior that imply that a states-man can totally avoid normal standards of morality because of the allegedly amoral nature of international politics or the license which is implied by too simplistic a view of the trustee's role. Quite the contrary, we have seen that total skepticism about ethics in international politics is not justified, and that the statesman's role does not provide full exoneration from normal moral standards. While the states-man must be considered as a trustee whose ultimate appeal is to a critical level of institutional utilitarian reasoning, the grounds on which he justifies his transition from normal rules to consequences must be held up to careful scrutiny. Simple consequentialist arguments are not enough.

Finally, in answering the question of how we judge moral arguments in foreign policy, one-dimensional moral reasoning makes it too easy to rationalize what is convenient. And grand appeals to national ideals or ideological motives ("democracy, human rights, stopping totalitarianism") can blind one to relevant facts and the two other dimensions of moral choice. All three dimensions of motives, means and consequences are important and the task of weighing competing moral claims cannot be solved by application of a simple formula, but must be reasoned in the light of facts in particular cases. The importance of facts and careful causal analysis to good moral reasoning does not mean that morality is merely the same as prudence. While there is a good deal of overlap between sound prudential and moral reasoning about foreign policy, a moral position includes basic assumptions about impartiality which establish certain minimal obligations to foreigners (e.g., negative duties, responsibility for consequences, Samaritanism) which must be weighed in any moral calculations.

Dealing with multidimensional moral judgments is not easy. The presumptivist approach helps us to avoid sliding too quickly down a convenient and slippery consequentialist slope by requiring a strong burden of proof which places the benefit of doubt in favor of the rules when the facts are highly uncertain. Procedures for protecting impartiality and structures which encourage serious moral reasoning are equally important – though often inconvenient for statesmen. Approaches such as just war theory, which combine rules and consequentialism, provide a device which can force attention to facts that are relevant to all three moral dimensions. We would have been better served before intervening in Vietnam had we turned to just war theory, rather than to the amoral theories of counter-insurgency and limited war popular at the time. Those in government who feared to appear soft by raising moral issues, in retrospect, might have appeared realistic. Ethical choice is part of our foreign policy. The unrealism is to ignore it. One of the critical tasks for statesmen is to structure situations in advance so that there is occasion for serious moral reasoning. Left till too late, there may often be no choice.

International politics is not like domestic politics and ethical considerations in foreign policy are more complex than in domestic policy. But they arise. The role of ethics in foreign policy is modest, but it is also inescapable. Neither politics nor morality stops at the waters' edge. They just become more complicated. The dangers of simplistic moralism do not justify equally simplistic cynicism. What is required are further efforts to refine the scope and methods of our moral reasoning in this particularly difficult domain.

Notes

* This essay was written for discussion at an Aspen Institute seminar.
1 R.M. Hare, *Moral Thinking* (Oxford, Clarendon Press, 1981), Ch. 10; see also J.L. Mackie, *Ethics* (Harmondsworth, Penguin, 1977), p. 192.
2 Paul Ramsey, "Force and Political Responsibility," in Ernest W. Lefever (ed.), *Ethics and World Politics* (Baltimore, Johns Hopkins, 1972), p. 72.
3 See Michael Walzer's discussion in *Just and Unjust Wars* (New York, Basic Books, 1977), pp. 82–85.
4 Arnold Wolfers, "Statesmanship and Moral Choice," in *Discord and Collaboration* (Baltimore, Johns Hopkins, 1962), Ch. 4.

5 See Reinhold Niebuhr, *Moral Man and Immoral Society* (New York, Scribner, 1932), and the criticism in J.E. Hare and Carey B. Joynt, *Ethics and International Affairs* (N.Y., Saint Martins, 1982), pp. 27–33.

6 See W.D. Hudson, *A Century of Moral Philosophy* (London, Lutterworth, 1980), Bernard Williams, *Morality* (N.Y., Harper & Row), and R.M. Hare, cited, for discussion of these issues.

7 See William Frankena, *Ethics* (Englewood Cliffs, Prentice Hall, 1973), pp. 63 ff.

8 J.J.C. Smart and Bernard Williams, *Utilitarianism: For and Against* (Cambridge, Cambridge University Press, 1973), pp. 98 ff.

9 On remorse vs. regret, see Hare, cited, pp. 28–29.

10 I am indebted to Russell Hardin for the term "institutional utilitarianism" which avoids some of the reductio ad absurdism objections that can be levelled against "rule utilitarianism."

11 *Lying, Moral Choice in Public and Private Life* (N.Y., Random House, 1978), Ch. 7.

12 See Jonathan Glover, *Causing Death and Saving Lives* (Harmondsworth, Penguin, 1977), Ch. 6 and 7.

13 Norman Podhoretz, *Why We Were in Vietnam* (N.Y., Simon and Schuster, 1982).

14 This section draws on work done jointly with Richard N. Cooper for the 25th Anniversary Conference of the Harvard Center for International Affairs.

15 Peter A. French, "Morally Blaming Whole Populations," in Virginia Held et al., *Philosophy, Morality and International Affairs* (N.Y., Oxford, 1974). See also Dennis Thompson, "Moral Responsibility of Public Officials," *American Political Science Review*, 74 (December 1980), pp. 905–915.

16 Arthur Schlesinger, Jr., "National Interests and Moral Absolutes," in Ernest Lefever, ed., cited p. 22.

17 Reinhold Niebuhr, cited. See also Robert Osgood and Robert Tucker, *Force, Order and Justice* (baltimore, Johns Hopkins, 1967), p. 281.

18 Stanley Hoffmann, *Duties Beyond Borders* (Syracuse, Syracuse University Press, 1981), p. 17 ff.; see also Michael Walzer, "Political Action: The Problem of Dirty Hands," *Philosophy and Public Affairs*, Winter 1973, 2:2.

19 See James Bamford, *The Puzzle Palace* (New York, Penguin, 1982), pp. 34–35.

20 Wolfers, cited; see also Hoffmann, cited, pp. 14–17.

21 See Charles Beitz, "Bounded Morality," *International Organization* 33, Summer 1979, pp. 405–424.

22 Hans J. Morgenthau, *Politics Among Nations* (N.Y., Knopf, 1955), p. 9.

23 John Rawls, *A Theory of Justice* (Cambridge, Harvard, 1971), p. 378.

24 Michael Walzer, "The Moral Standing of States," *Philosophy and Public Affairs*, 9 (Spring 1980), p. 211.

25 Stanley French and Andres Gutman, "The Principle of Self-Determination," in Held *et al.*, cited.

26 Gerald Doppelt, "Statism Without Foundations," *Philosophy and Public Affairs*, 9 (Summer 1980), pp. 401–403.

27 David Luban, "The Romance of the Nation State," *Philosophy and Public Affairs*, 9 (Summer 1980), p. 392; see also Robert Amdur, "Rawls Theory of Justice: Domestic and International Perspectives," *World Politics* (April 1977), pp. 438–461.

28 *Duties Beyond Borders*, cited, p. 155.

29 For a challenge of this distinction see Peter Singer, *Practical Ethics* (Cambridge, Cambridge University Press, 1979).

30 Michael Walzer, "The Distribution of Membership," in Peter G. Brown and Henry Shue, eds., *Boundaries* (Totowa, N.J., Rowman and Littlefield, 1981), p. 1.

31 See for example, Charles Beitz, "Cosmopolitan Ideals and National Sentiment," and Henry Shue, "The Burdens of Justices," *The Journal of Philosophy*, Volume LXXX, No. 10 (October 1983).

32 See the critique of Rawls in Michael J. Sandel, *Liberalism and the Limits of Justice* (Cambridge, Cambridge University Press, 1982).

33 Gerard Elfstrom, "On Dilemmas of Intervention," *Ethics*, Volume 93, No. 4 (July 1983), p. 711.

34 For examples see Robert O. Keohane and J.S. Nye, "Transgovernmental Relation and International Organization," *World Politics* XXVII (October 1974).

35 See Richard Cooper, "A New International Economic Order for Mutual Gain," *Foreign Policy* 26, Spring 1977, pp. 81 ff.

36 Walzer, "The Distribution of Membership," cited, p. 3.

37 Elfstrom, cited, p. 719.

38 *Causing Death and Saving Lives*, cited, p. 74.

39 R.J. Vincent, *Nonintervention and International Order* (Princeton, Princeton University Press, 1974), p. 13.

40 See the discussion of just war and intervention in Hare and Joynt, cited Chs 3 and 7.

11 NPT

The logic of inequality*

When the third conference to review the 1968 Treaty on the Non-Proliferation of Nuclear Weapons (NPT) convenes in Geneva this September, the halls and headlines will be filled with acrimony. Diplomats from non-nuclear-weapons states will charge the superpowers with discrimination, hypocrisy, and failure to live up to their commitments to disarm. Should this drama be taken seriously? No and yes. Excessive rhetoric is a hallmark of such conferences, and it will not necessarily signify an imminent collapse of the treaty. Yet these charges underscore a more basic, longrun security problem that the superpowers have tended to neglect in recent years and that could lead to the failure of the NPT when it comes up for renewal in 1995.

In the 40-year history of nuclear weaponry two remarkable facts stand out. The first is that in a world of sovereign states in which the right of self-defense is enshrined in the United Nations Charter as well as in international law, many countries have agreed to forgo acquiring the most destructive weapons of self-defense. The second is that although nuclear weapons technology has spread somewhat over four decades, it has not spread as widely as expected. In 1963 President John Kennedy envisaged a world in the 1970s with 15 to 25 nuclear weapons states posing "the greatest possible danger." Instead, today there are about seven: five declared weapons states, one state that has exploded a nuclear device but not produced weapons, and one or two that may have produced weapons but that have not yet set off an explosion.

Nuclear reality has been less alarming than predicted for several reasons, including the restrictive policies of the weapons states; the calculated self-interest of many nonweapons states in forgoing nuclear weapons; and the development of an international regime of treaties, rules, and procedures that establishes a general presumption against proliferation. The main norms and practices of this regime are found in the NPT and in regional counterparts such as the Treaty of Tlatelolco, which aims to keep Latin America non-nuclear; in the safeguards, rules, and procedures of the International Atomic Energy Agency (IAEA); and in various U.N. resolutions. With a few important exceptions, the great majority of states adhere to at least some of these norms. But can such a situation last?

Some charge that the nonproliferation regime is doomed because of its discriminatory nature; they view the regime as an artificial superpower creation that must sooner or later give way to the principle of equality among states. Some countries will argue in Geneva that the policy of nonproliferation is pure hypocrisy. In the abstract, much less than in its imperfect practice, the NPT regime cannot be expected to last if this view is correct.

In the abstract, however, it is quite possible to justify nuclear inequality. Imagine that an international security conference convened without publicity and that the diplomats did not know in advance which countries they would represent. If they knew nothing of world politics today or of the probable consequences of acquiring nuclear weapons, they might reason that if sovereign states have an equal right to self-defense, then either all or none should have nuclear weapons. But if they were informed that, in current circumstances, the efforts to create either of these two conditions might significantly increase the risk of nuclear war, they may well, under certain conditions, accept nuclear inequality. Such conditions might include: the limitation of nuclear weapons use to self-defense; the unusually careful treatment of such weapons in order to reduce risk of use; some compensation for non-nuclear-weapons states that preserves their independence and benefits created by the nuclear balance of power; and concrete steps to reduce the risks – particularly to third parties – of reliance on nuclear deterrence, including weapons dismantlement when circumstances permit. In other words, the abstract justification for the uneven possession of nuclear weapons would depend on the existence of limits on ends and means, as well as on continued attention to the relative risks created by deterrence and its alternatives.

Treaties, norms, and taboos

In fact, the current nonproliferation regime closely resembles such an imaginary compact. Notwithstanding their equal right to self-defense, the great majority of sovereign non-nuclear-weapons states – 121 to be precise – have adhered to the NPT. The treaty creates two categories of states: five that are recognized as nuclear weapons states and the rest, which promise not to follow suit. The treaty, notably, also involves two articles that imply compensation and risk reduction: Article IV, which mandates assistance in the development of peaceful uses of nuclear energy, and Article VI, which requires the nuclear weapons states to take steps toward disarmament. Moreover, in various U.N. forums the superpowers have made limited pledges not to use nuclear weapons to threaten non-nuclear-weapons states unless the latter are acting in accord with other weapons states. In this vein, during the Falkland/Malvinas war, Great Britain made no nuclear threats against non-nuclear Argentina. Nor did the United States seriously consider the use of nuclear weapons to avert its defeat by non-nuclear North Vietnam. Such behavior, of course, derived from prudence more than from U.N. resolutions. Nonetheless, it reinforces a strong taboo against using these weapons that has lasted for 40 years. At the same time, the superpowers have made little progress toward the arms reductions called for in Article VI, and some analysts argue that this "vertical proliferation" will soon justify horizontal proliferation.

But as the Vietnam example reveals, the current nonproliferation regime of treaties, norms, and taboos rests not only on formal and abstract considerations, but also on self-interest and prudence. Even though superpower compliance with Article VI of the NPT has been inadequate, many states will continue to adhere because they believe their security will be diminished if more states – particularly their regional rivals – obtain nuclear weapons. The treaty helps them by providing for international inspections by the IAEA to assure that ostensibly peaceful nuclear programs are not being used to develop weapons. And many states realize that the robust deterrence postures created by the two superpowers have discouraged many of the 40-odd states that possess nuclear technology today from building nuclear weapons. The credibility of the nuclear umbrella extended by Washington and Moscow over their allies is a major reason why proliferation has been much slower than Kennedy feared.

These calculations have not impressed the handful of major nuclear threshold countries – such as Argentina, Brazil, India, Israel, Pakistan, and South Africa – that have rejected the NPT. They consider it unacceptably discriminatory and hypocritical for the superpowers to maintain weapons denied to other states. Moreover, some analysts argue that the superpowers are wrong to try to stop others from gaining access to nuclear weapons technology. They contend that just as the existence of nuclear weapons has produced prudence that has stabilized the U.S.–Soviet relationship, the spread of nuclear weapons to other countries would stabilize regional rivals. A world of nuclear porcupines would be a more cautious world.

Other things being equal, this argument might have some merit. But other things are not equal, and contrary to the rhetoric that will be heard in Geneva, nuclear inequality has nothing to do with racism on the part of weapons states or with the irrationality that some claim to see in Third World leaders. The key difference between weapons and nonweapons states concerns the possibility that deterrence will fail. Although superpower relations and arsenals create this risk also, it is likely to be much higher in most regional situations because of the shaky political conditions found in most states seeking nuclear weapons as well as their limited experience with nuclear command and control systems. These risks are even greater in the early stages of a nuclear program, when new weapons are tempting and vulnerable targets for pre-emptive attack. The frequency of civil wars and overthrown governments in these countries, their embryonic procedures for civil control of the military, and their shortage of advanced electronic safety locks and secure battlefield communications networks all indicate that the danger of nuclear weapons use by new proliferators far exceeds that embedded in the U.S.–Soviet relationship. Nonproliferation is not an inconsistent or hypocritical policy if it is based on impartial and realistic estimation of relative risks.

Some might argue that a nonweapons state nonetheless has every moral and legal right in today's anarchic world to accept large risks. But the decision to build a nuclear weapon can impose significant new risks on third parties. If new proliferators are more likely to use nuclear weapons – even inadvertently – the breaking of a 40-year nuclear taboo becomes that much more likely, as does the chance that others might be drawn into the nuclear conflict. The inadequacies of the new proliferators' procedures for controlling weapons or weapons-usable fuels, such as plutonium or highly enriched uranium, multiply the chances that terrorists will steal nuclear devices. And finally, one must reckon with the simple but plausible proposition that the more nuclear weapons proliferate, the greater the prospects for accidental use and the greater the difficulty in eventually establishing controls and reducing the role of nuclear weapons in world politics.

Yet if the superpowers have the right to hold potential proliferators responsible for the likely effects of their actions on third parties, third countries may hold the superpowers similarly accountable. And the superpowers have not adequately fulfilled the obligations imposed on them by the nonproliferation regime. Even though the regime does not rest primarily on Article VI of the NPT, this American and Soviet failure could ultimately contribute to its collapse. Nevertheless, the key role played by their alliance guarantees in stemming proliferation indicates that their Article VI obligations cannot be interpreted as simple disarmament.

Stabilizing deterrence

The relation between nonproliferation and other arms control regimes is not as simple as it first appears. Ironically, the superpowers have seen deterrence stabilize even as their arsenals have greatly expanded. Over time, their high levels of weaponry have instilled prudence in their relationship and permitted their allies to eschew the nuclear option. Changes in the balance that allies perceive as weakening the credibility of deterrence not only threaten the stability of the central relationship, they also reduce the sense of security that helps slow the pace of proliferation. Paradoxically, under many circumstances the introduction of a single bomb in some non-nuclear states may be more likely to lead to nuclear use than the addition of a thousand more warheads to the U.S. and Soviet stockpiles.

On the other hand, professing indifference to the superpower nuclear arms relationship can weaken the nonproliferation regime in two ways. First, a disdain for the arms control institutions and concerns expressed by nonweapons states can aggravate the discrimination issue that is a central problem in nonproliferation policy. Second, nuclear doctrines and deployments that stress the military usefulness of nuclear weapons may help bolster deterrence, but they also tend to make nuclear weapons look more attractive to others. If states that have deliberately eschewed nuclear weapons see them treated increasingly like conventional defensive weapons, they may one day reconsider their decisions. In short, the relation between nonproliferation and general nuclear arms control efforts will require the nuclear states to be sensitive to both issues.

The idea of a comprehensive test ban (CTB) treaty became the ultimate symbolic issue of the previous two NPT review conferences. But the prospect that the Reagan administration will pursue a CTB is virtually nil. The administration contends that a test ban would deprive defense planners of vital information about the reliability of the stockpile and about the effects of nuclear radiation on new systems. And U.S. officials claim to doubt that such an accord could be verified. In addition, a CTB would hinder strategic modernization plans, including some elements of the Strategic Defense Initiative (SDI).

In the absence of serious CTB negotiations, superpower hopes of defusing charges of bad faith on Article VI will depend on whether the conferees feel optimistic about the other set of talks that will be under way in Geneva – over strategic arms. The American argument that the SDI is designed to rid the world of nuclear weapons and permit the implementation of Article VI is unlikely to carry much weight in either Geneva conference. Not only have scientists' doubts about a perfect defense been widely publicized, but also many countries know that without U.S.–Soviet agreement, unilateral defensive efforts are likely to reheat the offensive arms race. But whatever the short-run situation in September 1985, a perpetual increase in superpower arsenals can soon be expected to be perceived as inconsistent with the basic intuitive compact underlying the NPT, and eventually may undercut the regime. That is the serious long-term message that should not be lost as the nuclear states properly discount the exaggerated short-term rhetoric that will blare forth from Geneva.

Vertical proliferation, however, will not be the only source of acrimony at the review conference. Regional rivalries and charges against Israel and South Africa – both NPT nonsignatories – will be raised. Some will also charge that the supplier countries have not lived up to their full obligations under Article IV to assist developing countries' nuclear energy programs. Complaints are especially likely about the Nuclear Supplier Group Guidelines, published in 1978, which urge restraint in the export of sensitive facilities and equipment such as enrichment and reprocessing plants.

But these charges can be answered impartially by adopting an evolutionary approach to energy programs. As the International Nuclear Fuel Cycle Evaluation concluded in 1980, such technologies make little economic sense for countries with modest nuclear programs. Yet they could provide capabilities that would contravene the purposes of the treaty. Such transfers to larger programs may properly be considered in the context of a region's stability and of the susceptibility of the technology to safeguards. Yet few such national programs exist, and they are unlikely to generate much friction at the conference.

Moreover, the NPT is only part of what is needed for an effective nonproliferation policy. Bilateral diplomacy, cooperation among suppliers, coordination with the Soviet Union, efforts to induce second-tier suppliers – including China – to observe the guidelines, improvements in IAEA safeguards, and studies of the sanctions best able to respond to the next case of proliferation are merely a few of the critical elements of a successful policy. But maintaining the NPT regime will remain at the heart of an effective policy.

The question still remains of how long the great majority of states possessing nuclear technology will abjure nuclear weaponry. Obviously, political and technical trends will shift over time, but the prospects that proliferation may destabilize many regions, that nuclear weapons will not enhance the security of many states, and that superpowers will not fully escape proliferation's effects all generate a strong common international interest in the nonproliferation regime. For the present, most states are likely to accept some ordered inequality in weaponry because anarchic equality appears more dangerous.

Realistically, an international regime does not need perfect adherence to have a significant constraining effect any more than domestic laws require an end to deviant behavior in order to be effective. Nevertheless, there is a tipping point beyond which the accumulated weight of violations will upset today's balance of nuclear incentives and disincentives. Moreover, the police function is traditionally the domain of the great powers in international politics. If their preoccupation with the competitive issues in their relationship distracts them from this responsibility, the proliferation balance could approach this tipping point.

The consequences of further proliferation cannot be confidently predicted. The answer depends in part on the variables "who" and "when." Stable deterrence might be possible in some regions. And the rate of spread makes a big difference. The slower the pace of proliferation, the easier it will be to manage its destabilizing effects and contain the risk of nuclear use. Still, given the dangers of increased risks of nuclear use that would follow any proliferation, it would be wise to err on the safe side and try to prevent it.

A good, impartial case can be made for a strong nonproliferation policy, but it is important to remember that the obligations bind in two directions. Although much of the rhetoric of the NPT review conference will be exaggerated and will not necessarily indicate an imminent collapse, ignoring it completely would be foolish. Hidden among the excesses will be an important message about global security in the longer term of the nuclear age.

Note

* This essay reflected my State Department experience with non-proliferation policy.

Part 4

Interdependence, globalization, and governance

12 Independence and interdependence*

For two centuries, American foreign policy has been marked by a cyclical pattern in which decades of involvement have been followed by decades of isolationism. Now, on the two-hundredth anniversary of our independence, although the cycle watchers have us scheduled to turn inward, we find our leaders proclaiming that interdependence has entangled us with other nations.

Have we finally buried George Washington and the isolationist tradition he fathered? Not yet. As the Vietnam debacle punctuated the end of an era of hyper-involvement, public debate and public opinion polls became transfixed, right on cycle, by the shadowy ghost of isolationism. Our foreign policy leaders have turned from the tarnished talisman of "national security" that served them so well in the cold war to the rhetoric of interdependence in order to exorcise Washington's ghost and try to rebuild the public consensus for a foreign policy of involvement. Our thirty-fifth president announced that "the age of interdependence is here." Our thirty-eighth president warns us that "we are all part of one interdependent economic system."

Wrestling with Washington's ghost is not the best way to enter the third century. The slogan "isolationism" both misleads us about our history, and creates a false debate that hinders the making of relevant distinctions among types, degrees, and directions of American involvement with the rest of the world. The choices that confront us as we enter our third century are not between isolationism and interdependence. Both slogans contain a large mixture of myth. We were never all that isolated from the rest of the world and we are not now fully interdependent with the rest of the world. Mexicans, Nicaraguans, Filipinos, and Japanese, among others, must be permitted an ironic smile when they hear about our isolationist history. Isolation was our posture toward the European balance of power, and for a century that posture of independence rested on our tacit military dependence on British naval power. Even in the interwar period of this century, our independence from Europe was a military posture while we tried to influence events through dollar diplomacy.

It is ironic that the end of the Vietnam war stimulated neoisolationist arguments: A strong case can be made that, with only a quarter of our trade and investment involved in the militarily weak, poor countries, American economic welfare and military security depend rather little on what kinds of domestic political regimes rule such countries; exports to less developed countries represent about 1 per cent, and earnings on direct investments in such countries represent about one half of 1 per cent of our gross national product; less developed countries have limited – in some cases, negligible – military importance; except for ideologues, the interests of Americans were poorly served by a foreign policy that involved the Third World as an arena in which to combat communism; Americans do not really know what the best regimes for less developed countries are. Neoisolationist arguments such as these were badly needed a decade ago. Now they are like an innoculation against a disease from which we have largely recovered: helpful against recurring symptoms of the past, but possibly harmful as a prescription for the future.

The right bicentennial medicine

Does this mean that a declaration of interdependence is the right bicentennial medicine for our foreign policy aches and pains? Not if it is left at the rhetorical level. The rhetoric of interdependence risks creating a new myth that will be regarded with cynicism abroad and will make our own policy choices more difficult. Interdependence means a situation of reciprocal effects or mutual dependence. The sources of interdependence are both physical – for example, the spread of ocean pollutants or depletion of the earth's protective ozone shield – and social – for example, the economic, political, and perceptual effects that events in the Middle East and the United States have had upon each other. Reciprocal effect, however, is rarely equal on all parties and degrees of dependence are almost always uneven. Such uneven dependence can be a source of power. Where one of two countries is less dependent than the other, it can play upon this fact to manipulate the relationship. We must not let the rhetoric of interdependence blind us to the fact that others sometimes feel that the word "interdepend" is conjugated "I depend; you rule."

Overreliance on the rhetoric of interdependence not only may blind us to the legitimate concerns of other nations, but it can obscure our own choices at home. Rhetoric often makes interdependence sound like a good thing or an inexorable force toward cooperation. In fact, interdependence is neither good nor bad, and is just as easily a source of conflict as of cooperation. In some instances, the best policy response is to try to *diminish* rather than to extend interdependence. Take American energy policy for example. Whatever its many faults, the most trivial is the frequently heard criticism that Project Independence is inconsistent with our declarations of global interdependence. Rather than rhetoric, we need careful analysis of the effects and degree of choice presented by different types of interdependence. Even the physical effects of ecological interdependence, such as pollution, can be amplified or diminished by social and political choices. Rhetoric must not obscure such choices.

It is currently fashionable, in the aftermath of the oil crisis of 1973, to regard raw materials as an important source of power. Even a traditional realist like Hans Morgenthau sees an historically unprecedented divorcement of military power from economic and political power resulting from "the monopolistic or quasi-monopolistic control of raw materials." [1] One frequently encounters political judgments about American dependence supported by references to lists of raw materials that America imports, such as the following:

> Of the thirteen basic industrial raw materials required by a modern economy, the United States was dependent on imports for more than one half of its supplies of four of these in 1950: aluminum, manganese, nickel and tin. By 1970 the list had increased to six, as zinc and chromium were added. Projections indicate that by 1985 the United States will depend on imports for more than one half of its supplies of nine basic raw materials, as iron, lead and tungsten are added. By the end of the century it will be dependent primarily on foreign sources for its supply of each of the thirteen raw materials except phosphate.[2]

Sensitivity and vulnerability

We are often told that we are too dependent to risk antagonizing the countries that provide these imports. But such arguments rest on confusion about two aspects of interdependence – sensitivity and vulnerability. Sensitivity means liability to costly effects imposed from outside in a given situation – in other words, before any policies are devised to try to change the situation. Vulnerability means continued liability to costly effects imposed from outside, even after efforts have been made to alter or escape the situation. In the 1973 oil crisis, for example, the rapid rise in domestic prices and long lines at gasoline stations showed that the United States was very *sensitive* to the Arab states' embargo, but the degree of our direct *vulnerability* was limited by the fact that 85 per cent of the energy we consumed was produced at home. Japan, on the other hand, which relied almost entirely on imported energy, was both highly sensitive *and* highly vulnerable to the Arab embargo.

In the case of our "dependence" on imported raw materials, the fact, for example, that we import 85 per cent of our bauxite makes the price of aluminum *sensitive* to foreign changes in price or interruptions of supply. We are dependent in the sense that changes abroad can quickly cause costly changes at home. But we are not necessarily dependent in the sense of being vulnerable. Vulnerability is determined by whether we have reasonable alternatives. If we have alternative suppliers of bauxite, or if we could substitute domestic alumina-bearing clay for bauxite at relatively low cost, then we are not very vulnerable. Stockpiles could be held to tide us over the period of transition. The fact that we import a raw material may merely be a sign that it is cheaper abroad rather than an indication of our vulnerability. Of course vulnerability is a matter of degree and varies with the costs and time involved in developing alternatives. This implies hard policy choices about acceptable degrees of dependence and how willing we are to sacrifice the economic benefits of cheaper foreign supplies. That is what the foreign policy of raw material interdependence is about, not some magical transformation of power that supposedly occurred in 1973 or some force beyond our control. And that is why a policy of interdependence needs more analysis, not more rhetoric.

What will be the problems of a policy of interdependence in the third century? Not even our era's astrologers, the futurologists who convert large amounts of gold into paper, can really tell us. But though we cannot peer very far into the third century, we can as we cross the threshold identify certain characteristics and trends which appear deeply rooted enough to be important parameters of foreign policy well into the century. After sketching five such characteristics, I will turn to the critical question of how to organize ourselves to cope with the world we are entering.

A new foreign policy agenda

Protection against military threats will remain a major foreign policy problem, but national security can also be endangered by events outside the political-military sphere. A melting of the Arctic ice cap because of a three degree rise in the earth's temperature resulting from industrial growth; a depletion of the earth's ozone layer because of widespread use of refrigerants, fertilizers, or nuclear tests; theft of plutonium by terrorist groups; ill-fated experiments with weather modification; or a prolonged world population explosion could threaten the security of American (and other) people as seriously as many occurrences that could arise in the traditional political-military realm. Even such a traditionalist as Secretary of State Kissinger said in his 1975 speech in Los Angeles:

> Progress in dealing with our traditional agenda is no longer enough .... The problems of energy resources, environment, population, the uses of space and the seas, now rank with questions of military security, ideology, and territorial rivalry which have traditionally made up the diplomatic agenda.

Many of the possible threats arising from environmental and resource interdependence may never come about. But the new agenda does not depend upon the dramatic oversimplifications of the Club of Rome. Rather it rests on the age-old proposition that the proper task of foreign policy is to reduce uncertainty and insure against events that despite a small chance of occurring would have enormous potential costs if they did. For instance, a recent government-sponsored conference of atmospheric scientists could not agree on the extent or immediacy of "threats ranging from a Soviet proposal to reverse the direction of north-flowing rivers to possible depletion of stratospheric ozone by spraycan propellants, fertilizers, nuclear weapons, and high-flying aircraft." Nonetheless, the assembled scientists were in full agreement that "some man-induced changes could occur so soon that it would be dangerous to wait until entirely satisfactory scientific evidence is in hand." [3]

While many of the new agenda items will grow out of interdependencies in which effects are physically transmitted across borders, many effects will also be socially transmitted. The rapid rise in population and likely inability of South

Asians to grow enough food to avert a famine may appear as a South Asian problem from which we can isolate ourselves if we consider it in purely physical terms. It is highly likely, however, in an age of modern satellite communications that many Americans will demand a major U.S. policy response after watching people starve on the evening news before sitting down to ample dinners. The new items on the agenda will affect even the staunchest neoisolationist who never sets foot outside our borders and professes to care little about the rest of the world.

Blurring domestic and foreign policy

One of the characteristics of the new interdependence issues is that they often cut across the traditional distinction between domestic and foreign policy. During the cold war era, politics was supposed to stop at the water's edge. While this maxim was frequently breached in practice, the basic distinction between domestic and foreign concerns was generally accepted. Many of the new issues do not even appear to be foreign policy concerns at all. Decisions to strip mine coal in Montana, to permit or prohibit the production of freon, or to maintain a free market in grain appear to be purely domestic issues; but they are closely related to three of the examples of new foreign policy issues cited by Kissinger.

Thus it is not surprising that many of the institutions that handle the new issues on the foreign policy agenda are traditional domestic agencies. Nearly all the major executive departments have little foreign offices of their own. In 1973, for example, of 19,000 Americans abroad on diplomatic missions, only 3,400 were from the State Department[4] and less than half of the government

Table 12.1 U.S. transgovernmental contacts

Accredited Government Delegates to Conferences and Agencies			
	1964	*1968*	*1974*	*1974 as % of 1964*
Total government (46 agencies)	2,378	2,137	3,656	154
State Department as percentage of total government	52	48	44	
Overseas Stationing of Civilian Bureaucrats			
	1962	*1968*	*1974*	*1974 as % of 1964*
State (including AID, Peace Corps)	10,819	12,573	7,621	70
10 major agencies	1,567	2,410	1,259	80
Agriculture, Treasury, Justice	490	901	833	170

Sources: U.S. State Department, Bureau of International Organization; Raymond Hopkins, "The International Role of Domestic Bureaucracy" (manuscript).

delegates accredited to international conferences came from the State Department. Nor, as the table opposite indicates, have budgetary restrictions changed the trend.

These miniature foreign offices that domestic agencies have developed for dealing with the international aspects of issues with which they are concerned are not merely bureaucratic nuisances. They are needed in the management of interdependence issues that are both domestic and foreign. As the entire government becomes involved in "international" affairs, it becomes more difficult to reserve a separate section of the agenda for the State Department. An analogous situation exists in Congress where much of the "foreign policy" agenda comes under the jurisdiction of domestic committees rather than the Foreign Relations and International Relations committees. Isolation will not be a very meaningful concept for those third century issues that know no water's edge.

Transnational communications

One of the remarkable changes in the past two decades has been in communications technology. The jet plane has made Asia a day away, rather than several days' journey. Synchronous-orbit satellites have brought the cost of intercontinental communication into the same range as intercity calls. The price of a three minute call from New York to London was once $75; today it is only $5.40.[5]

The extent and rapidity of communications across borders will continue to grow in the third century but, profits and prophets notwithstanding, the world is not about to become a global village. On the contrary, transnational communications will affect different people in different ways here at home, while exposing the enormous disparities in global distribution and development. Even using the most optimistic assessments, there will be an enormous gap between the incomes of Americans and South Asians in the third century. Rather than developing a sense of village-like community, transnational communications will create different patterns of moral consciousness and new moral dilemmas as Americans try to reconcile differing moral claims. It is becoming fashionable to proclaim that equality is to our century what liberty was to the nineteenth century. But the problems of thinking clearly about equality in a world organized into national states (a condition likely to persist long into the third century) are not simple ones. As Robert Tucker has written, "if a large portion of Western liberal elites finds no more difficulty in distinguishing between the United States and Bangladesh than it does between California and Mississippi, it is safe to say that the general public continues to find a great deal of difficulty and that democratic governments will continue to prove responsive to the distinction the public draws between its collective welfare and the welfare of those outside the state."[6]

Nevertheless, it will be increasingly difficult to screen out the poor part of the world and the moral discomfort it creates. Even as some Americans will respond to the ugly television pictures of starving people by turning off the set, others will respond with moral outrage or act out of a sense of total alienation from our society. Is it unrealistic to imagine a small group of MIT-trained sons and daughters of Indian, Japanese, and American middle-class parents threatening to detonate a crude plutonium bomb in Boston unless American aid to Asia is immediately increased? Rather than the pacific image of a global village, the growth of transnational communication in a world of enormous inequality may merely bring us the Patty Hearst case with a global dimension. And the more we try to isolate ourselves from the problem now, the less leverage we will have over it in the future.

Erosion of hierarchy

As military force has become more costly for large powers to apply, power has become less fungible and the traditional hierarchy of states has been weakened. There is an increased discrepancy between power measured in military resources and power measured in terms of control over the outcome of events. Although American power is great in the first sense, our capacity for control is diminished. The need for leadership remains, but the capacity for hegemony is absent. The risk of a stalemate system, unable to respond flexibly to change, is likely to be further increased by the proliferation of nuclear capabilities.

Power has always been an elusive concept in international affairs, but it has become increasingly slippery as we enter our third century. The traditional view was that military power dominated, and that the states at the top of the hierarchy of military power controlled world affairs. But the nature of the resources that produce power capabilities has become more complex, and the international power hierarchy more difficult to determine. In the era of American independence, when a good infantry was the crucial power resource, European statesmen could calibrate the classical balance of power by counting the populations of conquered and transferred territories. The industrial revolution complicated such calculations, and nuclear weapons, as a power resource too costly to use except in an extreme situation, further weakened the relationship between power measured in military resources and power in the sense of control over the outcome of events. For many of the new interdependence items on the foreign policy agenda, calculating the balance of military power does not predict the pattern of outcome of events. And while uneven dependence can be relevant in such situations, judgment and measurement are still complicated. It is difficult to calculate asymmetries, and where there are many of them, to understand the linkages among them. Moreover, even if we felt fairly comfortable in our assessment, measurable power resources are not automatically translated into effective power over outcomes. Translation is by way of a political bargaining process where relative skill, relative intensity of concern, and relative coherence can belie predictions based on the supposed hierarchy of international power – witness the outcome of the Vietnam war.

This is not to say that military force has become obsolete as we enter our third century. Quite the contrary. Military deterrence is likely to remain a central concern of our foreign policy well into the future. But military force is difficult to apply to many of the new interdependence issues on the agenda, particularly for the major military states. The use of force is made more costly for major states by three conditions: (1) risks of nuclear escalation; (2) uncertain and possible negative effects on the achievement of economic goals; and (3) domestic opinion opposed to the human costs of the use of force. Even those states relatively unaffected by the third condition, such as Communist countries, may feel some constraints from the first two. On the other hand, lesser states involved in regional rivalries and terrorist groups may find it easier to use force than before. The net effect of these contrary changes in the role of force is to reduce hierarchy based on military power.

The erosion of the international hierarchy is sometimes portrayed as a decline of American power – as though the causes lay in our aging process. Admittedly, from the perspective of a policy-maker of the 1950s there has been a decline. But American power in the sense of resources has not declined as dramatically as is often supposed. U.S. military spending was roughly a third of the world total in 1950 and it still is today. Over the same period, the American gross national product has declined from slightly more than a third to slightly more than a quarter of the world total, but the earlier figure is a reflection of the wartime destruction of Europe and Japan, and the current figure still remains twice the size of the Soviet economy, more than three times the size of Japan's economy, and four times the size of West Germany's economy. In terms of power resources, America enters the third century as the most powerful country in the world – a condition likely to persist well into the century.

To understand what is changing, we must distinguish power over others from power over outcomes or over the system as a whole. What we are experiencing as we enter our third century is not so much an erosion of power resources compared to those of other countries (although there has been some), but an erosion of our power to control outcomes in the international system as a whole. The main reason is that the system itself has become more complex. There are more issues, more actors, and less hierarchy. We still have leverage over others, but we have far less leverage over the whole system.

The situation is illustrated by the changes in the international monetary system. Contrary to the prophets of American decline, the weakness of the dollar in the 1960s turned out to be partly an artifact of a particular institutional system. In 1976, the dollar is still the key currency. But the monetary system is far more complex in terms of the important governmental and nongovernmental players involved. As *The Economist* put it, "a simpler way of looking at it is that while America could fix the system it wanted at Bretton Woods in 1944, now it seems able only to block what it does not like." America remains powerful, but without a hegemonic capability. The problem is nicely summed up in the title of Marina Whitman's article in FOREIGN POLICY 20, "Leadership Without Hegemony."

Multilateral diplomacy

In such a world, multilateral diplomacy, often through international institutions, grows far more important. This is true not only because hegemonic power has declined, but because much of the agenda is concerned with organizing collective action. The number of international conferences in which the United States officially participated rose from an annual figure of 141 in 1946 to 308 in 1956, 625 in 1966, and 817 in 1975. Nor are the effects always trivial. On the tenth anniversary of our vehement opposition to tariff preferences for less developed countries at the first U.N. Conference on Trade and Development, Congress enacted just such a measure as American law. Similarly, in the process of negotiating in the Law of the Sea Conference, the United States has come to accept the idea of a 200 mile economic zone which it had strongly opposed at the beginning of the negotiations.

The fact that multilateral diplomacy is becoming more important does not mean that we are about to see a global re-enactment of our Constitutional Convention of 1787. It is highly unlikely that we will be faced with the opportunity (or the danger) of submerging our sovereignty. In fact, analogies drawn from our history are an impediment to understanding the political roles that international organizations play. To envisage international organizations as incipient world governments having supranational authority above states is to focus on a small (and frequently inaccurate) aspect of their political roles. More important is the way they affect the political process – for example, the ways by which agendas are set in world politics. The choice of organizational arena often determines which interdependence issues get priority on the interstate agenda. For example, the massive U.N. conferences on the environment, food, population, and women, with their accompanying nongovernmental tribunes and press attention, were largely exercises in agenda setting.

Moreover, the different jurisdictional scope and differing composition of delegations to different organizations frequently result in quite different distributions of influence and outcomes. The same issue may come out quite differently in GATT than in UNCTAD. Government officials shop among forums as they try to steer issues to arenas more favorable to their preferred outcomes; and they use international organizations as instruments to bring pressure on other governments as well as other departments of their own governments.

Indeed, as more bureaucracies once considered "domestic" become involved in international affairs, they sometimes discover a similarity of interests that is greater across national boundaries than it is with competing bureaus at home. International conferences and organizations provide the physical contact and aura of legitimacy that allow the translation of some of these potential transgovernmental coalitions into actual ones. The more technical the organization, the more likely it is that this process will occur. The political importance of international organization, particularly on interdependence issues, is less in their power *above* states than in their role in coordinating bits and pieces of power *across* states. One obvious example will suffice: the reinforcement various national offices of environmental protection received from the Stockholm Conference of 1972 and the subsequent activities of the U.N. Environment Program.

Organizing for interdependence

If the preceding projection is correct, Americans will confront a new type of foreign policy agenda consisting of issues which blur the traditional distinction between domestic and foreign policy while posing difficult moral dilemmas. At the same time, our power over outcomes in the international system will diminish and we will have to resort to multilateral diplomacy to organize collective action. If these five characteristics do indeed continue well into our third century, what are their implications for the design and management of a policy of interdependence? Two things at least are clear. We will need to pay more attention to the interconnection of domestic politics and foreign policy, and we will need to think more imaginatively about the relation of our institutions with international institutions.

One of the most basic questions is, given the erosion of the classical distinction between domestic and international politics, how will we determine the national interest? What will be the basis for judging our foreign policy? Cynics regard the term as meaningless and the question as irrelevant. But so long as the world's peoples define their political identities in relation to national communities – and that seems likely to continue well into our third century – the idea of a national interest is not vacuous.

There are clearly differences in the degree to which policies affect each American and how their costs are distributed. Clear threats to military security probably come closest to affecting all of us. Though there may be disagreements about the clarity of the threat and the way it is met, maintaining the central balance in the overall military security system of world politics remains a necessary (though not sufficient) condition for the normal functioning of other processes and thus will continue to be a central component of the national interest.

There are some aspects of economic and social issues that touch nearly all citizens in the aggregate (e.g., inflation and recession) and others that hurt or benefit particular groups. There is a long tradition in foreign policy that such groups try to blur the differences and cloak their concerns with the national interest. Their ability to do so is affected by the general concepts that symbolize consensus – such as it is at any time – on the general orientation of American foreign policy. During the height of the cold war and American leadership in the Atlantic Alliance, domestic economic interests were subordinated. For example, it has been estimated that in 1961, deflationary policies designed to strengthen the balance of payments and the position of the dollar cost the American economy some $45 billion. During the 1960s, key policy positions were filled by financial men. In 1971, the Soviet threat seemed less imminent, and our allies themselves seemed to pose an economic challenge. Thus, policy advisers from manufacturing and domestic political backgrounds defined American interests with less concern for preserving the Bretton Woods monetary system.

The benefits – and the costs

The point is not that one or the other of these definitions was necessarily right or wrong, but that as the overriding security symbolism weakens, it will become more difficult to establish an American consensus on priorities. The rhetoric of interdependence is an imperfect substitute because economic interdependence and, sometimes, ecological interdependence, more so than national security issues, tend to affect different groups in different ways. Take, for example, the 1975 debate over grain sales to the Soviet Union. Such sales were said to help détente. In the United States, the sales boosted farmers' (and grain-exporting companies') incomes, but had an inflationary effect on food prices across the nation. Thus, in this case, economic interdependence between the Soviet Union and the United States imposed an uneven pattern of costs and benefits on the American population.

Moreover, in terms of the distinction drawn earlier, it was unclear whether the increased mutual sensitivity was really leading to increased Soviet vulnerability that could provide the United States with a useful foreign policy tool in its relations with the Soviet Union. Indeed, some critics argued that the United States itself could become more vulnerable because domestic groups with an interest in maintaining the profitable transactions would lobby to maintain the relationship. In situations where one society is more liberal and pluralistic than another, the political vulnerability patterns cannot be determined by simple statistics. Moreover, where the domestic burdens fall unevenly leaders will find it difficult to obtain the leeway they need to make such subtle calculations and indulge their finely balanced judgments. It is more likely that they will be constrained by the view expressed by AFL-CIO president George Meany at the time of the 1975 Russian grain sales: "Foreign policy is too damned important to be left to the secretary of state!"

Many of the relevant policy decisions in the future will appear to be domestic rather than foreign. We can think of sensitivity interdependence, whether through a market relationship or a flow of goods or people, as a transnational system crossing national boundaries. To affect such a system, governments can intervene at different policy points: domestically, at their own borders; through international organizations at another country's border; or inside the domestic jurisdiction of another country. Different points of policy intervention impose different costs and benefits. Political struggles will arise over who pays the costs of any change. Such leaders as the president or secretary of state will often prefer policies proposing equitable international sharing of costs or even, as a price for retaining international leadership, a disproportionate American share. But leverage will be held by bureaucrats and congressmen whose democratic responsibilities are to a narrower and more immediate range of interests.

This means that foreign policy leaders dealing with these new issues will have to pay even more attention than usual to domestic politics. Foreign policy strategy will have to include a domestic political strategy designed with enough leeway to focus on long-term systemic interests of the United States. Different issues – for example, trade and money – have different political characteristics. Even though they may have the same effect on employment, trade issues tend to involve a broad number of political groups while monetary issues rarely do. Strategies will have to be formulated in terms of such political patterns.

Leaders will have to pay special attention to the way that their international bargaining linkages, threats of retaliation, and choice of international forum affect domestic politics as well as the creation of transnational alliances. They will have to anticipate points of strain. At home, they will have to pay more attention to the groups that bear the heaviest costs of adjustment to change. A good example is the comparative generosity of the adjustment assistance in the 1974 trade legislation designed to stave off the restrictive alternative Burke-Hartke bill, compared to the narrow adjustment assistance provision of the Trade Expansion Act that President Kennedy pressed as part of a grand security design in the early 1960s.

A greater congressional role

While it may be painful to the executive branch, the role of Congress in foreign policy decisions on economic and ecological issues is likely to continue to loom large. While part of the current activism of Congress in foreign policy may be a cyclical reaction against its passive role during the cold war and Vietnam years, a deeper cause lies in the fact that there is a domestic side to the issues described. *The choice confronting the executive branch is not between a large and a small congressional involvement, it is a choice between a cooperative and an antagonistic involvement.* The State Department is going to have to learn to work more closely with Congress and at an earlier stage in the development of issues in order to encourage longer-range perspectives. Otherwise, the congressional agenda will most likely be set by groups with short-term interests.

Too often, plans for coping with interdependence focus almost entirely on the role of the president and the executive. But while it is true that the president is often capable of having a longer and broader perspective than a congressman, we cannot simply assume that presidential interests are the national interest – particularly in regard to interdependence issues that involve long-term planning. Presidential political incentives are also short-term. For example, scientific reports on the impending energy and food crises were submitted to the White House in the mid-1960s, but failed to capture adequate presidential attention.

Focusing attention on problems of long-range national interest will require interaction of the executive, Congress, and private sector institutions. Congress has a vital role to play on these interdependence issues. First, of course, congressional activity helps to legitimize the hard trade-offs involved in many of these issues, and to develop the consensus needed for an effective foreign policy. Second, congressional hearings provide for structured public involvement – an open multiple-advocacy procedure which can facilitate the orderly participation of a broad range of groups including scientists, professionals, and special interest organizations. This public interaction of technical and political interests can amplify the political resonance of certain long-run interdependence issues and thus help to set the president's agenda.[7] Obviously, congressional involvement and politicization is no panacea. It can create as well as cure problems. But the choice in dealing with interdependence issues will not be between politicization or not, but between systematic politicization and the ad hoc politicization we now know all too well.

In order to play a more positive role in policy, Congress will have to pay more attention to improving its own procedures, particularly to accommodate the international effects of domestic legislation. While it is true that "foreigners don't have votes," on many interdependence issues they do have capabilities to respond to American legislation in ways our voters later regret. State's "constituents" may live overseas, but they are not irrelevant to Congress.

Domestic rule making in the United States has often meant rule making for the world. Once those rules are diffused and imitated internationally they become much more difficult to change or control. For example, President Truman's 1945 unilateral declaration of jurisdiction over the continental shelf unlocked a Pandora's box. Similarly, current proposals before Congress for legislation on off-shore harbors, coastal zones, and fishery jurisdiction may serve as the basis for international law – good or bad, depending on how it is formulated. To ensure that the international implications of "domestic" legislation are taken into account will require an early and close relationship between the executive and Congress and a reorganization of congressional procedures and committees.

The central consideration in organizing for interdependence is to insure that collectively shared interests prevail over narrowly defined interests, and that both domestic and foreign constituencies are taken into account. This can be exceptionally difficult when the number of groups or agencies affected by policy is very large, and when decisions must be made without interminable delay. Coordination is especially difficult when the issues are not generally perceived as posing foreign policy problems at all. But the solution does not rest in handing such issues to the secretary of state. Effective organization must recognize *both* the foreign and domestic aspects of the issues.

Setting an example

Our international leadership will be affected by the domestic examples we set, as well as by the ability of Americans to work with and understand people from other cultural and political backgrounds. Government officials – well beyond the State Department – will need to understand both the limits of our abilities as a nation to control events and the importance of our efforts as the most powerful state to provide leadership toward solutions from which all parties can gain. It will not be enough for a president or secretary of state to appear briefly and make an appeal to Europeans to agree on energy policy or to offer economic concessions to poor countries if there are not informed supporters in Congress and in other countries who understand the policy and are willing to follow through. Transgovernmental contacts and multilateral diplomacy are part of the process of generating that understanding and support.

This perspective affects the way one reacts to the proliferation of international activities of apparently "domestic" branches of the bureaucracy. If these contacts were an aberration, the solution might be simple. But given the technical complexity of many of the issues involved and the domestic problems that arise, the technical agencies must be intimately involved in the process. Thus, as I mentioned earlier, the miniature foreign offices that have evolved in many United States' domestic agencies are not merely a bureaucratic nuisance, as many career State Department officers have charged.

Policy coordination

At the same time, it is important to distinguish two types of transgovernmental behavior. Transgovernmental *policy coordination* is activity designed to implement or adapt policy in the absence of detailed higher policy directives. Transgovernmental policy coordination is essential to effective management of complex interdependence issues. There may be very beneficial results when officials from technical agencies of different governments work together to solve joint problems, or when interactions facilitate the exchange of information. In occasional instances, a sense of "collegiality" leads to especially effective problem solving. Sophisticated attitudes toward international cooperation and increased sensitivity to the international aspects of problems may thereby increase in the government.

Since international organizations often provide the arena for policy coordination, officials of operating agencies might develop mutually beneficial relationships with those organizations and their secretariats, as well. The role of central foreign policy organs, such as the State Department, should be to encourage constructive transgovernmental contacts of this type, and to orient the agencies involved toward broader views of world order rather than toward their narrowly defined problems. There should be no attempt to cut off such contacts. (This would be futile even if attempted.) On the contrary, one of the roles of technical assistance programs administered by the Agency for International Development should be to encourage the strengthening of "counterpart" agencies concerned with interdependence issues in foreign governments.

Coalition building

Transgovernmental coordination, however, can shade into *coalition building*. Transgovernmental coalition building is the construction of coalitions between like-minded agencies in various governments, for policy purposes, against elements of their own governments. Transgovernmental coalitions bear close watch, since they can make American policies incoherent. If separate agencies not only coordinate policies directly with their counterparts but adopt their own independent foreign policies through informal alignments with foreign counterparts, the prospect of achieving a relatively rational American policy as a whole disappears. Close monitoring by the State Department and relevant White House agencies is necessary to keep a check on this; but coordination efforts must be subtle enough to avoid repressing legitimate transgovernmental behavior and thus driving the whole process "underground." Coordination has its own costs, and coherence is not valuable in and of itself. The White House staff should identify in advance those areas where coordination is essential and those where the costs of coordination would probably be greater than the benefits. Whether transgovernmental contacts will have a beneficial or pathological effect will depend on the framework within which they occur.

In short, while transgovernmental contacts can present problems of coherence and control, transgovernmental coordination, carried on by operating agencies with their counterparts abroad, is a permanent and essential aspect of interdependence policy. "Collegia" of experts and officials from a variety of countries form around different issues and their associated international organizations, and can work effectively together. Frequently, delegations to international organizations are composed largely of such people; and the United States would do well to pay more attention to placing more of them in international organizations, as members of secretariats, to facilitate cooperation between the United States and these organizations.

Effectiveness in international organizations is not just a matter of voting or elegant speeches. Indeed, if elegant speechmakers signal their basic disinterest by failing to appear in the corridors, their efforts may be to little avail. One day was neither enough time to build ancient Rome nor to charm the 1975 Rome Food Conference. To be effective in international institutions, we have to take them seriously. This does not mean that we must accept meaningless votes as legislation or accept all current institutions. On the contrary, we need to be more imaginative about creating institutions that do not follow the pseudo-parliamentary model which stresses voting by states and gives a citizen of Gabon one thousand times as much voting power as a citizen of India.

There are several tasks that international organizations perform in world politics. These can be crudely ranked in ascending order of difficulty, as follows: (1) provision of information; (2) formation of general norms; (3) regulation and monitoring of state behavior in accordance with specific norms; and (4) operation of technologies or elaborate monitoring or planning systems.

The current trend in the U.N. system is toward large conferences characterized by bloc confrontation. In general, large conferences have positive value in the first two tasks. Even when we do not like the message, they are sometimes useful messengers. On the other hand, such conferences are poorly suited for organizing or regulating collective action.

States have a variety of concerns and adapt their political behavior to the nature of the arena. For example, Brazil was a leader against U.S. positions at the Stockholm Conference on the environment, the Law of the Sea Conference, and the Bucharest Conference on population. In bilateral dealings on these issues, however, the Brazilians have adopted more conciliatory positions.

We need to think of international organization in terms of the networks that are associated with them, and what kinds of behavior different arenas encourage. We need to consider ways in which nongovernmental and quasi-governmental institutions, such as the Institute for Applied Systems Analysis in Vienna, can complement and supplement intergovernmental institutions. Rather than being overly concerned about the existence of competing and overlapping institutions, we should think in terms of the flexibility of networks that such overlap allows.

In short, international institutions are one but not the only point of policy intervention in transnational systems of interdependence. Effective policy will have to be based on a combination of instruments. Organizing internationally for interdependence issues does not mean disposing of policy issues by turning them over to international institutions. Leadership will not come from such institutions, but such institutions will play an important role in international leadership.

Some conclusions

Can we finally bury George Washington? Is isolationism totally irrelevant? Not if it is taken in small doses. One of the obstacles to thinking clearly about a policy of interdependence is to ignore the range of choice that we face. One of the fashionable bicentennial themes portrays America as a declining empire such as Britain was a century ago.[8] The two situations, however, are quite different. Britain in 1876 was no longer the largest economy in the world (the United States had already surpassed her), while, as we saw earlier, the American economy today is equal to the next three largest economies in the world combined. Even more important, America is less dependent in the sense of vulnerability than Britain was at the end of its era of leadership. Whereas exports were 25 per cent and repatriated profits on foreign investment were 8 per cent of Britain's gross national product in 1914, the comparable figures for America today are 7 per cent and approximately 1 per cent. The American problem may be that we have too much, not too little, freedom of choice in the short run. We may not exercise sufficient leadership now to affect problems that will increasingly concern us in the future.

Indeed, if taken separately, one can imagine independence strategies that the United States could follow in regard to most of the particular issues of economic and ecological interdependence. If we are concerned about other countries' refusals (or inability) to sell us energy or materials, we can restrict total imports to a level we could live without if we had to; diversify sources of imports; build up stockpiles and design contingency plans for rationing supplies to lessen the impact of sudden deprivation; and invest heavily in technologies to produce new sources and substitutes. Given time, technology can change the seemingly inexorable dependence supposedly implied by figures about known reserves.

Any statement about resources is also an implicit statement about technology. For example, copper ore is being mined today that would have been discarded as waste half a century ago. The technology for mining seabed nodules, a vast new source of minerals, has only recently been developed. America eats up a large share of current world resources, but it also creates the technology that generates new resources.

Those who base arguments against neoisolationism on the finiteness of the earth's resources – either on raw material inputs or on the supposed limits of the earth's ability to tolerate pollutants or heat outputs – do a disservice by focusing on the wrong aspects of the problem. They simply challenge those who believe in technology to show how technological changes can relax some of the supposedly inexorable limits to independence that arise from environmental interdependence. Heat generated by energy consumption can be diminished by more energy-efficient technologies. If manmade heat nonetheless threatens to melt the polar ice caps, technological fixers will argue that they can develop ways to alter the earth's albedo so that we absorb less solar heat. The problem is not finite resources causing interdependence; it is our social and governmental ability to respond in time and in common with others. Will the right technology be available in time? Will we know enough about its possible adverse effects to be sure that we do not create technological Frankenstein monsters? Will we be able to work with others to ensure that they do not inadvertently do so?

Thus, to cast the issue of interdependence in terms of whether independence will still be technically possible in the third century is to focus attention on the wrong questions. The important question is not whether independence will be technologically feasible, but what such independence will cost, and whether we can organize ourselves to minimize such costs. Taken separately, each Project Independence that neoisolationists might propose to reduce our vulnerability to interdependence might be tolerable in terms of costs. But when we add up the list, it will represent a heavy burden on the American people. We can, however, avoid many of these costs by an earlier and larger role in world affairs. Moreover, if the environmental alarmists are even partly correct, the burden will grow heavier as our third century unfolds. And the costs must not be conceived in narrow economic terms. An "independence" solution to the social interdependence transmitted by transnational communications or transnational terrorism that involved censorship of television programs or restriction of civil liberties would be an ironic and tragic means of preserving the independence declared in 1776.

On the other hand, to declare on the two-hundredth anniversary of our independence that the third century will be an era of interdependence is true but trivial. Interdependence does not provide clear guidelines for a new foreign policy. There is still a "necessity for choice." Interdependence just makes the choices harder. The choices will be about how to organize ourselves so that both the "domestic and foreign" aspects of interdependence issues receive their share of attention.

Difficult choices will also have to be made about how to exercise leadership without the capability for hegemony. British hegemony over the world's oceans and monetary system in the last century rested on the twin pillars of restraining domestic interests and applying preponderant power (including an occasional touch of force) abroad. American leaders will encounter the same need to set a good domestic example, but will find the application of power more difficult. We will have to learn both how to live with interdependence and how to use it for leadership. Our lesser degree of vulnerability than other countries and our occasional ability to credibly threaten to opt out can be a source of strength and leadership if carefully used. That is about all that will remain of George Washington's legacy in our third century. Just as a pinch of salt in the hands of an able chef is often essential to a successful dish, so an occasional small dose of American independence may be an essential ingredient of leadership for interdependence. But if we swallow too much of the neoisolationists' offerings now, our children will be choking well before the end of the third century.

Notes

* This essay was written for the American bicentennial.
1 Hans J. Morgenthau, "The New Diplomacy of Movement," *Encounter*, August 1974.
2 Lester Brown, *World Without Borders* (New York: Random House, 1972), p. 194.

3 Walter Sullivan, "World Aid Urged for Environment," *New York Times*, November 1, 1975.
4 I am indebted to Peter Szanton for this statistic, taken from the State Department's submission to the Commission on the Organization of the Government for the Conduct of Foreign Policy.
5 William H. Read, "The U.S. and International Communication Policymaking," Harvard Program in Information Technologies and Public Policy, Working Paper 75–11.
6 Robert Tucker, "A New International Order?" Commentary, February 1975, pp. 49–50.
7 Such a procedure is sketched in greater detail in Robbert O. Keohane and J. S. Nye, "Organizing for Global Environmental and Resource Interdependence," Report to the Commission on the Organization of the Government for the Conduct of Foreign Policy, 1975.
8 Norman Macrae, "America's Third Century: A Survey," *The Economist*, October 25, 1975.

13 Transgovernmental relations and international organizations*

with Robert O. Keohane

"Realist" analyses of world politics have generally assumed that states are the only significant actors; that they act as units; and that their military security objectives dominate their other goals.[1] On the basis of these assumptions it is easy to conclude that international organizations – defined as intergovernmental organizations – are merely instruments of governments, and therefore unimportant in their own right. Compared with the hopes and dreams of world federalists, the Realist position reflects reality: international organizations in the contemporary world are not powerful independent actors, and relatively universal organizations such as the United Nations find it extraordinarily difficult to reach agreement on significant issues. It is therefore not surprising that students of world politics have paid relatively slight attention to these entities, particularly after hopes for a major United Nations peacekeeping role were dashed in the early 1960's.

The Realist model on which the above conclusions about international organizations are based is now being called into question. Faced with a growing complexity of actors and issues, a number of analysts have begun to pay more attention to transnational relations. In this article we will contend that if critiques of Realist models of world politics are taken seriously, they not only call into question state-centric conceptions of "the international system," but also throw doubt upon prevailing notions about international organizations. If one relaxes the Realist assumptions, one can visualize more significant roles for international organizations in world politics.

In an important recent contribution to the literature on transnational relations, Samuel P. Huntington argues explicitly that international organizations are relatively insignificant in contemporary world politics:

> internationalism involves agreement among nation-states.
>   . . . every international organization at some points finds itself limited by the very principle which gives it being.
> The international organization requires *accord* among nations; the transnational organization requires *access* to nations. . . . International organizations embody the principle of nationality; transnational organizations try to ignore it.

While national representatives and delegations engage in endless debate at UN conferences and councils, however, the agents of the transnational organizations are busily deployed across the continents, spinning the webs that link the world together.

Internationalism is a dead end.[2]

Like Huntington, we begin with the proposition that transnational relations are increasingly significant in world politics. But we reach very different conclusions about the roles of international organizations.

Before making that argument systematically in the remainder of this paper, we must briefly deal with the issue of how transnational relations should be defined. Huntington defines "transnational organizations" as organizations sharing three characteristics: they are large bureaucracies; they perform specialized functions; and they do so across international boundaries. He explicitly includes governmental entities, such as the United States Agency for International Development (AID) or the Central Intelligence Agency (CIA) and intergovernmental entities such as the World Bank, along with nongovernmental organizations such as multinational enterprises, the Ford Foundation, and the Roman Catholic Church. Although this definition has the virtue of pointing out similarities between governmental and nongovernmental bureaucracies operating across national boundaries, it obscures the differences. Some of Huntington's observations are clearly meant to apply only to nongovernmental organizations. He argues, for instance, that "The operations of transnational organizations . . . usually do not have political motivations in the sense of being designed to affect the balance of power within the local society."[3] But this hardly applies to the Agency for International Development or the Central Intelligence Agency, both of which he designates as "transnational." He contends, on the basis of literature about multinational enterprises, that personnel arrangements of transnational organizations move toward dispersed nationality patterns, in which country subdivisions are primarily managed by local personnel; yet no evidence is presented that this is true for AID or the CIA, much less for the Strategic Air Command – another "transnational" organization by Huntington's definition. Furthermore, the trends over time seem to diverge, and when Huntington discusses these trends, he finds himself distinguishing between "U.S. Government-controlled transnational organizations" and private groups.[4]

The anomalies into which Huntington is led convince us that for most purposes it is useful to retain the governmental–nongovernmental distinction, thus facilitating the task of examining both the differences between patterns of governmental and nongovernmental activity and the effects of each on the other. Only if one were to use organization theory in a sustained way to explain behavior of large bureaucracies that operate across international boundaries would it seem wise to adopt Huntington's definition.

The argument leads us also to reconsider some of our own past usage. In this article we will restrict the term "transnational" to nongovernmental actors, and the term "transgovernmental" to refer to sub-units of governments on those occasions when they act relatively autonomously from higher authority in international politics.[5] In other words, "transnational" applies when we relax the assumption that states are the only actors, and "transgovernmental" applies when we relax the assumption that states act as units.

Our choice of definition is not a matter of semantics but is related directly to the argument of this paper. Transnational activity makes societies more sensitive to one another, which may lead governments to increase their efforts to control this nongovernmental behavior. Such efforts, if pursued by more than one government, make governmental policies sensitive to one another: since one government may deliberately or inadvertently thwart the other's purposes, governments must design their own policies with the policies of others in mind. The result of this may well be attempts at policy coordination, which will increase direct bureaucratic contacts among governmental sub-units, and which may, particularly in a multilateral context, create opportunities for international organizations to play significant roles in world politics.

In the argument that follows we will first elaborate our concept of transgovernmental relations. In succeeding sections we will discuss the role of international organizations in facilitating or promoting various types of transgovernmental relations and the utility of international organizations as points of policy intervention in transnational systems. In our conclusions we will return to the question of the complexity of the connection among transnational relations, transgovernmental relations, and international organizations over time.

Transgovernmental relations

During the last century, governments have become increasingly involved in attempting to regulate the economic and social lives of the societies they govern. As a result, they have become more sensitive to external disturbances that may affect developments within their own societies. For instance, integration of money markets internationally, in the context of governmental responsibility for national economies, has made government policy sensitive both to changes in interest rates by other governments and central banks, and to movements of funds by nongovernmental speculators. These sensitives are heightened further by the expanding decision domains of transnational organizations such as multinational business firms and banks, reinforced by decreases in the cost of transnational communications.

As the agenda broadens, bureaucracies find that to cope effectively at acceptable cost with many of the problems that arise, they must deal with each other directly rather than indirectly through foreign offices.[6] Communications among governments increase. International conferences and organizations facilitate direct contacts among officials of what were once considered primarily domestic government agencies. In the words of a former White House official, "it is a central fact of foreign relations that business is carried on by the separate departments with their counterpart bureaucracies abroad, through a variety of informal as well as formal connections. (That is especially true in alliance politics. But to a point, it also applies elsewhere.)"[7] There have always been such contacts. What seems to be new is the order of magnitude of transgovernmental relations, as bureaucracies become more complex and communications and travel costs decrease.[8]

We define transgovernmental relations as sets of direct interactions among sub-units of different governments that are not controlled or closely guided by the policies of the cabinets or chief executives of those governments. Thus we take the policies of top leaders as our benchmarks of "official government policy." Lack of control of sub-unit behavior by top leadership is obviously a matter of degree, and in practice by no means free of ambiguity. The policy of the central executive is often unclear, particularly on details, and policy means different things at different organizational levels. "One man's policy is another man's tactics."[9] As one observer has put it, "Central policy is always waffled; actors latch on to the waffled parts and form coalitions to shift policy at their level."[10] Nonetheless, to treat all actors as equal and to ignore the existence of a political hierarchy charged with "course-setting" and maintaining some hierarchy of goals is to misrepresent both constitutional and political reality.[11] It is precisely because this central policy task has become more difficult in the face of greater complexity that both the opportunities and the importance of transgovernmental interactions may be expected to have increased.

It is quite conceivable that executives entrusted with responsibility for central foreign policy, such as presidents and prime ministers, will themselves attempt to collaborate with one another in ways that conflict with the behavior of their respective bureaucracies. Yet we will regard only the relatively autonomous activities of the lower-level bureaucracies, as opposed to those of top leadership, as being transgovernmental. Otherwise, we would find ourselves in the anomalous position of regarding a head-of-state meeting, at which new initiatives that deviate from established policy are taken, as an example of "transgovernmental politics" when indeed it is almost the paradigm case for the state-centric model whose inadequacies we are criticizing. The point of our terminology is to focus attention on bureaucratic contacts that take place below the apex of the organizational hierarchy – rather than merely to apply a new label to behavior that is easily subsumed by traditional models.

In view of our interest in the opportunities that transgovernmental relations may create for international organizations, we will concentrate in this essay on *cooperative* behavior among governmental subunits. It should be recognized, however, that conflict is not excluded from transgovernmental relations any more than from other aspects of world politics. Occasionally, direct contacts among sub-units may themselves be conflictual. A case in point is "close surveillance" of each other's activities by the American and Soviet navies in the 1960's, which higher-level officials sought with some difficulty to control. Our emphasis on cooperative direct contacts does not, therefore, exclude the possibility of transgovernmental clashes of interests.

We will distinguish two major types of essentially cooperative transgovernmental behavior. Transgovernmental *policy coordination* refers to activity designed to facilitate smooth implementation or adjustment of policy, in the absence of detailed higher policy directives. Another process, *transgovernmental coalition building*, takes place when subunits build coalitions with like-minded agencies from other governments against elements of their own administrative structures. At that point, the unity of the state as a foreign policy actor breaks down. Although transgovernmental policy coordination and transgovernmental coalition building are analytically distinct processes, they merge into one another at the margin. While bearing in mind that the distinction is in some sense an artificial convenience, we will look at the two processes in turn.

Transgovernmental policy coordination

The most basic and diffuse form of transgovernmental policy coordination is simply informal communication among working-level officials of different bureaucracies. Such communication does not necessarily contradict the conventional conceptualization of states as coherent coalitions vis-à-vis the outside world, although it may have side effects that influence policy. Face-to-face communications often convey more information (intended or unintended) than indirect communications, and this additional information can affect policy expectations and preferences. It is well known that international organizations frequently provide suitable contexts for such transgovernmental communication. As one official said INTERPOL, "What's really important here are the meetings on a social level – the official agenda is only for show."[12]

Where patterns of policy coordination are regularized, it becomes misleading to think of governments as closed decision-making units. It has been argued, for example, that in the 1960's Canadian officials in Washington were "often able to inject their views into the decision making process at various stages, almost as if they were American, and to actually participate, particularly in the economic sector, in the formulation of American policy."[13] In the Skybolt affair of 1962, British complacency about American planning, before cancellation was announced, was reinforced by "a steady stream of reassurances [that] flowed back and forth between the Air Forces. The USAF saw a staunch ally in Her Majesty's Government, and *vice versa*."[14]

From regularized coordination over a period of time, changes in attitudes may result. When the same officials meet recurrently, they sometimes develop a sense of collegiality, which may be reinforced by their membership in a common profession, such as economics, physics, or meteorology. Individual officials may even define their roles partly in relation to their transnational reference group rather than in purely national terms. Thus, in discussing trade discrimination in the 1950's, Gardner Patterson argued that "an important cost of discrimination was the necessity of reporting on it and defending it periodically in semi-public forums. . . . It was costly not just in terms of time and effort, but perhaps more important, in terms of the embarrassment of having many members of the 'club' – professional colleagues – charge that another member was not living up to some of its international commitments. . . ."[15]

Regularized patterns of policy coordination can therefore create attitudes and relationships that will at least marginally change policy or affect its implementation. This has been evident particularly in relations among close allies or associates, for instance between the United States and Canada[16] or among countries of the British Commonwealth. Even in relations among countries that are politically more distant from one another, policy coordination between bureaucracies with similar interests may occasionally take place. According to press reports, at any rate, United States and Soviet space officials who were engaged in technical talks on space cooperation in 1971 went considerably further than the National Security Council had authorized at that time.[17]

Patterns of regularized policy coordination have a significance that is not limited to the examples we have cited. As such practices become widespread, transgovernmental elite networks are created, linking officials in various governments to one another by ties of common interest, professional orientation, and personal friendship.[18] Even where attitudes are not fundamentally affected and no major deviations from central policy positions occur, the existence of a sense of collegiality may permit the development of flexible bargaining behavior in which concessions need not be requited issue by issue or during each period. James Coleman has suggested that the development of "political bank accounts," where a mental reckoning of political credits and debits relaxes the need for all payoffs to be immediate, is dependent on the existence of small-group collegiality.[19] When such behavior – once the prerogative of monarchs and diplomats – spreads throughout governments, the policy structure becomes more complex and decentralized. Some of the clearest examples of such behavior have been reported by students of the political processes of common markets, such as the European Community or the Central American Common Market, where the development of a sense of collegiality enabled officials and ministers in many instances to press policy coordination beyond what would otherwise have been the case.[20]

Transgovernmental coalition building

Transgovernmental policy coordination shades over into transgovernmental coalition building when sub-units of different governments (and/or intergovernmental institutions) jointly use resources to influence governmental decisions.[21] To improve their chances of success, governmental sub-units attempt to bring actors from other governments into their own decision-making processes as allies. When such coalitions are successful, the outcomes are different than they would be if each coalition partner were limited to his own nationality. The politics of such situations are more subtle and the rules less clear than in the classical coalition theorists' cases of electoral coalitions where resources are directly transferable into influence through a set of generally accepted rules, or national bureaucratic coalitions in which players hold formal positions that legitimize their rights to participate.

Transgovernmental coalitions may be employed by sub-units of powerful states such as the United States as means by which to penetrate weaker governments. U.S. aid agencies in the 1950's and 1960's frequently played a large role in writing requests for aid from the U.S. on behalf of potential recipients, and on occasion even served a liaison function among several ministries of a foreign government.[22] In Turkey, where the Planning Office and the Finance Ministry had equal authority but contradictory views on a U.S. aid project to bring local officials together, a *de facto* coalition developed between AID officials and Finance Ministry officials.[23] The Chilean military under Allende was willing to bear possible domestic opprobrium in order to receive American military aid. To some observers, the American strategy appeared to be an attempt to use transgovernmental politics to keep the Chilean Government divided.[24]

Transgovernmental coalitions, however, can also help agencies of other governments penetrate the U.S. bureaucracy. In 1961, when the U.S. Weather Bureau disagreed with the State Department's position at the United Nations on the control of the World Weather Watch, the Director of the U.S. Weather Bureau telephoned his Canadian counterpart and they discussed the common interests of their respective weather bureaus. The position of the two weather bureaus became the official Canadian position, which led in turn to defeat of the State Department's proposals.[25] In the late 1960's, a U.S. Defense Department official, worried that delay in returning Okinawa to Japanese control might harm United States–Japanese relations, worked out with a Japanese counterpart how to phrase Japanese messages to ensure that they would enter the right channels and trigger the desired response in the U.S. bureaucracy.[26] In 1968, an Air Force general, to whom the responsibility for negotiating with Spain about military bases had been delegated, conferred secretly with his Spanish counterparts without informing civilian officials of the progress of his negotiations, and agreed to a negotiating paper that proved to be unacceptable to the Department of State. As this last case indicates, transgovernmental coalitions are not always successful: the agreement reached, which would have been favorable to the Spanish Government, was disowned by the United States, and a negative reaction against Spain took place in the Senate.[27]

It is obviously a necessary condition for explicit transgovernmental coalitions that sub-units of government have broad and intensive contacts with one another. In some sense, a degree of transgovernmental policy coordination is probably a precondition for such explicit transnational coalitions. A second set of necessary conditions has to do with conflict of interest among sub-units and the degree of central control by top executive leaders. For a transgovernmental coalition to take place, a sub-unit of one government must perceive a greater common interest with another government, or sub-units of another government, than with at least one pertinent agency in its own country; and central executive control must be loose enough to permit this perception to be translated into direct contacts with the foreign governments or agencies in question. Figure 13.1 illustrates four types of political situations based on these two dimensions.

Sub-units in a governmental system of Type 1 are most likely to seek, or be amenable to, transgovernmental coalitions. High conflict of interest among sub-units of the government suggests that there may be sub-units of other governments with which advantageous coalitions can be made; low executive power indicates that the central officials' ability to deter such coalitions is relatively small. In the other three types, by contrast, the conventional assumption of unitary actors is more likely to be valid for external affairs, although for different

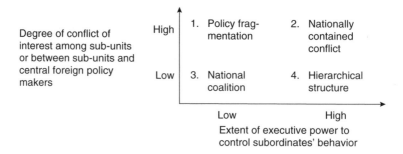

Figure 13.1 Conflict of interest and executive power in foreign policy: four types.

reasons. In Type 2, conflict is contained by a strong executive; sub-units may perceive potentially advantageous transgovernmental coalitions, but they do not dare attempt to consummate them directly. In Type 3, low conflict of interest among domestic governmental sub-units ensures that the option of national coalition generally seems more attractive than the transgovernmental alternative, even in the absence of strong central control. Type 4, of course, exemplifies the traditional situation: national coalition reinforced by effective hierarchy.

Relatively frequent contacts among governmental sub-units, looseness of governmental hierarchies (low executive control), and relatively high conflict of interest within governments are all necessary conditions for the development of explicit transgovernmental coalitions. But they are not in themselves sufficient. In the first place, for coalitions to be feasible, actors with common interests must be able to combine their resources effectively. That means that political resources (such as funds, prestige, information, and consent – where required, for instance, by the rules of an international organization) of actors outside a government must be valuable to at least some actors within it. This requires a political context that is relatively open and free of xenophobia, since in a xenophobic society foreign resources are heavily devalued, or regarded negatively, by virtue of their origin. Even in democratic societies, the borderline between legitimate transgovernmental behavior and treason may be unclear.

The need for resources that can be aggregated suggests that transgovernmental behavior may be particularly important in issue areas in which functionally defined international organizations operate. The procedures of the organization itself, for reaching agreement among its members, insure that the resources of one actor – at least its votes – may be useful to another; insofar as the organization has a specialized, functional orientation, the activities of national representatives may not be closely supervised by top leaders or their agents. More generally, the greater the natural sensitivity of governmental policies and the wider the acceptance of joint decision making on issues that cross national lines, the greater the legitimacy of transgovernmental bargaining is likely to be. An international organization, by symbolizing governments' beliefs in the need for joint decision making, tends to strengthen the legitimacy of this activity.

International organizations and potential coalitions

Recurrent international conferences and other activities of international organizations help to increase transgovernmental contacts and thus create opportunities for the development of transgovernmental coalitions. The number of intergovernmental organizations more than tripled between 1945 and 1965. Nongovernmental organizations have grown even more rapidly.[28] In Europe, the Commission of the European Communities has played a major role in the growth of such contacts, with the result that "there is a steady flow of national economic and administrative elites to the seat of Community decision-making."[29] These elites are drawn from many sectors of national bureaucracies, by no means entirely from foreign offices. The pattern is not confined to Europe: In 1962, of some 2,786 people who represented the United States at international conferences, more came from other departments of the government than from the State Department.[30]

Governments must organize themselves to cope with the fact that the flow of business, including such conferences, is often transacted under the auspices of international organizations. The organizations' definitions of which issues cluster together and which should be considered separately may help to determine the nature of interdepartmental committees and other arrangements within governments. In the long run, therefore, international organizations will affect how government officials define "issue areas." The existence of the International Monetary Fund and the General Agreement on Tariffs and Trade, for example, helps to focus governmental activity in the monetary and trade fields, in contrast to the area of private direct investment, in which no comparable international organization exists.

The fact that international organizations bring officials together should alert us to their effect in activating *potential* coalitions in world politics. Many sub-units of governments, which do not as a matter of course come into contact with each other, may have common or complementary interests. Indeed, we may speak of some potential coalitions as *de facto* "tacit coalitions" if the independent actions of one member seem to serve the interests of others and vice versa. One of the important but seldom-noted roles of international organizations in world politics is to provide the arena for sub-units of governments to turn potential or tacit coalitions into explicit coalitions characterized by direct communication among the partners. In this particular bit of political alchemy, the organization provides physical proximity, an agenda of issues on which interaction is to take place, and an aura of legitimacy. Informal discussions occur naturally in meetings of international organizations, and it is difficult, given the milieu, for other sub-units of one's own government to object to these contacts.

It is intriguing to ask specifically why some potential coalitions become active while others remain merely potential. It is easy to see why the parallel interests of the American and Soviet armed forces (in large military budgets) are not reflected in transgovernmental coalitions between military officers in the superpowers; but it may be more difficult to determine whether the common interests of central bankers in a stable currency system have been implemented as fully by transgovernmental contacts as they might have been. To take another example, the natural allies of the American farmer – and therefore of the Department of Agriculture – in seeking access to European markets are the European urban dwellers and European finance- and consumer-oriented ministers, rather than the European farmers and agriculture ministers. However, this kind of potential coalition between agriculture officials in the United States and non-agriculture officials in Europe is difficult to organize, since regular contacts have not been established. The contrast between the difficulty involved here and the close ties existing among European agriculture ministries is instructive. Where analogous agencies with close patterns of working relationships have common interests and participate in the same international organizations, it is likely to be much easier to create coalitions on the basis of those common interests than where the potential coalitions include a variety of actors that are not used to working closely with one another.

Even without an active secretariat, therefore, international organizations are of considerable relevance in many issue areas of world politics because they help to transform potential or tacit coalitions into explicit ones. When issues are linked or dealt with in institutional arenas with broad mandates, heterogeneous coalitions can be formed. Narrow institutional mandates discriminate against such coalitions. Thus, by defining the issues to be considered together, and by excluding others, international organizations may significantly affect political processes and outcomes in world politics, quite apart from active lobbying by their secretariats.

The second important role for international organizations, however, is the active one. Most intergovernmental organizations have secretariats, and like all bureaucracies they have their own interests and goals that are defined through an interplay of staff and clientele. International secretariats can be viewed both as catalysts and as potential members of coalitions; their distinctive resources tend to be information and an aura of international legitimacy. As Robert Cox has put it, "the executive head needs to fortify his position by alliance with domestic pressure groups. He must not limit himself to 'foreign' politics but know how to make domestic politics work in favor of his policies."[31] To the extent that the conditions enumerated in the first part of this article permit sub-units of governments to engage in transgovernmental coalitions, we would expect international secretariats or components of secretariats to form explicit or implicit coalitions with sub-units of governments as well as with nongovernmental organizations having similar interests.

Examples of alliances between parts of secretariats and governments are not hard to find. Many organizations have divisions that are regarded as fiefdoms of particular governments.[32] In a number of cases, lower-level officials of a secretariat have lobbied with governments in efforts to thwart the declared policy of their secretaries-general.[33] Representatives of UN specialized agencies in developing countries often strengthen old-line ministries against their rivals in central planning offices.[34] Chilean conservatives have used IMF missions to bolster their political positions.[35] With reference to the World Health Organization (WHO), Harold Jacobson argues that "many government representatives to WHO almost can be viewed as the director-general's agents or lobbyists within country sub-systems."[36] In some cases, international organizations initiate the formation of transgovernmental coalitions; in others, they or their own sub-units are recruited to the coalitions by sub-units of governments.

It must be recognized, however, that this activist, coalition-building role of international organizations is usually closely circumscribed. By no means is it a sure recipe for success. Yet the alternatives of passivity or of frontally challenging traditional notions of national sovereignty are usually less attractive. Secretariat officials often find the only feasible alternative to be to help governments, or sectors of governments, to perceive problems differently and to use their own resources in innovative ways. For example, as Ruggie points out, the World Weather Watch is not a supra-national operation but a set of national activities that the World Meteorological Organization (perceived as an ally by most weather bureaus) helps to coordinate, and the distribution of whose results it encourages.[37] Similarly, Maurice Strong has defined the role of the UN Environmental Office as one of stimulating the creation of new environmental units in member states, serving as an ally providing information and prestige for them, and thus encouraging a redefinition of "national interests."[38]

Coalition-building shades down into transgovernmental policy coordination in this example, as is frequently the case. On a long-term and somewhat diffuse basis, the communications that take place as a result of policy coordination and conferences may be as important as the coalitions that form on particular issues. As we have seen earlier, international organizations facilitate face-to-face meetings among officials in "domestic" agencies of different governments who would have little to do with each other in traditional interstate politics. Strategically-minded secretariats of international organizations could very well plan meetings with a view toward this transgovernmental communications function. Recurrent interactions can change officials' perceptions of their activities and interests. As Bauer, Pool, and Dexter have pointed out in their discussion of the United States politics of foreign trade, concentrating only on pressures of various interests for decisions leads to an overly mechanistic view of a continuous process and neglects the important role of communications in slowly changing perceptions of "self-interest."[39]

Conditions for the involvement of international organizations

To the extent that transgovernmental relations are common in a given issue area, under what conditions should we expect international organizations, in the sense of intergovernmental organizations, to be involved in them? One set of cases is obvious: where the international organization itself has created the network of elites. Thus, both the International Labor Organization (ILO) and the World Health Organization (WHO), as described by Cox and Jacobson, are characterized by extensive "participant subsystems" that link national trade unions, employers, and government officials to the ILO secretariat, and health-care professionals to WHO's bureaucracy.[40]

More generally, however, we would expect international organizations to become involved in transgovernmental politics on issues requiring some central point or agency for coordination. This implies that international organizations are likely to be most extensively involved on complex, multilateral issues in which major actors perceive a need for information and for communication with other actors, in addition to the traditional functions, as listed by Skolnikoff, of "1) provision of services, 2) norm creation and allocation, 3) rule observance and settlement of disputes, and 4) operation."[41] Insofar as patterns of politics follow the transgovernmental mode, increasing the number of actors will tend to create greater demands for communication with other actors (often of different types), as well as for information about both technical and political conditions. International secretariats staffed with knowledgeable individuals, even without traditional sources of power, have the opportunity to place themselves at the center of crucial communications networks, and thereby acquire influence as brokers, facilitators, and suggestors of new approaches. They will continue to be dependent on governments for funds and legal powers; but the relevant agencies of governments may be dependent on them for information and for the policy coordination, by a legitimate system-wide actor, which is required to achieve their own objectives.

International organizations and intervention in transnational systems

Thus far we have discussed two ways in which international organizations are relevant in world politics – as arenas and as members of transgovernmental coalitions. They may also be important as points of potential governmental intervention in predominantly nongovernmental transactional systems.

Analysts of world politics have begun to talk less about *the* international system, and to realize that there are significant variations among systems in different issue areas.[42] There are differences in degree of interdependence of units, in hierarchy among units, and in clarity of the demarcation of the systems' boundaries.[43] There are also differences in degree of governmental participation. In many issue systems, nongovernmental actors account for a major portion of activities that cross national boundaries. To the extent that this is the case, we can refer to the issue system as a transnational one. The more transnational a system, the more likely it is that nongovernmental actors constitute the basic initiating and compelling forces in it. That does not imply that governments are absent from these systems. On the contrary, they may be very important actors. But their actions will be largely focused on regulation and control of transnational activities.

Governments frequently attempt to use international organizations to achieve this regulation. Secretariats of international organizations may themselves perceive problems in the operation of these systems, as well as opportunities for their organizations to act effectively. The same is true of nongovernmental actors or sub-units of governments that may have interests at stake. Thus, the control of important transnational systems is and will remain a significant political focus for the activity of international organizations.

Analysis of this struggle for control, and the implications it has for international organizations, may be facilitated by thinking of transnational systems as having five key points of policy intervention insofar as any two states are concerned, with correspondingly more as additional states are included:

1. internal measures in country A;
2. border measures by country A;
3. international or transnational organizational measures;
4. border measures by country B;
5. internal measures in country B.

As a simple example, consider the following hypothetical incident in a transnational system based on a free market for skilled labor. Filipino doctors leave their native country to work in American hospitals for much higher salaries, with the consequence that a Filipino peasant dies from a simple disease because his village has no doctor, while there is a relative abundance of Filipino doctors in some American hospitals.

Table 13.1 illustrates the five points at which policy can affect this transnational system: two (1 and 5) are generally considered purely "domestic"; two (2 and 4) are "border controls" where the interdependence of states is recognized but jurisdiction lies with only one state; and one (3) is an operating intergovernmental bureaucracy. Similar diagrams could be drawn for other transnational systems, including those involving monetary relations, trade, environmental pollution, and international investment. In all these cases, movements of people, funds, goods, or pollutants across national boundaries can be affected at any of these five points of intervention, insofar as two countries are concerned. As the two examples labeled

Table 13.1 A transnational system of "Brain Drain"

	Village in Philippines	*Manila (port of exit)*		*Boston (port of entry)*	*U.S. hospital staffed by foreigners*
Points of policy intervention, with possible strategies to reduce "brain drain" counterstrategies lending to facilitate it:	1 *Phil. Internal* (persuade doctors to stay through financial or other incentives)	2 *Phil. Border* (deny exit visas or impose exit levies)	3 *I.O.* (WHO sends doctors to Philippines)	4 *U.S. Border* (restrict entry visas)	5 *U.S. Internal* (discriminate against foreign doctors)
				(*counter*: encourage entry of skilled personnel)	(*counter*: recruit foreign doctors)

"counter" in Table 13.1 indicate, state policies may tend to thwart as well as to complement one another.[44]

In principle, domestic measures, border controls, and international organizations can complement, countervail, or substitute for each other. From a system-wide point of view, therefore, the policy problem in the abstract is merely one of finding the most efficient point or combination of points of intervention. For the monetary system, an economist may ask which combination of fiscal and monetary policy changes, exchange controls and/or trade barriers, and changes in IMF or GATT rules will produce the desired equilibrium. In practice, however, different groups generally have different interests and different degrees of influence at various points of policy intervention. Although there may be more or less common interest in system management, there are also likely to be conflicts. The holders of certain sets of interests may prefer that only certain potential points of policy intervention be used, and only in particular ways. Others may be opposed to all controls on transnational systems from which they benefit. Thus the choice of points of intervention is itself an important policy decision that imposes constraints on subsequent action. Insofar as control over an international organization confers influence over a transnational system, or a means to discourage intervention at some other policy point in the system, the organization can be an important stake in political conflict.

Actors' strategies and the uses of international organizations

If transnational relations are important in a set of issues, an explanation of outcomes made simply in terms of "sovereignty" and "national interests" will be insufficient. There is also, however, a distributional question. Some actors may believe that they are adversely affected by transnational activities and will seek strategies to cope with these perceived problems.

The most obvious response by disadvantaged groups is to use the weapons of sovereignty against the transnational adversary. Insofar as national regulation can be effective, groups with national political strength can redress the balance. In the field of international trade, tariff and non-tariff barriers are familiar strategies. To curb direct investment, nationally oriented groups may resort to expropriation, strict regulation, or bans on the flow of capital or technology. For example, the AFL-CIO in the United States supported the restrictive Burke-Hartke bill as a means of legislating relief from problems of "runaway plants" and the "export of jobs."

The chief difficulty with national solutions in the context of interdependence is that they may not only be ineffective, but may lead to policy conflicts among states, as governments attempt to counter the adverse effects of other governments' actions. This is the familiar "beggar-thy-neighbor" problem, applicable to a wide variety of issues in which interdependence is high. National actions to reduce the adverse effects of *societal* interdependence may have the paradoxical effect of increasing *policy* interdependence: that is, such measures may increase the extent to which governments depend on the actions of other governments for the achievement of their own goals.

In such a situation of policy interdependence, sub-units of governments are likely to resort to transgovernmental policy coordination or transgovernmental coalition building, as discussed above, making use of existing international organizations to facilitate these relationships. Yet in the context of intense transnational activity by nongovernmental actors, this may lead not merely to transgovernmental coalitions but to mixed coalitions including nongovernmental as well as governmental agents. According to one description of a preparatory session for the Conference on the Law of the Sea, for instance, officials of the United States Department of the Interior and representatives of certain multinational enterprises (both of which favored a definition of a wide continental shelf) lobbied with representatives of foreign governments against the declared U.S. policy (preferred by the Departments of State and Defense) of a narrow shelf.[45]

Such a strategy is inappropriate for actors whose political resources are predominantly domestic. Having perceived that national self-encapsulation is a futile strategy, or having tried such a strategy unsuccessfully, actors may seek to politicize (i.e. increase the controversy over) an issue. By increasing controversy, they would hope to raise the level in the government at which the issue is considered – in order to reduce the scope for transgovernmental and transnational political strategies. Central political officials – responsible directly to the public in one way or another – would then negotiate internationally in the interests of nationally based groups. This could be called a nationalassertion strategy (represented by the Nixon-Connally policies of 1971), as distinguished from a national protection strategy (illustrated by the Burke-Hartke bill). Thus, as Robert Russell has shown, transgovernmental coalitions among central bankers and working-level officials were increasingly constrained even before the events of 1971, as monetary issues became more controversial.[46] Such a strategy may well lead to the decline of international organizations which were established on different premises. In some cases, however, issues may be politicized partly by using international organizations to bring them to the attention of higher-level officials. The point is illustrated by the examples of UNCTAD in the trade field, and by UN investigations into operations of multinational firms.

Issues are unlikely, in general, to remain indefinitely at the top level of governmental attention. Politicization may facilitate the resolution of issues, or at least the establishment of new structures and new assumptions within which particular questions can be settled at lower levels of the governmental hierarchy. International organizations may also be important at this "depoliticization" stage, in once again facilitating transgovernmental coalitions. But the important point here is that if substantial restructuring has taken place, the coalitions that form will be different than they were before. Potential coalitions that could not be actualized in earlier periods may become possible now, and different groups may benefit. Thus, an international monetary organization set up to monitor floating exchange rates would look quite different from the IMF of the 1960's, which was premised on fixed but adjustable rates. An international organization established to keep non-tariff barriers within stated limits might give more leeway to coalitions of protectionist groups than GATT, with its prohibition on quantitative restrictions.

It is therefore too simple to contend, as is often done, that the basic strategic choice is between national encapsulation and internationalism. Internationalism has many dimensions, with very different implications for group interests as well as for normative values. International strategies by interested groups, as we have indicated, may take any of three forms: (1) exploitation of transgovernmental or mixed transnational-transgovernmental coalitions within an established framework of policy, and through established international organizations; (2) politicization of issues to remove them from transgovernmental bargaining, reemphasizing the role of responsible top officials of governments; and (3) restructuring of issues, as a result of a period of politicization, so that new transgovernmental and mixed coalitions can become effective, perhaps under the aegis of new or substantially altered international organizations. The second and third strategies, in particular, are not mutually exclusive but may reflect different phases in a cycle. When internationalization as a strategy for dealing with transnational issues is considered, distinctions such as these should be made.

Conclusions

It should be clear from the examples we have chosen that we do not regard the involvement of international organizations in transnational and transgovernmental coalitions as necessarily contributing to global welfare or equity. Like other political institutions, international organizations reflect the interests as well as the attitudes of actors that are powerful in them. Opportunities for impact by international organizations by no means assure their autonomy or their dedication to the commonweal. Increased opportunities for certain international organizations may in some cases lead to the fragmentation of an international effort, which Sir Robert Jackson criticized, or to the pursuit of the interests of well-placed groups at the expense of the interests of less fortunate but larger sectors of the population. The effects of transgovernmental politics on the efficacy of democratic control may be very serious.[47] In some circumstances, an expansion of the influence of international organizations in ways such as we have suggested here may be undesirable. There is no magic wand that makes it unnecessary to undertake detailed, case-by-case normative analyses of the actions of international organizations.

With respect to empirical projections, our prognosis differs from that of the international functionalists and others who see transnational systems and societal interdependence as making national governments obsolete.[48] While there are some valid elements in the functionalist scenario, we suggest the following alternative view as somewhat more plausible.

The development of transgovernmental relations, as well as the involvement of international organizations in them, is generally stimulated by the activities of elites trying to cope with increased *societal* interdependence. Dynamic nongovernmental forces frequently provoke increased governmental efforts at control. However, as a side effect of increasing interchange among elites, transgovernmental politics and the activities of international organizations are likely to increase *policy* inter-dependence. That is, the policies of relevant actors – central foreign policy organs of governments, other governmental agencies, transnational actors, or secretariats of international organizations – will increasingly depend for their success on actions and reactions of other actors. Succumbing to one form of interdependence may be the price one pays for avoiding another. Efforts to cope with policy inter-dependence will in turn further broaden the scope of interstate agendas, involve more bureaucracies (national, international, and transnational), and thus provide more occasions for transgovernmental relations. For top leaders this leads to the further problem of losing effective control of their own sprawling and transgovernmentally active bureaucracies. A continuing struggle between groups favoring transgovernmental policy patterns and those supporting a return to strategies of national assertion or national protection is likely to ensue. Figure 13.2 provides a highly simplified sketch of some of the causal relations that may contribute to political struggles of this type.

This is not an argument for the superiority of international or transnational as opposed to national solutions, nor does it suggest a general view of the merits of international institutions. We have simply sought to establish the political signifi-cance of international organizations in certain issue areas – as arenas and members of transgovernmental coalitions, and as potential points of intervention in transna-tional systems. International organizations are not necessarily weak "because they are inherently the arenas for national actors," or because they require "*accord* among nations."[49] Which bureaucracies represent the nation? Who defines the "national interest," and how does it change over time? Is there transgovernmental coordination? Are there mixed coalitions of transgovernmental, transnational, and international actors? Viewed from the perspective of these questions, it is not always – or only – the transnational organizations that are "busily deployed across the continents spinning the webs that link the world together."[50]

A major policy task for those who create and manage international institutions is to ask themselves whether there are areas of activity in which international organizations could make an impact by aligning their activities with sub-units of governments. As Ruggie points out, traditional images of interstate politics and international organizations as entities "above" states unduly constrain institutional imagination.[51] Understanding the transnational and transgovernmental politics of an issue as well as the technical, economic, or military nature of the problem may

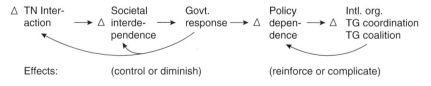

Figure 13.2 Hypothetical causal relations involving transnational systems and transgov-ernmental relations.

permit a wider choice of organizational strategy and structure, and in some cases more constructive outcomes.

International organizations are rarely optimally efficient, and they are frequently quite unsatisfactory. Some improvements are possible, but many government officials will always find them hard to live with. For the foreseeable future, however, it seems that they will be impossible to live without. And if that is true, their political role and impact on various issues in world politics deserve both more and a new type of attention.

Notes

* We profited from discussions of this subject with Hayward Alker, Graham Allison, Robert Dickerman, Samuel Huntington, Alex Inkeles, Peter J. Katzenstein, Stephen Krasner, John Ruggie, Robert Russell, Harrison Wagner, and other members of the Transnational Relations Study Group at the Harvard Center for International Affairs. Support for this research was provided by the Ford Foundation.

1 For a general discussion, see Robert O. Keohane and Joseph S. Nye, Jr., eds., *Transnational Relations and World Politics* (Cambridge, Mass. 1972). For documentation of the point based on a survey of the literature, see John R. Handelman, John A. Vasquez, Michael K. O'Leary, and William D. Coplin, "Color it Morgenthau: A Data-Based Assessment of Quantitative International Relations Research," paper delivered to the International Studies Association, March 1973.

2 Samuel P. Huntington, "Transnational Organizations in World Politics," *World Politics*, xxv (April 1973), 333–68; quotations from pp. 338, 339, and 368 respectively.

3 *Ibid.*, 358.

4 *Ibid.*, 348–49.

5 This is a slight modification of our usage in the volume cited above. We used the term "transnational interactions" to refer to "interactions in which one actor was nongovernmental," and the term "transnational relations" as a generic category that included both "transnational and transgovernmental interactions." We have become convinced that this was unnecessarily confusing. For a stimulating critique of our language as well as our ideas, see R. Harrison Wagner, "Dissolving the State: Three Recent Perspectives on International Relations," *International Organization*, xxviii (Spring 1974).

6 Karl Kaiser has been a pioneer in developing arguments about what he calls "multibureaucratic politics." See in particular his "Transnational Politics: Toward a Theory of Multinational Politics," *International Organization*, xxv (Autumn 1971), and "Transnational Relations as a Threat to the Democratic Process," in Keohane and Nye (fn. 1).

7 Testimony of Francis Bator before the Subcommittee on Foreign Economic Policy, Committee on Foriegn Affairs, House of Representatives, July 25, 1972. *U.S. Foreign Economic Policy: Implications for the Organization of the Executive Branch*, 110–11.

8 See John F. Campbell, *The Foreign Affairs Fudge Factory* (New York 1971), 204 ff., for figures on the United States. On Britain, see Anthony Sampson, "The Institutions of British Foreign Policy," in Karl Kaiser and Roger Morgan, eds., *Britain and West Germany: Changing Societies and the Future of Foreign Policy* (London 1971).

9 Raymond Bauer, "The Study of Policy Formation," in Raymond Bauer and Kenneth Gergen, eds., *The Study of Policy Formation* (New York 1968), 2.

10 M. S. Hochmuth, comments at Transnational Relations Study Group Seminar, Center for International Affairs, Harvard University, February 8, 1972.

11 Stephen Krasner, "Are Bureaucracies Important?" *Foreign Policy*, VII (Summer 1972).
12 *New York Times*, October 1, 1972.
13 Dale Thompson, Testimony before Standing Committee on External Affairs and National Defense, House of Commons (Canada), *Minutes of Proceedings and Evidence*, April 28, 1970.
14 Richard E. Neustadt, *Alliance Politics* (New York 1970), 37.
15 Gardner Patterson, *Discrimination in International Trade: The Policy Issues* (Princeton 1966), 36.
16 See K. J. Holsti, "The United States and Canada," in Steven Spiegel and Kenneth Waltz, eds., *Conflict in World Politics* (Cambridge, Mass. 1971).
17 *New York Times*, December 4, 6, and 16, 1971.
18 Our thinking on the subject of elite networks was stimulated by our friend and valued colleague, the late Ivan Vallier, who was undertaking systematic research on elite networks in Latin America until his death in January 1974.
19 James Coleman, "Political Money," *American Political Science Review*, LXIV (December 1970), 1074–87.
20 See Leon Lindberg and Stuart Scheingold, *Europe's Would-Be Polity* (Englewood Cliffs, N.J. 1970); Lawrence Sheinman, "Some Preliminary Notes on Bureaucratic Relationships in the EEC," *International Organization*, XX (Autumn 1966); and Joseph S. Nye, Jr., "Central American Regional Integration," *International Conciliation*, No. 562 (March 1967).
21 This definition is based on the article by William A. Gamson on "Coalitions," in the *International Encyclopedia of Social Science*.
22 Theodore Geiger and Roger Hansen, "The Role of Information in Decision Making on Foreign Aid," in Bauer and Gergen (fn. 9).
23 Based on conversations with a participant (1973).
24 *New York Times*, December 9, 1972.
25 Edward Miles, "Transnationalism in Space: Inner and Outer," in Keohane and Nye (fn. 1).
26 Based on conversations with a participant (1972).
27 In the cases of the weather bureau and the Spanish bases, the United States Government was divided while the smaller state apparently had a relatively unified policy. In terms of coherence, these relationships were asymmetrical in favor of Canada and Spain, respectively. Spain, Nationalist China, Israel, and Canada are among the countries that have taken advantage of the size and diversity of the United States Government to create asymmetries of coherence in their favor to counter asymmetries of power in favor of the United States. See Robert O. Keohane, "The Big Influence of Small Allies," *Foreign Policy*, II (Spring 1971). For Canadian cases, see Roger Swanson, "The United States Canadian Constellation I: Washington, D.C.," *International Journal*, XXVII (Spring 1972), 185–218; Holsti (fn. 18); and J. S. Nye, "Transnational Relations and Interstate Conflict: An Empirical Analysis," *International Organization*, XXVIII (Autumn 1974).
28 J. David Singer and Michael Wallace, "Intergovernmental Organization in the Global System, 1815–1964," *International Organization*, XXIV (Spring 1970); Robert C. Angell, *Peace on the March: Transnational Participation* (New York 1969).
29 Lindberg and Scheingold (fn. 20), 80.
30 Arnold Beichman, *The "Other" State Department* (New York 1967), 92.
31 Robert W. Cox, "The Executive Head," *International Organization*, XXIII (Spring 1969), 225.
32 See, for example, J. S. Nye, "UNCTAD: Poor Nations' Pressure Group," in Robert W. Cox and Harold K. Jacobson, eds., *The Anatomy of Influence: Decision Making in International Organization* (New Haven 1973).
33 James Magee discusses a situation in which FAO bureaucrats conspired with African governments to thwart the director's decision to relocate two offices. "ECA and the

Paradox of African Cooperation," *International Conciliation*, No. 580 (November 1970).

34 See Leon Gordenker, "Multilateral Aid and Influence on Government Policies," in Robert W. Cox, ed., *International Organization: World Politics* (London 1969). A related example is provided by the Jackson Report, which indicated that its investigations "revealed example after example where Departmental Ministers have advocated policies in the governing bodies of the particular agency which concerned them (e.g. a Minister of Agriculture in FAO, or a Minister of Education in UNESCO) which were in direct conflict with his government's policies toward the UN system as a whole." United Nations, *A Study of the Capacity of the United Nations Development System*, Vol. I (Geneva 1969), v.

35 See Albert Hirschman, *Journeys Toward Progress* (New York 1965), 291 ff.

36 Harold K. Jacobson, "WHO: Medicine, Regionalism, and Managed Politics," in Cox and Jacobson (fn. 32), 214.

37 John G. Ruggie, "The World Weather Watch," unpub., 1972.

38 Based on conversations with Strong during 1972.

39 Raymond Bauer, Ithiel de Sola Pool, and Lewis Dexter, *American Business and Foreign Policy* (New York 1963), chap. 35, esp. pp. 472–75.

40 See Harold K. Jacobson, "WHO: Medicine, Regionalism, and Managed Politics," pp. 194–205; and Robert W. Cox, "ILO: Limited Monarchy," pp. 114–27, in Cox and Jacobson (fn. 32).

41 Eugene B. Skolnikoff, "Science and Technology: The Implications for International Institutions," *International Organization*, XXV (Autumn 1971), 772.

42 James N. Rosenau, "Pre-Theories and Theories of Foreign Policy," in R. Barry Farrell, ed., *Approaches to Comparative and International Politics* (Evanston, Ill. 1966), 73–74. For another suggestive discussion of world politics in terms of networks of systems, see John Burton, *Systems, States, Diplomacy and Rules* (Cambridge 1968), esp. pp. 6–10.

43 For a discussion of the conditions of existence for a system, see the article by Anatol Rapoport on "Systems," in the *International Encyclopedia of the Social Sciences*, p. 452.

44 Where a larger number of countries is involved, problems of effectiveness become much more complex, and interdependence is likely to be more intricate.

45 This situation was described to us by two government officials. See also Ann Hollick, "Seabeds make Strange Politics," *Foreign Policy*, IX (Winter 1972–73).

46 Robert W. Russell, "Transgovernmental Interaction in the International Monetary System, 1960–1972," *International Organization*, XXVII (Autumn 1973).

47 See Kaiser in Keohane and Nye (fn. 6).

48 See, for example, Angell (fn. 28); and David Mitrany, *A Working Peace System* (Chicago 1966).

49 Huntington (fn. 2), 338.

50 *Ibid.*, 339.

51 John G. Ruggie, "The Structure of International Organization: Contingency, Complexity, and Post-Modern Form," *Peace Research Society*, Papers, XVIII, 1971, 73–91.

14 Globalization*

What's new? what's not?
(and so what?)

with Robert O. Keohane

"Globalization" emerged as a buzzword in the 1990s, just as "interdependence" did in the 1970s, but the phenomena it refers to are not entirely new. Our characterization of interdependence more than 20 years ago now applies to globalization at the turn of the millennium: "This vague phrase expresses a poorly understood but widespread feeling that the very nature of world politics is changing." Some skeptics believe such terms are beyond redemption for analytic use. Yet the public understands the image of the globe, and the new word conveys an increased sense of vulnerability to distant causes. For example, as helicopters fumigated New York City in 1999 to eradicate a lethal new virus, the press announced that the pathogen might have arrived in the bloodstream of a traveler, in a bird smuggled through customs, or in a mosquito that had flown into a jet. Fears of "bioinvasion" led some environmental groups to call for a reduction in global trade and travel.

Like all popular concepts meant to cover a variety of phenomena, both "interdependence" and "globalization" have many meanings. To understand what people are talking about when they use the terms and to make them useful for analysis, we must begin by asking whether interdependence and globalization are simply two words for the same thing, or whether there is something new going on.

The dimensions of globalism

The two words are not exactly parallel. Interdependence refers to a condition, a state of affairs. It can increase, as it has been doing on most dimensions since the end of World War II; or it can decline, as it did, at least in economic terms, during the Great Depression of the 1930s. Globalization implies that something is increasing: there is more of it. Hence, our definitions start not with globalization but with "globalism," a condition that can increase or decrease.

Globalism is a state of the world involving networks of interdependence at multicontinental distances. The linkages occur through flows and influences of capital and goods, information and ideas, and people and forces, as well as environmentally and biologically relevant substances (such as acid rain or pathogens). Globalization and deglobalization refer to the increase or decline of globalism.

Interdependence refers to situations characterized by reciprocal effects among countries or among actors in different countries. Hence, globalism is a type of interdependence, but with two special characteristics. First, globalism refers to networks of connections (multiple relationships), not to single linkages. We would refer to economic or military interdependence between the United States and Japan, but not to globalism between the United States and Japan. U.S.–Japanese interdependence is part of contemporary globalism, but is not by itself globalism.

Second, for a network of relationships to be considered "global," it must include multicontinental distances, not simply regional networks. Distance is a continuous variable, ranging from adjacency (between, say, the United States and Canada) to opposite sides of the globe (for instance, Great Britain and Australia). Any sharp distinction between long-distance and regional interdependence is therefore arbitrary, and there is no point in deciding whether intermediate relationships – say, between Japan and India or between Egypt and South Africa – would qualify. Yet globalism would be an odd word for proximate regional relationships. Globalization refers to the shrinkage of distance on a large scale [see box on pages 110]. It can be contrasted with localization, nationalization, or regionalization.

Some examples may help. Islam's rapid diffusion from Arabia across Asia to what is now Indonesia was a clear instance of globalization, but the initial movement of Hinduism across the Indian subcontinent was not. Ties among the countries of the Asia Pacific Economic Cooperation forum qualify as multicontinental interdependence, because these countries include the Americas as well as Asia and Australia; but ties among members of the Association of Southeast Asian Nations are regional.

Globalism does not imply universality. At the turn of the millennium, more than a quarter of the American population used the World Wide Web compared with one hundredth of 1 percent of the population of South Asia. Most people in the world today do not have telephones; hundreds of millions live as peasants in remote villages with only slight connections to world markets or the global flow of ideas. Indeed, globalization is accompanied by increasing gaps, in many respects, between the rich and the poor. It implies neither homogenization nor equity.

Interdependence and globalism are both multidimensional phenomena. All too often, they are defined in strictly economic terms, as if the world economy defined globalism. But there are several, equally important forms of globalism:

- *Economic globalism* involves long-distance flows of goods, services, and capital, as well as the information and perceptions that accompany market exchange. It also involves the organization of the processes that are linked to these flows, such as the organization of low-wage production in Asia for the U.S. and European markets.
- *Military globalism* refers to long-distance networks of interdependence in which force, and the threat or promise of force, are employed. A good example of military globalism is the "balance of terror" between the United States and the Soviet Union during the cold war. The two countries' strategic interdependence was acute and well recognized. Not only did it produce world-straddling alliances, but either side could have used intercontinental missiles to destory the other within 30 minutes. Their interdependence was distinctive not because

it was totally new, but because the scale and speed of the potential conflict arising from it were so enormous.

- *Environmental globalism* refers to the long-distance transport of materials in the atmosphere or oceans, or of biological substances such as pathogens or genetic materials, that affect human health and wellbeing. The depletion of the stratospheric ozone layer as a result of ozone-depleting chemicals is an example of environmental globalism, as is the spread of the AIDS virus from west equatorial Africa around the world since the end of the 1970s. Some environmental globalism may be entirely natural, but much of the recent change has been induced by human activity.
- *Social and cultural globalism* involves the movement of ideas, information, images, and people (who, of course, carry ideas and information with them). Examples include the movement of religions or the diffusion of scientific knowledge. An important facet of social globalism involves the imitation of one society's practices and institutions by others: what some sociologists refer to as "isomorphism." Often, however, social globalism has followed military and economic globalism. Ideas, information, and people follow armies and economic flows, and in doing so, transform societies and markets. At its most profound level, social globalism affects the consciousness of individuals and their attitudes toward culture, politics, and personal identity. Indeed, social and cultural globalism interacts with other types of globalism, because military, environmental, and economic activity convey information and generate ideas, which may then flow across geographical and political boundaries. In the current era, as the growth of the Internet reduces costs and globalizes communications, the flow of ideas is increasingly independent of other forms of globalization.

This division of globalism into separate dimensions is inevitably somewhat arbitrary. Nonetheless, it is useful for analysis, because changes in the various dimensions of globalization do not necessarily occur simultaneously. One can sensibly say, for instance, that economic globalization took place between approximately 1850 and 1914, manifested in imperialism and increased trade and capital flows between politically independent countries; and that such globalization was largely reversed between 1914 and 1945. That is, economic globalism rose between 1850 and 1914 and fell between 1914 and 1945. However, military globalism rose to new heights during the two world wars, as did many aspects of social globalism. The worldwide influenza epidemic of 1918–19, which took 30 million lives, was propagated in part by the flows of soldiers around the world. So did globalism decline or rise between 1914 and 1945? It depends on what dimension of globalism one is examining.

Contemporary globalism

When people speak colloquially about globalization, they typically refer to recent increases in globalism. In this context, comments such as "globalization is fundamentally new" make sense but are nevertheless misleading. We prefer to speak of globalism as a phenomenon with ancient roots and of globalization as the process of increasing globalism, now or in the past.

The issue is not how old globalism is, but rather how "thin" or "thick" it is at any given time. As an example of "thin globalization," the Silk Road provided an economic and cultural link between ancient Europe and Asia, but the route was plied by a small group of hardy traders, and the goods that were traded back and forth had a direct impact primarily on a small (and relatively elite) stratum of consumers along the road. In contrast, "thick" relations of globalization, as described by political scientist David Held and others, involve many relationships that are intensive as well as extensive: long-distance flows that are large and continuous, affecting the lives of many people. The operations of global financial markets today, for instance, affect people from Peoria to Penang. Globalization is the process by which globalism becomes increasingly thick.

Globalism today is different from globalism of the 19th century, when European imperialism provided much of its political structure, and higher transport and communications costs meant fewer people were directly involved. But is there anything about globalism today that is fundamentally different from just 20 years ago? To say that something is "fundamentally" different is always problematic, since absolute discontinuities do not exist in human history. Every era builds on others, and historians can always find precursors for phenomena of the present. Journalist Thomas Friedman argues that contemporary globalization goes "farther, faster, deeper, and cheaper . . ." The degree of thickening of globalism may be giving rise to three changes not just in degree but in kind: increased density of networks, increased "institutional velocity," and increased transnational participation.

Density of networks

Economists use the term "network effects" to refer to situations where a product becomes more valuable once many people use it – take, for example, the Internet. Joseph Stiglitz, former chief economist of the World Bank, has argued that a knowledge-based economy generates "powerful spillover effects, often spreading like fire and triggering further innovation and setting off chain reactions of new inventions." Moreover, as interdependence and globalism have become thicker, systemic relationships among different networks have become more important. There are more interconnections. Intensive economic interdependence affects social and environmental interdependence; awareness of these connections in turn affects economic relationships. For instance, the expansion of trade can generate industrial activity in countries with low environmental standards, mobilizing environmental activists to carry their message to these newly industrializing but environmentally lax countries. The resulting activities may affect environmental interdependence (for instance, by reducing cross-boundary pollution) but may generate resentment in the newly industrializing countries, affecting social and economic relations.

The worldwide impact of the financial crisis that began in Thailand in July 1997 illustrates the extent of these network interconnections. Unexpectedly, what first appeared as an isolated banking and currency crisis in a small "emerging market" country had severe global effects. It generated financial panic elsewhere in Asia, particularly in South Korea and Indonesia; prompted emergency meetings at the highest level of world finance and huge "bail-out" packages orchestrated by the International Monetary Fund (IMF); and led eventually to a widespread loss of confidence in emerging markets and the efficacy of international financial institutions. Before that contagious loss of confidence was stemmed, Russia had defaulted on its debt, and a U.S.-based hedge fund had to be rescued suddenly through a plan brokered by the Federal Reserve Bank of New York. Even after recovery had begun, Brazil required an IMF loan, coupled with a devaluation, to avoid financial collapse in 1999.

Economic globalism is nothing new. Indeed, the relative magnitude of cross-border investment in 1997 was not unprecedented. Capital markets were by some measures more integrated at the beginning than at the end of the 20th century. The net outflow of capital from Great Britain in the four decades before 1914 averaged 5 percent of gross domestic product, compared with 2 to 3 percent for Japan over the last decade. The financial crisis of 1997–99 was not the first to be global in scale: "Black Tuesday" on Wall Street in 1929 and the collapse of Austria's Creditanstalt bank in 1931 triggered a worldwide financial crisis and depression. In the 1970s, skyrocketing oil prices prompted the Organization of Petroleum Exporting Countries to lend surplus funds to developed and speed distinguish contemporary globalization from earlier periods. Whereas the debt crisis of the 1980s was a slow-motion train wreck that took place over a period of years, the Asian meltdown struck immediately and spread over a period of months.

The point is that the increasing thickness of globalism – the density of networks of interdependence – is not just a difference in degree. Thickness means that different relationships of interdependence intersect more deeply at more points. Hence, the effects of events in one geographical area, on one dimension, can have profound effects in other geographical areas, on other dimensions. As in scientific theories of "chaos," and in weather systems, small events in one place can have catalytic effects, so that their consequences later, and elsewhere, are vast. Such systems are difficult to understand, and their effects are therefore often unpredictable. Furthermore, when these are human systems, people are often hard at work trying to outwit others, to gain an economic, social, or military advantage precisely by acting in unpredictable ways. As a result, globalism will likely be accompanied by pervasive uncertainty. There will be continual competition between increased complexity and uncertainty, and efforts by governments, market participants, and others to comprehend and manage these increasingly complex interconnected systems.

Globalization, therefore, does not merely affect governance; it is affected by governance. Frequent financial crises of the magnitude of the crisis of 1997–99 could lead to popular movements to limit interdependence and to a reversal of economic globalization. Chaotic uncertainty is too high a price for most people to pay for somewhat higher average levels of prosperity. Unless some of its aspects can be effectively governed, globalization may be unsustainable in its current form.

Institutional velocity

The information revolution is at the heart of economic and social globalization. It has made possible the transnational organization of work and the expansion of markets, thereby facilitating a new international division of labor. As Adam Smith famously declared in *The Wealth of Nations*, "the division of labor is limited by the extent of the market." Military globalism predated the information revolution, reaching its height during World War II and the cold war; but the nature of military interdependence has been transformed by information technology. The pollution that has contributed to environmental globalism has its sources in the coal-oil-steel-auto-chemical economy that was largely created between the middle of the 19th and 20th centuries and has become globalized only recently; but the information revolution may have a major impact on attempts to counter and reverse the negative effects of this form of globalism.

Sometimes these changes are incorrectly viewed in terms of the velocity of information flows. The biggest change in velocity came with the steamship and especially the telegraph: The transatlantic cable of 1866 reduced the time of transmission of information between London and New York by over a week – hence, by a factor of about a thousand. The telephone, by contrast, increased the velocity of such messages by a few minutes (since telephone messages do not require decoding), and the Internet, as compared with the telephone, by not much at all. The real difference lies in the reduced cost of communicating, not in the velocity of any individual communication. And the effects are therefore felt in the increased intensity rather than the extensity of globalism. In 1877 it was expensive to send telegrams across the Atlantic, and in 1927 or even 1977 it was expensive to telephone transcontinentally. Corporations and the rich used transcontinental telephones, but ordinary people wrote letters unless there was an emergency. But in 2000, if you have access to a computer, the Internet is virtually free and transpacific telephone calls may cost only a few cents per minute. The volume of communications has increased by many orders of magnitude, and the intensity of globalism has been able to expand exponentially.

Markets react more quickly than before, because information diffuses so much more rapidly and huge sums of capital can be moved at a moment's notice. Multinational enterprises have changed their organizational structures, integrating production more closely on a transnational basis and entering into more networks and alliances, as global capitalism has become more competitive and more subject to rapid change. Nongovernmental organizations (NGOs) have vastly expanded their levels of activity.

With respect to globalism and velocity, therefore, one can distinguish between the velocity of a given communication – "message velocity" – and "institutional velocity." Message velocity has changed little for the population centers of relatively rich countries since the telegraph became more or less universal toward the end of the 19th century. But institutional velocity – how rapidly a system and the units within it change – is a function not so much of message velocity than of the intensity of contact – the "thickness" of globalism. In the late 1970s, the news cycle was the same as it had been for decades: People found out the day's headlines by watching the evening news and got the more complete story and analysis from the morning paper. But the introduction of 24-hour cable news in 1980 and the subsequent emergence of the Internet have made news cycles shorter and have put a larger premium on small advantages in speed. Until recently, one newspaper did not normally "scoop" another by receiving and processing information an hour earlier than another: As long as the information could be processed before the daily paper "went to bed," it was timely. But in 2000, an hour – or even a few minutes – makes a critical difference for a cable television network in terms of being "on top of a story" or "behind the curve." Institutional velocity has accelerated more than message velocity. Institutional velocity reflects not only individual linkages but networks and interconnections among networks. This phenomenon is where the real change lies.

Transnational participation and complex interdependence

Reduced costs of communications have increased the number of participating actors and increased the relevance of "complex interdependence." This concept describes a hypothetical world with three characteristics: multiple channels between societies, with multiple actors, not just states; multiple issues, not arranged in any clear hierarchy; and the irrelevance of the threat or use of force among states linked by complex interdependence.

We used the concept of complex interdependence in the 1970s principally to describe emerging relationships among pluralist democracies. Manifestly it did not characterize relations between the United States and the Soviet Union, nor did it typify the politics of the Middle East, East Asia, Africa, or even parts of Latin America. However, we did argue that international monetary relations approximated some aspects of complex interdependence in the 1970s and that some bilateral relationships – French–German and U.S.–Canadian, for example – approximated all three conditions of complex interdependence. In a world of complex interdependence, we argued, politics would be different. The goals and instruments of state policy – and the processes of agenda setting and issue linkage – would all be different, as would the significance of international organizations.

Translated into the language of globalism, the politics of complex interdependence would be one in which levels of economic, environmental, and social globalism are high and military globalism is low. Regional instances of security communities – where states have reliable expectations that force will not be used – include Scandinavia since the early 20th century. Arguably, intercontinental complex interdependence was limited during the cold war to areas protected by the United States, such as the Atlantic security community. Indeed, U.S. power and policy were crucial to the construction of postwar international institutions, ranging from NATO to the IMF, which protected and supported complex interdependence.

Since 1989, the decline of military globalism and the extension of social and economic globalism to the former Soviet empire have implied the expansion of areas of complex interdependence, at least to the new and aspiring members of NATO in Eastern Europe. Moreover, economic and social globalism seem to have created incentives for leaders in South America to settle territorial quarrels, out of fear both of being distracted from tasks of economic and social development and of scaring away needed investment capital.

Even today complex interdependence is far from universal. Military force was used by or threatened against states throughout the 1990s, from the Taiwan Strait to Iraq, from Kuwait to the former Yugoslavia, from Kashmir to Congo. Civil wars are endemic in much of sub-Saharan Africa and sometimes have escalated into international warfare, as when the Democratic Republic of Congo's civil war engulfed five neighboring countries. The information revolution and the voracious appetite of television viewers for dramatic visual images have heightened global awareness of some of these civil conflicts and made them more immediate, contributing to pressure for humanitarian intervention, as in Bosnia and Kosovo. The various dimensions of globalization – in this case, the social and military dimensions – intersect, but the results are not necessarily conducive to greater harmony. Nevertheless, interstate use and threat of military force have virtually disappeared in certain areas of the world – notably among the advanced, information-era democracies bordering the Atlantic and the Pacific, as well as among a number of their less wealthy neighbors in Latin America and increasingly in Eastern-Central Europe.

The dimension of complex interdependence that has changed the most since the 1970s is participation in channels of contact among societies. There has been a vast expansion of such channels as a result of the dramatic fall in the costs of communication over large distances. It is no longer necessary to be a rich organization to be able to communicate on a real-time basis with people around the globe. Friedman calls this change the "democratization" of technology, finance, and information, because diminished costs have made what were once luxuries available to a much broader range of society.

"Democratization" is probably the wrong word, however, since in markets money votes, and people start out with unequal stakes. There is no equality, for example, in capital markets, despite the new financial instruments that permit more people to participate. "Pluralization" might be a better word, suggesting the vast increase in the number and variety of participants in global networks. The number of international NGOs more than quadrupled from about 6,000 to over 26,000 in the 1990s alone. Whether they are large organizations such as Greenpeace or Amnesty International, or the proverbial "three kooks with modems and a fax machine," NGOs can now raise their voices as never before. In 1999, NGOs worldwide used the Internet to coordinate a massive protest against the World Trade Organization meeting in Seattle. Whether these organizations can forge a coherent and credible coalition has become the key political question.

This vast expansion of transnational channels of contact, at multicontinental distances, generated by the media and a profusion of NGOs, has helped expand the third dimension of complex interdependence: the multiple issues connecting societies. More and more issues are up for grabs internationally, including regulations and practices – ranging from pharmaceutical testing to accounting and product standards to banking regulation – that were formerly regarded as the prerogatives of national governments. The Uruguay Round of multilateral trade negotiations of the late 1980s and early 1990s focused on services, once virtually untouched by international regimes; and the financial crisis of 1997–99 led to both public and private efforts to globalize the transparent financial reporting that has become prevalent in advanced industrialized countries.

Increased participation at a distance and greater approximation of complex interdependence do not imply the end of politics. On the contrary, power remains important. Even in domains characterized by complex interdependence, politics reflects asymmetrical economic, social, and environmental interdependence, not just among states but also among nonstate actors, and through transgovernmental relations. Complex interdependence is not a description of the world, but rather an ideal concept abstracting from reality. It is, however, an ideal concept that increasingly corresponds to reality in many parts of the world, even at transcontinental distances – and that corresponds more closely than obsolete images of world politics as simply interstate relations that focus solely on force and security.

So what really is new in contemporary globalism? Intensive, or thick, network interconnections that have systemic effects, often unanticipated. But such thick globalism is not uniform: It varies by region, locality, and issue area. It is less a matter of communications message velocity than of declining cost, which does speed up what we call systemic and institutional velocity. Globalization shrinks distance, but it does not make distance irrelevant. And the filters provided by domestic politics and political institutions play a major role in determining what effects globalization really has and how well various countries adapt to it. Finally, reduced costs have enabled more actors to participate in world politics at greater distances, leading larger areas of world politics to approximate the ideal type of complex interdependence.

Although the system of sovereign states is likely to continue as the dominant structure in the world, the content of world politics is changing. More dimensions than ever – but not all – are beginning to approach our idealized concept of complex interdependence. Such trends can be set back, perhaps even reversed, by cataclysmic events, as happened in earlier phases of globalization. History always has surprises. But history's surprises always occur against the background of what has gone before. The surprises of the early 21st century will, no doubt, be profoundly affected by the processes of contemporary globalization that we have tried to analyze here.

Want to know more?

Interdependence became a buzzword in the 1970s, thanks in part to the landmark works of two economists: Richard N. Cooper's *The Economics of Interdependence: Economic Policy in the Atlantic Community* (New York: McGraw Hill, 1968) and Raymond Vernon's *Sovereignty at Bay: The Multinational Spread of U.S. Enterprises* (New York: Basic Books, 1971). Political scientists Robert O. Keohane and Joseph S. Nye Jr. have published a number of works on the topic, including *Transnational Relations and World Politics* (Cambridge: Harvard University Press, 1972) and *Power and Interdependence: World Politics in Transition* (Boston: Little, Brown, and Company, 1977; forthcoming third edition, New York: Longman, 2000).

Technological and economic change did not stop in the 1980s, even as the "little cold war" was refocusing public attention, foundation resources, and academic fashions on the more traditional security agenda. With the cold war's end, the resulting growth in interdependence became so clear that journalist Thomas Friedman's well-written book on globalization, *The Lexus and the Olive Tree* (New York: Farrar Straus and Giroux, 1999) became a bestseller. (Friedman engaged *Le Monde diplomatique's* Ignacio Ramonet in a lively debate over globalization in the Fall 1999 issue of FOREIGN POLICY.) William Greider presents a skeptical post-cold-war view in his *One World, Ready or Not: The Manic Logic of Global Capitalism* (New York: Simon & Schuster, 1997).

The most complete academic survey of globalization to date is the magisterial *Global Transformations: Politics, Economics, and Culture* (Stanford: Stanford University Press, 1999), by David Held, Anthony McGrew, David Goldblatt, and Jonathan Perraton. Saskia Sassen presents an interesting sociological perspective in *Globalization and Its Discontents: Essays on the New Mobility of People and Money* (New York: New Press, 1997). Frances Cairncross takes a somewhat breathless view of the information revolution in *The Death of Distance: How the Communications Revolution Will Change Our Lives* (Boston: Harvard Business School Press, 1997). Margaret E. Keck and Kathryn Sikkink's book *Activists Beyond Borders: Advocacy Networks in International Politics* (Ithaca: Cornell University Press, 1998) offers a historical perspective on the evolution of global norms, and Jared M. Diamond's *Guns, Germs, and Steel: The Fates of Human Societies* (New York: W.W. Norton & Company, 1997) examines the various dimensions of globalism over a span of centuries.

Karl Polanyi's *The Great Transformation* (New York: Farrar & Rinehart, 1944; Beacon Press, 1985) remains a classic account of the rise and fall of 19th-century economic globalism. Dani Rodrik's *Has Globalization Gone Too Far?* (Washington: Institute for International Economics, 1997) updates these concerns for the current era. Jeffrey G. Williamson's chapter, "Globalization and the Labor Market," in Philippe Aghion and Jeffrey G. Williamson, eds., *Growth, Inequality and Globalization: Theory, History, and Policy* (Cambridge: Cambridge University Press, 1998) is an excellent source for important historical data.

For links to relevant Web sites, as well as a comprehensive index of related FOREIGN POLICY articles, access www.foreignpolicy.com.

Note

* This article drew upon the third edition of our book *Power and Interdependence: World Politics in Transition* (New York: Longman, 2000).

15 Globalization's democratic deficit

How to make international institutions more accountable*

Seattle; Washington, D.C.; Prague; Québec City. It is becoming difficult for international economic organizations to meet without attracting crowds of protesters decrying globalization. These protesters are a diverse lot, coming mainly from rich countries, and their coalition has not always been internally consistent. They have included trade unionists worried about losing jobs and students who want to help the underdeveloped world gain them, environmentalists concerned about ecological degradation and anarchists who object to all forms of international regulation. Some protesters claim to represent poor countries but simultaneously defend agricultural protectionism in wealthy countries. Some reject corporate capitalism, whereas others accept the benefits of international markets but worry that globalization is destroying democracy.

Of all their complaints, this last concern is key. Protest organizers such as Lori Wallach attributed half the success of the Seattle coalition to "the notion that the democracy deficit in the global economy is neither necessary nor acceptable." For globalization's supporters, accordingly, finding some way to address its perceived democratic deficit should become a high priority.

It's a small world

Globalization, defined as networks of interdependence at worldwide distances, is not new. Nor is it just economic. Markets have spread and tied people together, but environmental, military, social, and political interdependence have also increased. If the current political backlash against globalization were to lead to a rash of protectionist policies, it might slow or even reverse the world's economic integration – as has happened at times in the past – even as global warming or the spread of the AIDS virus continued apace. It would be ironic if current protests curtailed the positive aspects of globalization while leaving the negative dimensions untouched.

Markets have unequal effects, and the inequality they produce can have powerful political consequences. But the cliché that markets always make the rich richer and the poor poorer is simply not true. Globalization, for example, has improved the lot of hundreds of millions of poor people around the world. Poverty can be reduced even when inequality increases. And in some cases inequality can even decrease. The economic gap between South Korea and industrialized countries, for example, has diminished in part because of global markets. No poor country, meanwhile, has ever become rich by isolating itself from global markets, although North Korea and Myanmar have impoverished themselves by doing so. Economic globalization, in short, may be a necessary, though not sufficient, condition for combating poverty.

The complexities of globalization have led to calls for a global institutional response. Although a hierarchical world government is neither feasible nor desirable, many forms of global governance and methods of managing common affairs already exist and can be expanded. Hundreds of organizations now regulate the global dimensions of trade, telecommunications, civil aviation, health, the environment, meteorology, and many other issues.

Antiglobalization protesters complain that international institutions are illegitimate because they are undemocratic. But the existing global institutions are quite weak and hardly threatening. Even the much-maligned World Trade Organization (WTO) has only a small budget and staff. Moreover, unlike self-appointed nongovernmental organizations (NGOs), international institutions tend to be highly responsive to national governments and can thus claim some real, if indirect, democratic legitimacy. International economic institutions, moreover, merely facilitate cooperation among member states and derive some authority from their efficacy.

Even so, in a world of transnational politics where democracy has become the touchstone of legitimacy, these arguments probably will not be enough to protect any but the most technical organizations from attack. International institutions may be weak, but their rules and resources can have powerful effects. The protesters, moreover, make some valid points. Not all member states of international organizations are themselves democratic. Long lines of delegation from multiple governments, combined with a lack of transparency, often weaken accountability. And although the organizations may be agents of states, they often represent only certain parts of those states. Thus trade ministers attend WTO meetings, finance ministers attend the meetings of the International Monetary Fund (IMF), and central bankers meet at the Bank for International Settlements in Basel. To outsiders, even within the same government, these institutions can look like closed and secretive clubs. Increasing the perceived legitimacy of international governance is therefore an important objective and requires three things: greater clarity about democracy, a richer understanding of accountability, and a willingness to experiment.

We, the people

Democracy requires government by officials who are accountable and removable by the majority of people in a jurisdiction, together with protections for individual and minority rights. But who are "we the people" in a world where political identity at the global level is so weak? "One state, one vote" is not democratic. By that formula, a citizen of the Maldive Islands would have a thousand times more voting power than would a citizen of China. On the other hand, treating the world as a single global constituency in which the majority ruled would mean that the more than 2 billion Chinese and Indians could usually get their way. (Ironically, such a world would be a nightmare for those antiglobalization NGOs that seek international environmental and labor standards, since such measures draw little support from Indian or Chinese officials.)

In a democratic system, minorities acquiesce to the will of the majority when they feel they are generally full-fledged participants in the larger community. There is little evidence, however, that such a strong sense of community exists at the global level today, or that it could soon be created. In its absence, the extension of domestic voting procedures to the global level makes little practical or normative sense. A stronger European Parliament may reduce the "democratic deficit" within a union of relatively homogeneous European states, but it is doubtful that such an institution makes sense for the world at large. Alfred, Lord Tennyson's "Parliament of man" made for great Victorian poetry, but it does not stand up to contemporary political analysis. Democracy, moreover, exists today only in certain well-ordered nationstates, and that condition is likely to change only slowly.

Still, governments can do several things to respond to the concerns about a global democratic deficit. First, they can try to design international institutions that preserve as much space as possible for domestic political processes to operate. In the WTO, for example, the procedures for settling disputes can intrude on domestic sovereignty, but a country can reject a judgment if it pays carefully limited compensation to the trade partners injured by its actions. And if a country does defect from its WTO trade agreements, the settlement procedure limits the kind of tit-for-tat downward spiral of retaliation that so devastated the world economy in the 1930s. In a sense, the procedure is like having a fuse in the electrical system of a house: better the fuse blow than the house burn down. The danger with the WTO, therefore, is not that it prevents member states from accommodating domestic political choices but rather that members will be tempted to litigate too many disputes instead of resolving them through the more flexible route of political negotiations.

Clearer connections

Better accountability can and should start at home. If people believe that WTO meetings do not adequately account for environmental standards, they can press their governments to include environment ministers or officials in their WTO delegations. Legislatures can hold hearings before or after meetings, and legislators can themselves become national delegates to various organizations.

Governments should also make clear that democratic accountability can be quite indirect. Accountability is often assured through means other than voting, even in well-functioning democracies. In the United States, for example, the Supreme Court and the Federal Reserve Board respond to elections indirectly through a long chain of delegation, and judges and government bankers are kept accountable by professional norms and standards, as well. There is no reason that indirect account-ability cannot be consistent with democracy, or that international institutions such as the IMF and the World Bank should be held to a higher standard than are domestic institutions.

Increased transparency is also essential. In addition to voting, people in democracies debate issues using a variety of means, from letters to polls to protests. Interest groups and a free press play important roles in creating transparency in domestic democratic politics and can do so at the international level as well. NGOs are self-selected, not democratically elected, but they too can play a positive role in increasing transparency. They deserve a voice, but not a vote. For them to fill this role, they need information from and dialogue with international institutions. In some instances, such as judicial procedures or market interventions, it is unrealistic to provide information in advance, but records and justifications of decisions can later be disclosed for comment and criticism – as the Federal Reserve and the Supreme Court do in domestic politics. The same standards of transparency should be applied to NGOs themselves, perhaps encouraged by other NGOs such as Transparency International.

The private sector can also contribute to accountability. Private associations and codes, such as those established by the international chemical industry in the aftermath of the Bhopal disaster, can prevent a race to the bottom in standards. The practice of "naming and shaming" has helped consumers hold transnational firms accountable in the toy and apparel industries. And although people have unequal votes in markets, the aftermath of the Asian financial crisis may have led to more increases in transparency by corrupt governments than any formal agreements did. Open markets can help diminish the undemocratic power of local monopolies and reduce the power of entrenched and unresponsive government bureaucracies, particularly in countries where parliaments are weak. Moreover, efforts by investors to increase transparency and legal predictability can spill over to political institutions.

New democrats

Rather than merely rejecting the poorly formulated arguments of the protesters, proponents of international institutions should experiment with ways to improve accountability. Transparency is essential, and international organizations can provide more access to their deliberations, even if after the fact. NGOs could be welcomed as observers (as the World Bank has done) or allowed to file "friend of the court" briefs in WTO dispute-settlement cases. In some cases, such as the Internet Corporation for Assigned Names and Numbers (which is incorporated as a nonprofit institution under the laws of California), experiments with direct voting for board members may prove fruitful, although the danger of their being taken over by well-organized interest groups remains a problem. Hybrid network organizations that combine governmental, intergovernmental, and non-governmental representatives, such as the World Commission on Dams or U.N. Secretary-General Kofi Annan's Global Compact, are other avenues to explore. Assemblies of parliamentarians can also be associated with some organizations to hold hearings and receive information, even if not to vote.

In the end, there is no single answer to the question of how to reconcile the necessary global institutions with democratic accountability. Highly technical organizations may be able to derive their legitimacy from their efficacy alone. But the more an institution deals with broad values, the more its democratic legitimacy becomes relevant. People concerned about democracy will need to think harder about norms and procedures for the governance of globalization. Neither denying the problem nor yielding to demagogues in the streets will do.

Note

* This article draws on my address to the March 2001 meeting of the Trilateral Commission in London and on my work with Robert O. Keohane in the book *Governance in a Globalizing World.*

16 Terrorism*

Introduction

Terrorism in not new. Nor is it an entity. Rarely is it an ideology. It is simply a method of conflict frequently defined as a deliberate attack on the innocent (outside the context of organized war) with the objective of spreading fear and intimidation. In the nineteenth century, Joseph Conrad drew an indelible portrait of the terrorist mind, and terrorism was a familiar phenomenon in the twentieth century. Whether homegrown or transnational, it was a staple of conflicts throughout the Middle East, in Northern Ireland, Spain, Sri Lanka, Kashmir, South Africa, and elsewhere. It occurred on every continent except Antarctica and affected nearly every Trilateral country. September 11, 2001 was a dramatic escalation of an age-old phenomenon.

But September 11 also began a divergence of perspectives about terrorism among the Trilateral countries. After an initial surge of solidarity illustrated by a headline in *Le Monde* declaring, "we are all Americans now," the differences between United States and the other countries began to widen. The United States declared a war on transnational terrorism, greatly increased its defense budget, fought a war in Afghanistan, declared a new strategy that expanded pre-emption into the realm of preventive war, and undertook the most massive reorganization of its government in more than half a century. Other countries, while cooperating with the United States on Afghanistan, intelligence sharing, and police work, began to express concern that the United States was over-reacting. In a description by the French analyst Therese Delpech, "most Europeans do not accept the idea of a 'war' on terrorism. They are used to dealing with this phenomenon with other methods (intelligence services, police, justice) . . . . The Europeans fear that the Americans are engaging in an endless war without considering all the possible consequences."[1] Similar attitudes could be encountered in many parts of Asia.

It is not surprising that attitudes diverged. After all, the tragedy of September 11 happened inside the United States and created a greater and longer lasting sense of urgency. Many governments were anxious not to frighten their populations or exacerbate relations with their Muslim minorities. Some people believed that American foreign policy was in part responsible for the disaster and that it would be wise to seek distance from the United States. But perhaps, most importantly, was the widespread feeling of déja vu. Europe, Japan, and other countries had lived through severe episodes of terrorism in the 1970s and 80s, yet managed to overcome it with their democracies intact. Terrorism was a nuisance that had to be managed, not a challenge requiring total change. Moreover, the political rhetoric of "evil" and "war" that helped to mobilize the American public seemed alien and alarming to many overseas who preferred a managerial approach.

Different perceptions are natural among the different political cultures of the Trilateral countries, but when these perceptions go unchecked they can have dangerous effects. European and Asian reactions could reduce incentives for cooperation. American irritation with its allies could reinforce unilateralist responses to problems that would benefit from more cooperative approaches. Over time, such friction could spill over into other areas as well. But most important, diverging perceptions could limit the cooperation that is necessary to address common vulnerabilities and leave everyone worse off.

What's new?

To what extent is terrorism today sufficiently different from the past to warrant a new approach? Until recently, the difference between allied and American attitudes toward terrorism was not that different. A number of studies pointed to new trends well before September 11, but they were often ignored. For example when the bipartisan Hart-Rudman Commission issued its warnings in the United States in March 2001, the *New York Times* did not report it nor did the White House embrace it. Yet two developments have made terrorism more lethal and more difficult to manage.

One set of trends grows out of progress in science and technology. First, there is the complex, highly technological nature of modern civilization's basic systems. As a committee of the National Research Council of the National Academy of Sciences pointed out, market forces and openness have combined to increase the efficiency of many of our vital systems – such as those that provide transportation, information, energy, and health care. But ironically such systems become more vulnerable and fragile as they become more complex and efficient. The result is that progress makes our infrastructures "vulnerable to local disruptions which could lead to widespread or catastrophic failures."[2]

At the same time, progress is "democratizing technology", making the instruments of mass destruction smaller, cheaper, and more readily available to a far wider range of individuals and groups. Where bombs and timers were once heavy and expensive, plastic explosives and digital timers are light and cheap. The costs of hijacking an airplane are sometimes little more than the price of a ticket. Finally, the success of the information revolution is providing inexpensive means of communication and organization that allow groups once restricted to local and national police jurisdictions to become global in scope. Thirty years ago, instantaneous global communication was sufficiently expensive that it was restricted to large entities with large budgets like governments, multinational corporations, or the Catholic Church. Today the Internet makes global communication virtually free for anyone with access to a modem.[3] Similarly, the Internet has reduced the costs of searching for information and making contacts related to instruments of wide scale destruction.

The second set of trends reflects changes in the motivation and organization of terrorist groups. Terrorists in the mid-twentieth century tended to have relatively well defined political objectives, which were often ill served by mass destruction. Many were supported and covertly controlled by governments. Toward the end of the century, radical groups grew on the fringes of several religions. Most numerous were the tens of thousands of young Muslim men who went to fight against the Soviet occupation of Afghanistan.[4] There they were trained in a wide range of techniques and many were recruited to organizations with an extreme view of the religious obligation of jihad. As Walter Laquer has observed, "traditional terrorists, whether left-wing, right-wing, or nationalist-separatists, were not greatly drawn to these opportunities for greater destruction. . . . Terrorism has become more brutal and indiscriminate since then."[5] This is reinforced when motivations change from the limited and political to unlimited or retributive objectives reinforced by promises of rewards in another world. Organization has also changed. For example, al Qaueda's network of tens of thousand of people in loosely affiliated cells in some sixty countries gives it a scale well beyond anything seen before. But even small networks can be more difficult to penetrate than the hierarchical quasi-military organizations of the past.

Both trends – technological and political – have created a new set of conditions that have increased the lethality and the difficulty of managing terrorism today. Because of September 11 and the unprecedented scale of al Qaeda, the current focus is properly on terrorism associated with Islamic extremists. But it would be a mistake to limit our attention or responses to Islamic terrorists, for that would ignore the wider effects of the democratization of technology and the broader set of challenges that must be met. Technological progress is putting into the hands of deviant groups and individuals, destructive capabilities that were once limited primarily to governments and armies. Every large group of people has some members who deviate from the norm, and some are bent on destruction. It is worth remembering that the worst case of terrorism in the United States before September 11 was Timothy McVeigh, a purely homegrown anti-government fanatic. Similarly, the Aum Shinrykio cult that spread sarin gas in the Tokyo subway system in 1995 had nothing to do with Islam.

Lethality has been increasing. In the 1970s, the Palestinian attack on Israeli athletes at the Munich Olympics or the killings by the Red Brigades that galvanized world attention and cost dozens of lives. In the 1980s, Sikh extremists bombed an Air India flight and killed 325 people. September 11, 2001 cost several thousand lives – and all of this escalation occurred without using weapons of mass destruction. If one extrapolates this lethality curve and imagines a deviant group gaining access to biological or nuclear materials within the coming decade, it is possible to imagine terrorists being able to destroy millions of lives. To kill so many people in the twentieth century, a deviant individual like Hitler or Stalin required the apparatus of a totalitarian government. Unfortunately, it is now all too easy to envisage extremist groups and individuals killing millions without the help of governments. This is truly the "privatization of war" and a dramatic change in world politics. Moreover, this next step in the escalation of terrorism would have profound effects on the nature of our urban civilization. What would happen to our willingness to locate in cities, to real estate prices, to museums and theatres if instead of destroying two office buildings, a future attack destroys the lower half of Manhattan? The new terrorism is not like the 1970s terrorism of the IRA, the ETA, or the Red Brigades.

Nor is the vulnerability limited to any one society. The "business as usual" attitude/approach towards curbing terrorism is not enough.

Common and diverging interests

If the new terrorism presents a profound challenge to the urban civilizations of the trilateral countries, then efforts to counter it approximate a global public good whose production benefits all countries, whether they pay for it or not. But even if there are common interests in producing a public good, there are diverging interests in defining and paying for it.

For example, politics has plagued efforts to agree on a common definition of terrorism at the United Nations. Terrorism is a method of violent conflict that is sometimes called the weapon of the weak against the strong. Some would argue that one man's terrorist is just another man's freedom fighter. Therefore treating suppression of terrorism as a global public good is merely the hypocrisy of the powerful trying to disarm the weak. But that need not be the case. Not all struggles for national liberation have turned to deliberate killing of the innocent. Deliberate killing of non-combatants (in war or not) is condemned by the moral code of most major religions, including Islam. Such behavior is unacceptable whether it is carried out by the powerful or the weak. While there are problems with any definition at the margins, the core of terrorism is clear enough to permit efforts to de-legitimize it. Indeed, many countries are parties to UN conventions that commit them to combating aspects of terrorist behavior, even though the UN has not agreed on one formal definition.

In a sense, terrorism is to the twenty-first century what piracy was to an earlier era. Pirates used violence against commerce for their private purposes, but some governments gave pirates and privateers safe harbor in order to earn revenues or to harass their enemies. As Britain became the dominant naval power in the nineteenth century, it suppressed piracy and most countries benefited from that situation. A multilateral convention outlawing piracy was agreed in Paris by mid-century. Today, some states harbor terrorists in order to attack their enemies or because they are too weak to control powerful groups. If a campaign to suppress terrorism is based on broad coalitions that focus on the core value of de-legitimizing attacks on innocent non-combatants, it has a prospect of success. While anti-terrorism will not be seen as a global public good by the groups that use it, the objective should be to isolate them in public opinion, and to reduce the minority of states that give them safe harbor.

Even when there is broad acceptance of the general nature of a public good, there can be conflicts over its production. Since all benefit and none can be excluded from the benefits, there is a great incentive to ride for free. When there are many small participants, most fear that they will not reap benefits in proportion to the costs they pay, and the public good is difficult to produce. One of the virtues of a situation of unequal power, like British naval pre-eminence in the nineteenth century or American pre-eminence today, is that the largest country has an incentive to take the lead in suppressing piracy or terrorism because it knows that it will gain a good part of the benefits.

Nonetheless, problems of burden sharing arise, and the temptation to free ride always exists. Countries may wish to avoid the budgetary burdens of military measures or of providing assistance in nation building. Even more dangerous is the temptation to divert terrorists to targets in other countries. Some countries may think that by appeasing terrorists or by distancing their policies from the United States they can remove themselves from the line of fire. Others may think that by tightening their domestic security systems, they can divert terrorists to softer targets in other countries.

In general, these calculations are mistaken. With regard to the specific threat from Islamic extremism, it is worth noting that citizens of many countries have suffered attacks. Many terrorists object to Western culture as well as American policies. For example, radical Islamist groups, such as those responsible for the bombing a nightclub in Bali, have local agendas and were around before they linked up with al Qaeda.[6] And although Osama bin Laden has complained about American troops in the land of the two holy mosques and American support for Israel, he also refers to the indignity that Muslims have suffered since Europeans dismantled the last caliphate eighty years ago. Policy issues are only part of the problem and only part of the solution. Moreover, opting out on policy issues would do nothing to deal with the deeper challenges represented by the democratization of technology. After al Qaeda is gone, deviants in many societies may be tempted by terrorism unless such methods of conflict are de-legitimized and steps are taken to make them harder to use. Countries still have to cooperate to discourage the next Timothy McVeigh or Aum Shinrykio. Free riding is always a temptation, but in a larger perspective, it provides no escape.

In fact, one of the lessons of the efforts since September 11 is that there is no way to avoid cooperation. In that sense the metaphor of war is misleading, since military force is not the major source of the solution. Afghanistan provides a good example. The United States' skillful use of force was necessary and effective in defeating the Taliban government which had provided a safe haven for terrorists, but the war destroyed only a quarter or so of al Qaeda, which is a network organization with cells in sixty countries. Precision bombing is not an option for countering cells in Hamburg, Singapor, or Detroit. Only close civilian cooperation in intelligence sharing, police work across borders, tracing financial flows, working to pre-clear cargo manifests, passenger lists, and so forth can cope with such a threat. Countries cooperate out of self-interest, but the degree of cooperation is affected by the degree of consultation in the definition of those interests. While American pre-eminence is instrumental in organizing cooperation, the temptation it creates for unilateralism can become a hindrance if it reduces the willingness of others to cooperate.

Elements of a strategy

Some who follow my reasoning thus far part company on the question of strategy. They adopt a fatalistic view and argue that there is not much more to be done in the future than in the past. It is impossible to detect, interdict, and prevent all deviants from using violence against innocent civilians, so we simply have to learn to live with it. Why make extraordinary efforts if they are bound to fail?

However, even though it may be impossible to eliminate the number of terrorist incidents, reducing their frequency and lethality will make a large difference in their impact on our societies. We can do that by (1) de-legitimizing attacks on innocent civilians as a method of conflict; (2) discouraging states from providing resources or safe harbor for those who use such methods; (3) hardening our targets at home to make it more difficult for deviants to use terrorism successfully; (4) denying terrorists easy access to means of mass destruction; and (5) addressing issues that reduce incentives to turn to terrorism. There are five major instruments we can use to pursue these objectives: military, diplomatic, intelligence and police, development assistance, and homeland security.

Military measures may not deal with the largest part of the problem, but they are essential in some instances, particularly regarding state sponsors of terrorism and failed states. Al Qaeda was able to reach its current scale because of the opportunities provided by its safe haven in Afghanistan. The military action that deprived them of that haven was not sufficient, but it was necessary. The number of states sponsoring terrorism has decreased over the past decade, and diplomacy backed by military threat can continue to reduce the number. Some failed states are so chaotically organized that they cannot be deterred from providing a haven for terrorists. In such instances, military assistance may be relevant: in others intervention may become necessary.

The Bush Administration has correctly argued that deterrence does not work where there is no return address, and pre-emption against terrorist groups is justifiable self-defense when deterrence is impossible. But if pre-emption of a clear and present danger is stretched to justify preventive wars against states that might help terrorists in the future, it creates a dangerous precedent that weakens international norms that govern the use of force. The best way to solve this dilemma is to restrict unilateral pre-emption to a narrowly constrained clear and present danger criterion, and to subject arguments for preventive war to multilateral scrutiny.

Intelligence sharing and police cooperation is often the most effective front line of counter-terrorism. Early warning can enhance prevention as well support police cooperation. It is often the only way to use force in situations where military action is not possible. Because of the sensitivity of sources and dangers of disclosure, much of this work will be carried out in a series of bilateral arrangements.

Diplomatic measures run a wide gambit. Conventions and norms at the United Nations and regional organization levels are important ways to help de-legitimize terrorism. (Equally important is that governments be scrupulous that their behavior does not deliberately kill non-combatants.) Diplomatic pressures and sanctions can be brought to bear both against countries and non-governmental organizations suspected of aiding terrorists. Public diplomacy is also an important dimension. It is essential that we not leave the presentation of our policies and culture to al Jazeera and others. Yet the United States spends on public diplomacy less than one quarter of one percent of what it spends on defense.[7]

Homeland Security is a critical part of any strategy, but there is always a question of cost and how much insurance is enough. Some people see homeland security as a secondary issue because they assume a constant supply of terrorism and argue that if you protect one target it simply diverts terrorists to another target. But by raising thresholds and hardening targets, it may be possible to lower the supply of terrorism. Some deviants will lack the skill or sophistication to surmount more difficult barriers and be discouraged from trying. Others will try, but will be caught before they can succeed. And since terrorism often engenders an imitation or copycat effect, preventing incidents can have a beneficial cumulative effect.

Working to raise the thresholds that terrorists must overcome requires a systematic approach since plugging one hole sometimes does divert them to others. Homeland security offices must work out strategic plans to plug the most glaring vulnerabilities at reasonable levels of cost. Since modern societies are similar in these vulnerabilities, the Trilateral countries should have a great deal to learn from each others' mistakes and best practices. Moreover, insofar as transnational systems are concerned, our Trilateral societies are as vulnerable as the weakest link. Once someone boards a plane in a country with weak security, they are in the system and it makes no sense to beef up security in, say, New York if a terrorist can enter the system easily in, say, Paris. On the other hand, overly costly and ineffectual security can seriously disrupt trade and commerce without really improving safety. Many of these transnational systems are largely in the private sector, as are many of the vulnerable domestic systems. It is crucial to work out ways to involve the private sector in improving homeland security.

Aid and assistance can be used to strengthen the capacities of poor countries that are involved in these transnational systems. Such investments are a clear case of coincidence between self-interest and charity. A particularly important type of assistance is in helping other countries to develop capabilities to deal with weapons of mass destruction. In the case of biological agents, assistance on world public health has become a security issue. Terrorists can obtain microbes and viruses from inadequately protected foreign laboratories, or by bribing underpaid scientists in the remnants of the Russian biological warfare system, or from natural sources. In addition, the World Health Organization reports that there were thirteen naturally occurring cases of anthrax last year alone. It has created a global network of national laboratories that do early detection work, and it manages all this on a meager budget of roughly $400 million per year.

Another crucial area for Trilateral assistance is the Cooperative Threat Reduction effort with Russia, through which the U.S. provides funds to help improve their control and destruction of weapons usable materials. Funding also goes to scientists from former nuclear, biological, and chemical weapons laboratories to help them turn to civilian work. These programs too are under-funded, although there was an agreement in principle at the G-8 summit in Canada last year for ten countries to provide $10 billion over the next ten years.

Somewhat more controversial is the question of whether development aid more broadly is an important counter-terrorist instrument. Advocates say that it is an important tool for "draining the swamps" or attacking the roots of terrorism. Skeptics challenge whether poverty is the root of terrorism. They argue that accusing the poor of terrorism is a libel, and that most of the terrorists on September 11 were middle class citizens of a relatively wealthy country. Moreover, if we have to wait for development assistance to raise the world from poverty as the answer to terrorism, we will all be dead. Both sides of this argument have a point. The time horizons of development policy are out of line with the time horizons of counter-terrorism, but terrorist groups are often led by well off deviants who (like Lenin or bin Laden) recruit followers by pointing to the injustices in the world. There are many reasons for development assistance by wealthy countries, but one is to deprive terrorist leaders of such arguments by showing that our policies are aligned with the long-term aspirations of the poor.

Notes

* Report for the Trilateral Commission meeting in Seoul, 2003.
1 Therese Delpech, *International Terrorism and Europe* (Paris, Institute for Security Studies, 2002), p. 31.
2 National Research Council, *Making the Nation Safer* (Washington, National Academies Press, 2002), p. 25.
3 See Nye, *The Paradox of American Power*, Chapter 2, for details. Oxford University Press, 2002.
4 Peter Bergen, *Holy War, Inc.: Inside the Secret World of Osama bin Laden*, estimates the numbers involved at about 50,000.
5 Walter Laquer, "Left, Right and Beyond: The Changing Face of Terror," in James Hoge and Gideon Rose, *How Did This Happen?* (New York, Public Affairs Press, 2001) p. 74.
6 Raymond Bonner, "Radical Islamists a Threat to Southeast Asia Even if al Qaeda is Eliminated, Singapore Says," *New York Times*, Jan 10, 2003, p. 11.
7 Council on Foreign Relations, *Report of the Task Force on Public Diplomacy* (New York, 2002).

Part 5

Praxis and theory

17 Essay on career choice*

> Two roads diverged in a yellow wood, and sorry I could not travel both and be one traveler, long I stood and looked down one as far as I could. . . .
>
> Robert Frost, "The Road Not Taken"

I have always loved Robert Frost's poem "The Road Not Taken," but in truth my career is one in which I have traveled two roads, both the academic and the governmental. Some who pursued only one road have gone further in achieving a high position or in the length of their list of publications, but I would not trade with them. I have found both halves of my career satisfying and cannot imagine my life without either. I would like to recommend such a course to others, but I must confess that it is not easy to plan to take two roads. In my case, serendipity played a large role.

I certainly had no fixed plan to take the roads I did. I grew up on a farm in Northwest New Jersey, and that childhood bequeathed me a lifelong love of the outdoors. As a teenager, I wondered about a career as a forester or a farmer. For a spell, I was influenced to think I might want to follow in the example of the friendly local minister. My father was in the securities business, and I often felt I would wind up following in his footsteps. He loved his work. He used to say that "in my business, you are in everybody's business," and he encouraged me with visits to his office on Wall Street. At the same time, he never tried to control my choice. It was a wise approach which allowed us to remain close without feeling tension or guilt about my decisions. I have followed his example with regard to my three sons, none of whom has chosen an academic path.

When I went to college "down the road" at Princeton, I had no idea what I wanted to major in, much less choice of career. I found psychology, history, politics, economics, and philosophy all interesting, so I chose an interdisciplinary major in the Woodrow Wilson School of Public and International Affairs. For my senior thesis, I wrote a history of a private firm in Philadelphia as an example of Schumpeter's theory of entrepreneurship. I was gratified to win a prize, but what the thesis taught me was the fascination of original research and trying to make order out of a chaos of empirical material. In retrospect, the most important thing I got from Princeton was a broad basis in liberal arts. I still find myself remembering lessons from my early science and philosophy courses. When students sometimes complain to me that their liberal arts education is not preparing them for anything, I respond that it is preparing them for life. College courses are like building blocks. An undergraduate business degree allows you to pile them into a tall tower quickly. Liberal arts is more like a pyramid with a broad base that does not reach the same early heights. But when the earth shakes, and it likely will more than once during the course of a career in today's world, pyramids are more stable than towers.

Career choices at age 21

Senior year arrived and I had no clear idea of what I wanted to do as a career. At that time, all healthy males faced a period of military service. I decided to join the Marine Corps. An older friend had just finished officer training for platoon leaders in the Marines and made it sound appealing. Friends encouraged me to apply for a Rhodes Scholarship, but I was uncertain about it. By chance, as I entered the library one day to work on my thesis, I bumped into a professor of English whose course I was taking. He asked what I intended to do next year. I replied, "Marine Platoon Leader's Corps." He shook his head and said I really should apply for the Rhodes. So I did. I remember in the Rhodes interview being asked what I wanted to do for a career. I had enjoyed writing a column for the student newspaper so I said that I wanted to try to understand society and write about it. "Oh, a pundit?" they asked. I looked puzzled, but they gave me the scholarship anyway. During the summer after graduation, I worked as a night reporter for a local newspaper. I found that writing as a reporter merely scratched the surface of what interested me. I went to Oxford cured of any desire to pursue a career in journalism, but with nothing in its place.

Besides postponing my career choice for two years, Oxford had several important effects. One was time to experiment and travel. I thought of becoming a novelist, but, I decided to postpone any such efforts for a later stage in life. (My novel, *The Power Game*, will finally be published in 2004.) Also important was the ethic of public service that went along with the Rhodes. I enjoyed my tutorials in philosophy, politics, and economics, but the most important aspect of Oxford was making foreign friends and expanding my interest in the rest of the world. In particular, I remember long discussions with a friend from Ghana over the future of democracy in Africa. To this day, I believe that making friends who help you see the world through the eyes of foreigners is as educational as any formal course in college. Even if you never want to work overseas, you do not really know what is "American" until you can compare it with what is not American. And in a world of growing globalization, distant events can have a powerful effect on your life and career.

By the end of my two years at Oxford, I was leaning toward a career in government, perhaps in the Foreign Service. At the same time, following the example of another friend, I decided to apply for the PhD program in government at Harvard. I thought a PhD would give me options if it turned out that I did not like the Foreign Service.

Career choices at age 24–28

Some people like graduate school. I found it a period of great anxiety and continual work. There was so much to learn and everyone seemed to know more than I did. In the first two years, impending oral exams loomed like a sword of Damocles. In addition to endless reading, I worked as a research assistant for a professor and taught sophomore tutorial. And I wanted to finish in four years. Perhaps that is why I do not recommend pursuing a PhD unless you need it. If you want to teach, it is a necessary union card. For most other purposes, it strikes me as a lot of pain for the amount of gain.

The best part of graduate work was writing my thesis. I wanted to get away from Harvard and feel creative again. I also wanted to find out what was happening in the newly independent countries in Africa. The idea for my thesis came from a seminar I took on economic development. Professor Ed Mason had just returned from chairing a World Bank mission to Uganda. He said that economic rationality argued for maintaining the East African Common Market, but it would take a political scientist to answer whether that was possible. That was my challenge. My new wife and I spent 15 months in Uganda, Kenya, and Tanzania collecting data, interviewing political leaders, and trying to understand how politics and economics interacted in new nations.

Life in Africa was exhilarating. Trying to make sense of what was happening around me proved to be an all-absorbing challenge. I decided to postpone the issue of a job search until I returned to Cambridge to write my material. One tropical evening in December, standing on the lawn of the East African Institute of Social Research at Makerere University, someone handed me a letter. I opened it and discovered that the government department at Harvard was offering me a teaching job. Since I had no other plan, I decided to accept and try it for a while, knowing I could always change if I did not like it. The while turned out to be quite long.

Early career choices

Having set my foot on the academic ladder, I quickly developed a desire to climb it. While I enjoyed teaching, all the signals I received made it clear that progress depended on research and publication. My thesis had won a prize and I worked hard to turn it into a book. I presented papers based on it at the American Political Science Association and the International Political Science Association. The idea of government service did not vanish, but it receded into the background for consideration at a later date. It was clear that I needed first to succeed as an academic. That meant I had to pay my dues.

I soon started to plan my second major research project. I had discovered that there was a thriving common market in Central America, though my thesis had explained why, despite their economic merits, common markets were difficult to maintain in less developed countries. So I polished up my Spanish (sitting in the same courses as some of the students I was teaching) and applied for a grant to spend six months in Central America. To explain the anomaly, a few years later I followed my intellectual curiosity to Geneva, teaching and researching regional organizations and the politics of trade more generally for a year. The result was a second book, *Peace in Parts*, which was necessary before the impending decision on tenure.

Tenure is the hurdle that looms in front of all academics at this stage of their careers. One tries to banish it from daily thought, but it is like sharing a bedroom with an elephant. I remember asking Richard Neustadt, a senior member of my department, whether I should try to take a leave from Harvard and pursue a policy job in Washington. His advice: save that for later. Focus on getting tenure first. Other mentors such as Stanley Hoffmann pointed out interesting areas for research and suggested my name for the editorial board of a journal, *International Organization*. That led to further contacts—the famous networking effect—which provided a sense of professional direction. Just as chickens have pecking orders, when academics meet they tend to discuss who is working on what research and how it ranks in the pecking order. It may seem odd, but it is hard to ignore.

One of the benefits of these early professional activities was making a number of new friends. In particular, Robert Keohane and I found that we shared common interests, common dissatisfaction with the field of international organization as it was then conceived, and enjoyed working together. This led to fruitful collaboration on a number of articles and on our book, *Power and Interdependence*. It also produced a lifelong friendship. I think the ideas of both of us were better for our collaboration. Tearing apart each other's drafts and rewriting them both refined and accelerated the work process. The important lesson is not to be afraid of collaboration and not to wear your ego on your sleeve.

Another satisfaction about focusing on an academic career at this stage of life is that it has more flexibility in terms of family. In the long run, being able to spend time with my wife and children as they were growing up was more important than any aspect of a career. I know that my wife, Molly, thinks that I spent too much time on work, but when I compare the flexibility of my hours during my academic years with the rigidity of my schedule when I was in government, the former has a much better fit with small children.

Molly and I celebrated tenure with a quiet dinner and a fine bottle of wine way above our budget. I would like to say that at age 33, I began to seek a role in government, but there was a complication. I was not a member of the political party then in power in Washington. That is the price one pays for waiting until after tenure. You never know when opportunities in government will arise. If you really want to go that route more than anything else, you should probably take advantage when lightning strikes. As it turned out, it was not until seven years later that I went to Washington, where I spent two years before returning to Harvard, mainly because I had promised my children that I would. I thought I would go back into government after a few years out. Thanks to choices of the American electorate, however, those few years turned out to be 12. Planning a career as an "in and outer" is not easy in a democracy!

Career choices at 40

Fortunately, I was excited by the work I was doing on transnational relations and interdependence. Some of the academic writing had policy relevance, and I began to write articles and op-eds in that style. I was invited to join the editorial board of *Foreign Policy*. I attended conferences and meetings on policy issues at places like the Council on Foreign Relations and Ditchley, where I developed another type of network. I also participated in a policy study on nuclear energy and trade in nuclear materials organized by the Ford Foundation. It was probably through these writings and contacts that I came to the attention of people involved in Jimmy Carter's 1976 campaign. I submitted a paper or two for the campaign, but played no significant role. After Carter won, I was quite surprised to be invited to join his transition team as a consultant on nuclear proliferation. Later, when Cyrus Vance was appointed secretary of state, he asked me to be a deputy undersecretary in charge of Carter's new initiatives on nonproliferation. It took me no time to say yes.

It took me a lot longer to become good at my job. Eventually, I was presented with the State Department's highest medal, the Distinguished Honor Award, but in my first months I thought I might not survive. At most, my administrative experience had been the management of one secretary, (and some might say that the other way round). Here I was in charge of 30 or 40 people and supposedly coordinating a major policy as chair of the interagency committee. Once again, everyone knew more than I did. There was no shortage of experienced bureaucrats who wanted to cut me out of the action. Because Carter's policy was unpopular in some quarters, figures in the nuclear industry and Congress said they would get me fired. I found myself going to work at 7 a.m. and returning near midnight. I sought advice from a wide variety of sources. It was my steepest learning curve since first grade.

In retrospect, I might have adjusted to a major policy job more quickly if I had had an earlier apprenticeship in government. Certainly, the second time I went into government years later was much easier. It is hard to overstate the difference in the two cultures. One of the big differences is the premium on time. In academic life, time is a secondary value. It is important to get things just right even at the price of being late. In government, an A+ briefing that reaches the president's desk after the foreign minister has arrived in the Oval Office is an F. Timing is everything. And brevity is a close second. I remember academic colleagues sending me seminar-length papers (like I used to write) with solutions to the proliferation problem. They could not envision a world in which I had to read overnight intelligence and press clips before the morning staff meeting with the secretary and, after that, was caught up in a whirlwind of events until I returned home that evening too exhausted to read anything.

I remember watching some academics who tried to maintain their old habits after they entered government. They either changed or were shunted aside as irrelevant. This does not mean that academic training is irrelevant. On the contrary, it provides the intellectual capital which sometimes allows an academic to set forth a strategy that might escape a career bureaucrat. It is vital to set and maintain priorities and not become a prisoner of one's in-box. But there is little time on the job to develop new intellectual capital.

Partly for those reasons, and mainly for family reasons, I returned to Harvard when my two-year leave expired. I found that there were many intellectual puzzles that arose when I was in government which I had no time to figure out. I was particularly intrigued by the ethical issues involved in foreign policy in general, and nuclear weapons in particular. When I returned to Harvard, I switched part of my teaching to the Kennedy School of Government where there was more concern for policy issues. There I found that teaching a course on ethics and foreign policy to a bright group of students was a great way to work out my ideas, eventually published as *Nuclear Ethics*. At the same time, I developed a large course on international conflicts for the core curriculum in the college and took pride in being able to explain foreign affairs to freshmen and sophomores. Later, the course became the basis for a popular textbook, *Understanding International Conflict*.

Choices at 55

Much as I enjoyed my teaching and writing. I still hoped to spend another period in government. In the late 1980s, I wrote a book, *Bound to Lead: The Changing Nature of American Power*, which argued that America was not in decline (as was then the academic fashion to predict). I also became very interested in the role of Japan, which some saw as a challenge to the United States. These intellectual puzzles gave me much to chew on, but I missed the chance to affect policy and to use the administrative talents I had belatedly discovered. At this stage in life, there are numerous offers of deanships and college and university presidencies. I had considered but resisted such opportunities a number of times. I preferred administration in government, but as such prospects faded after the election of 1988, I began to wonder about succumbing. I tried a period as an associate dean. Fortunately, I was rescued by the election of 1992.

In 1993, I returned to Washington as chair of the National Intelligence Council, the body which coordinates interagency intelligence estimates for the president. Much as I enjoyed it, I was tempted by a policy job which would let me implement some of the issues I had been writing about as academic. I moved to the Defense Department to become assistant secretary for international security affairs under William Perry, with whom I had helped to organize the Aspen Strategy Group in the 1980s. If ever I wanted to see the world, this was almost too much of a good thing. In one year, I visited 53 countries in 52 weeks!

I enjoyed the Pentagon so much that when my two-year leave from Harvard expired in January 1995, I decided to resign my tenure and stay on in government. Finally I cut the umbilical cord! Yet within the year, I was back at Harvard as dean of the Kennedy School, a job for which I had earlier said I did not want to be considered. The major consideration in my change of mind (which took more than a month to decide) was the aftermath of the bombing of the federal building in

Oklahoma City. The national debate about government struck me as polarized and confused. I worried about what was happening to public life in our country. I was struck by the irony of the fact that while I was working *in* government, I was too busy to think about what was happening *to* government. I decided that the Kennedy School, with its multidisciplinary faculty and its tradition of combining analytic excellence with policy relevance would provide a base for addressing my concerns. Since returning, I have organized a faculty study group that has addressed issues of declining trust in government (*Why People Don't Trust Government*), the effects of the information revolution on government (*democracy.com?*), and issues of a global nation (*Governance in A Globalizing World*). I do not regret my decision to return to academic life. I am now wise enough to realize that it is highly unlikely that I would ever return to government.

Summing up

If you are attracted to both analysis and action, a career as an "in and outer" has a lot to offer. Academic life allows you to follow your intellectual curiosity and to knaw on interesting bones. Writing provides a sense of creativity. Teaching is fun. Meeting your students in later years is enormously satisfying. In addition, you are able (within limits) to control your own time and agenda. With policy jobs in government, you do not control your own time or agenda. There is little opportunity to explore ideas, much less smell the flowers or read poetry. On the other hand, such jobs can be very exciting at times. Not only will you meet the great (and not so great) and be present at fascinating events, but occasionally you can put your own stamp on issues of considerable importance. That is a different sense of creativity: to feel that you have helped to shape an important policy outcome.

Focusing solely on one or the other may lead to higher achievement in that domain. There are trade-offs both in time and recognition from switching back and forth. Some people who choose one road will be jealous and some resentful of intruders and deserters who try to have their cake and eat it too. It all depends on what you want out of life. For me, the in and outer approach has been worth it, but I enjoyed my academic base in its own right. The biggest problem is the difficulty of planning such a career. Notice what a large role serendipity played in the story I have told above. You can walk in a field with a golf club in a thunderstorm and not be struck by lightning. There is no sense selling short your academic career in hope of being struck by political lightning. If you want both, make sure that you start with the one that will be most satisfying if the other does not happen. That way you cannot lose.

Note

* This is a revised version of my essay in a Career Services booklet for Kennedy School students.

Index